Christian Eagle-tis-ti-cal Dreamers

Christian Eagle-tis-ti-cal Dreamers

Itching Ears Lead to Sin and Chaos on Church Pews

GAILLEE SOLOMON

All scripture quotations are taken from
The King James Version – Holy Bible

Christian Eagle-tis-ti-cal Dreamers : Itching Ears Lead to Sin and
Chaos on Church Pews

Copyright © 2017 Gaillee Solomon
ISBN-13: 9780692030011
ISBN-10: 0692030018

Published by Bold Christians, Incorporated
Peoria, IL 61605

Special Dedication To Mom and Dad

This book is dedicated to my parents, Walt and Peggy. First, they taught God, then dreamer skills. Never forget God. "Train up a child in the way he should go: and when he is old, he will not depart from it." Proverbs 22:6. "Hear counsel, and receive instruction, that thou mayest be wise in thy latter end." Proverbs 19:20. "Cease, my son, to hear the instruction that causeth to err from the words of knowledge." Proverbs 19:27.

Education leads to better lives affording countless opportunities. Proudness, of my walk with the Lord, mentor programs, and dream accomplishments, bears lifelong, heartfelt, sentiments. Constantly, my parents' legacy tape recorder plays in my head saying: "Don't ever give up. Don't quit. You can accomplish anything you want."

Thankfully, when discouragement speaks, my parents' training and voices ring loudly in memory bank saying, "Keep moving; and do not stop." My parents trained their children in The Way (God's Way – Holiness). God's Word is powerful, never returns void. Righteous training sticks better than permanent glue. Combination of proper teachings, trainings, and persistence pays earthly and heavenly rewards for the entire family and heavenly eternality. During childhood and adulthood, encouraging, words were spoken with love and well-being in their voices and compassionate care. Throughout life, their lifestyle and excellent parenting legacy inspires.

Table of Contents

God's salvation resets and reconstructs lives putting souls on heaven's path – eternal life. God's reset and reconstruction buttons are true. Falsifications are disallowed in righteousness.

-GAILLEE SOLOMON

Preface

WHO ARE EAGLE-TIS-TI-CAL **Dreamers**? Christians, unashamed, bold warriors, serving in God's Army. Eagle-tis-ti-cal dreamers believe, plan, move, and speak on His commands – not men-pleasers. These leaders do not "fit in" wicked "status quos." Dreamers personify courage, compassion, and service. Vows are made and kept. Helping, others, helps self. Rightfully, selfishness is abhorred.

Several topics are discussed in the book; because, dreamers' high standards encounter positive and negative venues. Itching ears' drama, church pew clashes, scoffers' mediocrity, liberality, stinginess, intrusiveness, lying, thievery, slander, hypocrisy, governance, heavenly homegoing preparations, Jesus' return, etc., are discussed at length. Dreamer territories entail various responsibilities. Christian dreamers are noble and generous souls who enjoy helping others prosper.

Dreamers – leaders - are rarely afforded normalcy and incorrectly categorized as undiplomatic. Dreamers use blessings for helping others. Boldness and straightforwardness are requirements for dream attainment. Dreamer traits include holiness, wisdom, thankfulness, tactfulness, thoughtfulness, discretion, consideration, etc. Positively, dreamers utilize brain power and discipline, telling mouths and hands what to say and do. Contrastingly, nondreamers use mouths, hands, time, and resources, haphazardly. Dreamers take righteous center stages moving forward; however, nondreamers move backward. Envious nondreamers loiter in wildernesses and chicken yards. Eagle-tis-ti-cal dreamers soar high hoping to raise expectations. Without visions, nondreamers always follow, hang on margins, or are left behind. Jealousy toward dreamers' success stir non-dreamers' fights, animosities, and other opposition tactics. Their obstinate philosophies, ideals, and stances are purposely unfair and detrimental. In spite of numerous opposition tactics, dreamers succeed. Consider doings. Carefully consider mind and body exposures. Righteous exposures work. Wrongful exposures sometime alter minds making rightful recovery difficult and possibly impossible. Seemingly, nondreamers think sin works. Actually, sin steals, kills, and destroys. Satan tries glamorizing sin as prosperity. Satan is a liar headed to eternal punishment hoping souls join him in permanent torment. Jesus is the Right One to follow. Choosing Jesus makes eternal life inevitable! Righteousness marches forward.

This book is written, based on God's Word (unadulterated Gospel), not on flattery and itching ears. Layout includes precise, value, differences between dreamers and nondreamers. The twosomes' value traits and opposition tactics are expounded. Differences are enormous.

Dreamers are strong, stellar, leaders cherishing righteousness, godly ambitions, soaring in integrity skies. Sadly, nondreamers prefer wallowing in mediocrity valleys leading to inhibitions and unfulfilled dreams. Even though nondreamers' agitation demonstrates through opposition tactics, dreamers remain watchful and prayful. Change the psyche switch! Specifically, if travelling in the righteous direction, keep moving. If travelling in the wrong direction, stop! Turn on right avenue. Nondreamers' itching ears (naivety) put them at odds with righteousness; because, only smooth words are tolerated. Basically, realism is ignored, banished, and untaught. Apparently, naivety is dangerous. Through opposition tactics, enemies find easy prey used for their so-called gain. Unsuspecting souls disregard hate thus steadily moving in wrong, backward, directions. Nondreamers, sometimes called "useful idiots", are remarkably despicable toward dreamers' knowledge, visions, and success. Walk out of nondreamland into dreamland. "For a dream cometh through the multitude of business; and a fool's voice is *known* by multitude of words." Ecclesiastes 5:3.

Altogether, in mediocre arenas, focus, boldness, and wisdom, are despised and unappreciated. Backwardly, bravery is rewarded less than timidity and mediocrity; but, courage overrides weakness.

Confidence, for dream executions, is exemplary. This book is a gem for dreamers as well as inspiration for perspective dreamers. Never lose enthusiasm. Talk, without business (action), is a disastrous life formula. Procure winner confidence. "Be ye followers of me, even as I also *am* of Christ." I Corinthians 11:1.

1

Joseph Is a Dreamer

Joseph's life is a wonderful example for soaring dreamers' lifestyles. Although family and non-family problems exist, he continuously moves forward. Move forward with God.

Mission

- Structure life for eternal, heaven-bound, success. Dreamers realize _only knowing of God is insufficient_. _Heaven homegoing requires knowing God (having a personal relationship with Him)._
- Inspire dreamers to fulfill God's plan for their lives. Allow Him to retool according to His perfect plans and times.
- Encourage and help nondreamers become dreamers.

Responsibility

Keenly, dreamers' purpose-driven lifestyles demonstrate excellence propensities. When on wrong paths, **God intercedes**. "…I heard the voice of the Lord, saying, Whom shall I send, and who will go for us? Then said I, Here _am_ I; send me." Isaiah 6:8.

Joseph is believable, coachable and peaceable; however, his brothers are hostile, jealous, oppositionists. Jealousy is cruel. Oftentimes, life experiences coincide with family and pew challenges. Peaceful congregation settings require righteous value traits such as love, mercy, and charity.

Live for God. Cheerlead for God. Healthy dreaming involves loving God, business, and work. Stir Holy Ghost passion in hearts. Ungodly, wicked, involvements evaporate godly passions. Eagerness to learn, teach, and motivate, is crucial.

Nondreamers' opposition tactics indicate differences between good and evil, wise and unwise, excellence, and mediocrity. "And they have turned unto me the back, and not the face: though I taught them, rising up early and teaching *them* yet they have not hearkened to receive instruction." Jeremiah 32:33. "But they hearkened not, nor inclined their ear, but walked in the counsels *and* in the imagination of their heart, and went backward, and not forward." Jeremiah 7:24. "And now, because ye have done all these works, saith the Lord, and I spake unto you, rising up early and speaking, but ye heard not; and I called you, but ye answered not …" Jeremiah 7:13.

"Wise *men* lay up knowledge: but the mouth of the foolish *is* near destruction. The rich man's wealth *is* his strong city: the destruction of the poor *is* their poverty." Proverbs 10: 14-15. "Lo, *this is* the man *that* made not God his strength; but trusted in the abundance of his riches, *and* strengthened himself in his wickedness." Psalm 52:7. Assuredly, learning is one of life's most important opportunities, experiences, and tools. Some agree; although disappointingly, many disagree. Significant numbers of learning establishments receive disparagement and are viewed, and handled, as only game rooms. Bullies penetrate pews and most places. Assuredly, growth interests must be proactive. In many instances, knowledge is torpedoed. Dreamers consider sayings, but more importantly, intentional silences and doings. When learning is valued, adequate services, monetary funds, supports, and alliances are maintained. Knowledge inflates opportunities and stabilities. Fairness includes fair treatments for all, not for select groups only. Respecter of persons is unfairness, sinful. Reaching dreams envelopes pitfall mixtures. Some good; but, some bad.

Under fair conditions, more growth takes place. Mediocrity and injustice facilitates trouble in the land; namely, ungodliness, inhumanness, manipulation, hate, harassment, evil communications, and foolishness. "Unto the pure all things *are* pure: but unto them that are defiled and unbelieving *is* nothing pure; but even their mind and conscience is defiled. They profess that they know God; but in works they deny *him* being abominable, and disobedient, and unto every good work reprobate." Titus 1:15-16.

Eagle-tis-ti-cal Christian dreamers possess gateway propensities like vision, skills, and intellect. Eagle-tis-ti-cal Christian dreamers face life storms by soaring above them. Pettiness lowers expectations. Since difficulties come into God's peoples' lives, ample biblical preparations (knowing God intimately, faith, prayer) are essential. God never abandons His flock. He is always mindful. Reach the lost at whatever price necessary. Keeping company with Bible believers begets strength; whereas, overly indulging in unbelievers' company (evil communication) begets weakness.

Adversities come. Storms have consequences. God gives strength, skills, and abilities, enabling dreamers to cast cares on Him. In the midst of persecutions, dreamers press forward. Without faith, the devil overtakes souls. Faith is essential. Ongoing prayer helps every situation. Living for Our Father, and doing Our Father's business, is rewarding in this life and life to come. Eagle-tis-ti-cal Christian dreamers are good soldiers. Good soldiers discern predicaments and, in some cases, outcomes. God's paths go in right directions. Dreamers believe "If God is not in circumstances; I have no business in them."

Expectations

Dreamers anticipate opposition. Why? Life winners are stationed on righteousness frontlines - excellence and forward thinking – commanders and chiefs of goodwill. Leaders confront mediocrity daily. "Many *are* the afflictions of the righteous: but the Lord delivereth him out of them all." Psalm 34:19. Perseverance is required. "But the path of the just *is* as the shining light, that shineth more and more unto the perfect day." Proverbs 4:18.

Dreamers nurture biblical-proven, spiritual, character in their homes and communities. Salvation is daily commitment and fulfillment to God. Crystal clear, vital, roles are satisfied, living examples of godly professions.

Greatness glows. Cynically, dreamers' gifts are seen as threatening targets to nondreamers' facetious tactics. Dreamers are aware of "...many unruly and vain talkers and deceivers..."Whose mouths must be stopped, who subvert whole houses, teaching things which they ought not, for filthy lucre's sake." Titus 1:10-11. Constantly, these talkers cause damage, create confusion, make death threats, and spoil relationships. Vain talkers and deceivers are oppositionists, opportunists, and badwill dealers.

As many dreamers attest, Joseph probably felt like a stranger in his own family. He was a hated man. "And Joseph dreamed a dream, and told *it* his brethren: and they hated him yet the more. And he said unto them, Hear I pray you, this dream which I have dreamed: For behold, we *were* binding sheaves in the field, and lo, my sheaf arose, and also stood upright; and behold, your sheaves stood round about, and made obeisance to my sheaf. And his brethren said unto him, Shalt thou indeed reign over us? And they hated him yet the more for his dreams, and for his words." Genesis 37:5-8.

In order to destroy Joseph and his dreams, physical and mental, abuse is administered. His brothers' jealousy drive them to conspiracy. "And they said one to another, Behold, this dreamer cometh." Genesis 37:19. They plan to kill and throw him in a pit. Joseph's brother, Reuben, abhors bloodshed. Instead, they strip Joseph out of his coat of many colours and throw him in a pit (see Genesis 37:18-24).

Along comes a group of Ishmaelites and Midianites. Joseph, an Israelite, is sold for twenty pieces of silver and carried to Egypt. Meanwhile, Rueben returns to check the pit; but is troubled because his brother is not there. Judah, his father, is inconsolable because he presumes Joseph is dead.

Potiphar, an Egyptian officer, of King Pharaoh, purchases Joseph. The Lord prospers Joseph in everything he does. His master sees God is with him; so, he makes him boss over his property. In exemplary fashion, Joseph serves his master's house. Fields are blessed.

Unfortunately, his master's wife pursues Joseph trying to trap him. He runs from her advances. She lies to the household men saying Joseph tried to lie with her. Even though her husband imprisons Joseph, God stands with him. The prison keeper appoints Joseph over all prisoners and employs him as his business overseer. The Lord continues to prosper his hand.

While in prison, two of King Pharaoh's officers dream a dream; but they need interpretation. "…And Joseph said unto them, *Do* not interpretations *belong* to God? Tell me *them*, I pray you." Genesis 40:8. He interprets their dreams and asks them to shew him kindness by mentioning and pleading his case to King Pharaoh. He tells them that his master's wife lied and slandered his reputation (paraphrasing) and he was stolen from his land and imprisoned for a crime he did not do. Believably, not all prisoners are guilty. When Pharaoh's officers get out of prison, one goes back to work in King Pharaoh's palace. The other is hanged; therefore, Joseph's plight, or request, is not mentioned.

Dreamers embrace godly traits - righteousness. Bids for souls are at hand. Acceptance to God's call is the correct choice. Heaven is majestic.

Hell adjusts for God-rejecters' accommodations. Satan has the lowest bid, with the widest way. Satan's place is hot, tumultuous. Upon arrival, destination is sealed - irreversible. Dreamers take godly opportunities while available. Nondreamers follow worldliness, envy dreamers, and squander meaningful opportunities.

"For a dream cometh through the multitude of business; and a fool's voice is known by multitude of words." Ecclesiastes 5:3.

2

Joseph's Valleys Propel His Dreams

King Needs Help

Two years pass, King Pharaoh dreams twice. His spirit is troubled. All the magicians and wise men, of Egypt, cannot interpret his dreams.

While imprisoned, the chief butler tells King Pharaoh that Joseph interpreted his and the baker's dreams. Pharaoh thinks he should have mentioned Joseph's talent earlier. Again, he imprisons the butler. He sends for Joseph.

Basically, he says to Joseph, I need your help. When I dream no one interprets; but, I hear you interpret dreams. Immediately, Joseph acknowledges God. "And Joseph answered, Pharaoh, saying, *It is* not in me: God shall give Pharaoh an answer of peace." Genesis 41:16. Pharaoh told him the dreams. "And Joseph said unto Pharaoh…God hath shewed Pharaoh what *he is* about to do. Behold, there come seven years of great plenty throughout all the land of Egypt: And there shall arise after them seven years of famine; and all the plenty shall be forgotten in the land of Egypt; and the famine shall consume the land; and the plenty shall not be known…by reason of that famine following; for it *shall be* very grievous." Genesis 41:25, 29-31.

Exaltation in Affliction

Joseph advises Pharaoh to appoint officers to take up part of Egypt's land during plenteous years. They are to store food for the seven-year famine.

Pharaoh and servants agree. "And Pharaoh said unto his servants, Can we find *such a one* as this is, a man in whom the Spirit of God *is*? And Pharaoh said unto Joseph, Forasmuch as God hath shewed thee all this, *there* is none so discreet and wise as thou *art...*" Genesis 41:38-39. King Pharaoh's recognition of God's work – through Joseph - is unavoidable. At age 30, King Pharaoh appoints Joseph – second in command – over his house and all Egypt's land. He also gives him jewelry, fine clothing, and transportation in the second chariot.

Joseph goes throughout Egypt storing food in every city. Corn is extremely plentiful. "For God, said he, hath made me forget all my toil, and all my father's house...For God hath caused me to be fruitful in the land of my affliction." Genesis 41:51-52.

Seven years, of plenteousness, end. Seven years, of famine, start in all lands. Joseph has gathered countless numbers of corn. In all the land of Egypt, there is bread. (v.54). As time passes, Egypt famines and asks for King Pharaoh's help. He sends them to Joseph. Famine spreads over the earth. Joseph opens all storehouses, and sells to the Egyptians..."And all countries came into Egypt to Joseph to buy *corn...*" (see Genesis 41:56-57).

Unforeseen Family Circumstances

Keep in mind, jealousy, hatred, and rejection causes Joseph's whereabouts and predicaments; but, God has plans. "Jesus saith unto them, "Did ye never read in the scriptures, The stone which the builders rejected, the same is become the head of the corner: this is the Lord's doing, and it is marvelous in our eyes?" St. Matthew 21:42.

Admittedly, God's grace helped Joseph focus and enabled his perseverance. Endurance pays weighty dividends. Jacob, Joseph's father, heard there is corn in Egypt. "... Get you down thither, and buy for us from thence; that we may live, and not die." Genesis 42:2.

Sow and Reap

We all need God. Sow righteous seeds and reap glorious rewards.

Obviously, Joseph is a dreamer; but, his brothers are jealous, furious, nondreamers.

Each of Joseph's brothers, except one, goes to purchase food. Joseph is the governor, sole seller, in the land. He sees and recognizes his family members; but they are unaware of his identity. "… Joseph remembered the dreams which he dreamed of them, and said unto them, Ye *are* spies; to see the nakedness of the land ye are come. And they said unto him, Nay, my lord, but to buy food are thy servants come." Genesis 42:9-10.

Although he recognizes them, he still calls them spies and puts them in ward for three days. On day three, he bargains with them as follows: One man stays behind in prison. The other brothers carry food to their houses and bring the youngest brother back. This serves as verification that you are not spies; therefore, you will not be killed. They agree.

Family Dilemma

Without his brothers' realization, Joseph oversees their crisis. They reminisce among themselves. Admittance to guilt, concerning ill-treatment toward Joseph, is verbalized. Still, they do not recognize the man, with the food, is the brother they threw in the pit. Isn't God's Work amazing?

Through an interpreter; Joseph speaks to his brothers. They assume he does not understand their conversation. Reuben convinced his siblings not to become murderers. He says "…Spake I not unto you, saying, Do not sin against the child; and ye would not hear? therefore, behold, also his blood is required." Genesis 42:22-23. Secretly, Joseph weeps, but continues withholding his identity. He takes one brother, Simeon, bounds him; and gives provisions for the trip to his other brothers. The brothers leave.

Reconnection

When they return home, they inform their father, Jacob, of what happened. The seller, of the food, was rough, talkative and accusatory. He claims we are spies. To Joseph, the only acceptable confirmation of their return is to leave Simeon in prison for the time-being. In the meantime, they are to bring his youngest brother back to him. If not, he says Simeon dies. As time passes, the corn is eaten. Their father said "…Go again, buy us a little food." Genesis 43:2. Clearly, Joseph would not show himself unless his conditions are met.

Who can blame Joseph for – skepticism – setting conditions? After all, his brothers are responsible for the "pit problems." At this point, Joseph's father is yet unaware that his sons threw their brother in the pit. He is also unaware that Joseph is still alive and is the food seller. In other words, at this point, Joseph is the only one aware that he is dealing with his family. This situation is difficult. But, dreamers thrive in difficulty; because quitting is not a trait.

Their father instructs them to go back to the man, take gifts and their brother Benjamin. The brothers are still unaware the man with food is Joseph – their kin. They go back to Egypt and stand before Joseph. He sees – his youngest brother – Benjamin - with his brothers.

He has a party! The house steward brings the men into Joseph's home. Frighteningly, they predict slavery is befalling them because of returned money in their sacks – on the first trip. They talk to the house steward saying "…we cannot tell who put our money in our sacks. And he said, Peace *be* to you, fear not: your God, and the God of your father, hath given you treasure in your sacks …" Genesis 43:22-23.

He brings Simeon out. Food preparation is made to eat at noon. His brothers present gifts and bows to him to the earth. He inquires of their welfare as well as their father's. "And he lifted up his eyes, and saw his brother Benjamin, his mother's son, and said, *Is* this your younger brother, of whom ye spake unto me? And he said, God be gracious unto thee, my son." Genesis 43:29.

Joseph can hardly hold back tears; so he goes to his chamber and cries. He pulls himself together and goes out to eat with them. Food is served. Benjamin's food is several times as much as his brothers. They eat, drink, and are ecstatic.

Another Trip

Joseph commands "the steward of his house, saying, Fill the men's sacks with food…and put every man's money in his sack's mouth…put my cup… in the sack's mouth of the youngest, and his corn money…As soon as the morning was light, the men went away…*And* when they were gone out of the city, *and not yet* far off, Joseph said unto his steward, Up, follow after the men; and when thou dost overtake them, say unto them, Wherefore have ye rewarded evil for good?" Genesis 44:1-4. The brothers exclaimed, "God forbid that thy servants should do according to this thing." (see Genesis 44:7). The sacks are searched; and the cup is in Benjamin's sack. The stipulation is "withsoever of thy servants it be found, both let him die, and we also will be my lord's bondmen." Genesis 44:9.

The brothers return to Joseph's house. "And they fell before him on the ground." Genesis 44:14. He asked what have you done. "…Judah said… how shall we clear ourselves?…behold, we are my lord's servants, both we, and he also with whom the cup is found. (Genesis 44:16).

Joseph said "…the man in whose hand the cup is found, he shall be my servant …" Genesis 44:17. Judah comes close and asks Joseph to have a word with him. Joseph asks if they have a father or brother. They said, "we have a father…a little one; and his brother is dead…and he alone is left of his mother, and his father loveth him." (Genesis 44:20). The brothers are hard-pressed; because, they led their father to believe Joseph is dead. Now, the lad may encounter evil. Food shortage exposes jealousy, conspiracy, and lies among family members. Moreover, bullying, and self-esteem, is commonplace among nondreamers.

Identity Revealed

Joseph can no longer withhold his secret. He cries and divulges his identity to his brothers. He says "…I am Joseph; doth my father yet live? And his brethren could not answer him; for they were troubled at his presence." Genesis 45:3.

Brothers' Response

At this moment, Joseph's brothers seem terrified; because realization says this is our brother we contemplated murdering, but instead threw him in a pit. Reaping time stares us in our faces. But, Joseph's reactions are reconciliatory, loving, and absolutely positive. Instead of punishment and hate, he shows love, comfort, and kindness – brotherly love.

"...Joseph said unto his brethren, Come near to me, I pray you. And they came near. And he said, I am Joseph your brother, whom ye sold into Egypt. Now therefore be not grieved, nor angry with yourselves, that ye sold me hither: for God did send me before you to preserve life." Genesis 45:4-5. Even though Joseph is wronged, he encourages his family and does them no harm.

Five more years of famine is prospect. Joseph assures his family that "...God sent me before you to preserve you a posterity in the earth, and to save your lives by a great deliverance. So now it was not you *that* sent me hither, but God: and he hath made me a father to Pharaoh, and lord of all his house, and ruler throughout all the land of Egypt." Genesis 44:7-8.

Life Lessons

In the lives of all concerned, this moment is pivotal. God's plan is revealed. Joseph knows the "pit problems" are not about him only. God's plan continues to unfold. "Haste ye, and go up to my father, and say unto him, Thus saith thy son Joseph, God hath made me lord of all Egypt: come down unto me, tarry not..." Genesis 45:9.

New Chapter

Enjoyment time is here! Not scolding! For Joseph and his family, a new era is here. They are together and have plenty resources.

Now that his family is close to him, Joseph makes plans for them to reside in Goshen "...thou, and thy children, and thy children's children, and thy flocks, and thy herds, and all that thou hast...I will nourish thee;

for yet *there are* five years of famine; lest thou, and thy household, and all that thou hast, come to poverty." Genesis 45:10-11.

As a reminder, Joseph speaks to his brothers saying "…your eyes see, and the eyes of my brother Benjamin, that *it is* my mouth that speaketh unto you." Genesis 45:12. Quickly, Joseph wants them to bring his father to him. "Moreover he kissed all his brethren, and wept upon them: and after that his brethren talked with him." Genesis 45:15.

Not only is Joseph elated, his boss, Pharaoh, is also. When Pharaoh hears Joseph's brothers are here, he says, "Say unto thy brethren, This do ye; lade your beasts, and go, get you unto the land of Canaan…take your father and your households, and come unto me: and I will give you the good of the land of Egypt, and ye shall eat the fat of the land." Genesis 45:17-18.

Furthermore, Pharaoh commanded, "take you wagons out of the land of Egypt for your little ones, and for your wives and bring your father, and come." Genesis 45:19. According to Pharaoh's commands, Joseph gives Egypt's good things (provisions); such as clothing, food, and animals. They depart.

Upon arrival into Canaan, unto Jacob's (Joseph's father) home, the brothers relay Joseph's whereabouts and connections saying he is alive! Disbelief presents itself. When all the words of Joseph are shared, Jacob is uplifted, and goes to see his son before he dies.

Jacob Acknowledges God

Jacob takes his journey, to Egypt, with all his seed and belongings… "and offered sacrifices unto the God of his father Isaac." (Genesis 46:1). "And God spake unto Israel in the visions of the night, and said, Jacob, Jacob. And he said, Here *am* I. And he said, I *am* God, the god of thy father: fear not to go down into Egypt; for I will there make of thee a great nation: I will go down with thee into Egypt; and I will also surely bring thee up *again*: and Joseph shall put his hand upon thine eyes." (Genesis 46:1-4).

Joseph prepares to meet his dad, Jacob, in Goshen. When he presents himself, Jacob falls on his son's neck weeping. After a while, Joseph introduces his family to Pharaoh. Pharaoh asks Joseph's brethren their occupation. "And they said unto Pharaoh, Thy servants are shepherds, both we, *and* also our fathers...For to sojourn in the land are we come...for the famine *is* sore in the land of Canaan: now therefore, we pray thee, let thy servants dwell in the land of Goshen." (Genesis 47:3-4).

Pharaoh's behavior toward Joseph's family is impressively compassionate. "And Pharaoh spake unto Joseph, saying, Thy father and thy brethren are come unto thee: The land of Egypt *is* before thee; in the best of the land make thy father and brethren to dwell...and if thy knowest *any* men of activity among them, then make them rulers over my cattle." Genesis 47:5-6.

Joseph's family is welcome; because God is in this plan. When the pit problems started, does family members imagine Joseph's survival? Could they imagine he would be blessed to minister to them? Did they remember his dreams?

Jacob and his family is blessed. "...Joseph nourished his father, and his brethren, and all his father's household, with bread, according to *their* families." Genesis 47:12. Jacob lives in the land of Egypt seventeen years. Time draws closer for Jacob's (Israel's) death. He says to Joseph, "If now I have found grace in thy sight, put, I pray thee, thy hand under my thigh, and deal kindly and truly with me; bury me not, I pray thee, in Egypt: But I will lie with my fathers, and thou shalt carry me out of Egypt, and bury me in their burying place, And he said, Swear unto me, And he sware unto him..." Genesis 47:29-31.

Joseph loves God. Joseph's commitment to God, and disposition toward his family, is commendable. His family is greatly rewarded; because, God put Joseph in a place, and position, to save their lives. More people should love, live, and dream like Joseph.

"For God, said he, hath made me forget all my toil, and all my father's house…For God hath caused me to be fruitful in the land of my affliction." Genesis 41:51-52.

3

Dreamers' Value Traits

Dreamers Outshine

For DREAM FULFILLMENT, foundational traits are pivotal. Dreamers (do-gooders) walk in God's light, allowing His continuous cleansing, security, and heavenly homegoing. Joseph warns his family of upcoming events. He remains righteously adamant through ordeals; because, his dreams supersede him and his family. God has plans and purposes for lives.

God's love and purpose for Joseph's life is unstoppable. Dreamers' preparation to meet the Lord includes obeying the Holy Bible and focusing on doing His business. Final appointments come.

Joseph answers God's call. As a teenager, he shows leadership traits. Leadership and intellect interlock. Leadership is an enduring asset. Intellect encompasses strength, confidence, and courage. "...the lips of knowledge *are* a precious jewel." Proverbs 20:15. "He that getteth wisdom loveth his own soul: he that keepeth understanding shall find good." Proverbs 19:8. Feast at love, knowledge, goodness, charity, enrichment, and mercy, tables. Shun murmurings, complaining, and disputing. Embrace righteous dreaming.

Disappointingly, offence is common toward dreamers. "...But Jesus said unto them, A prophet is not without honour, save in his own country, and in his own house." St. Matthew 13:57. "…a man's enemies *are* the men of his own house." Micah 7:6. Still, Joseph's calling is fulfilled. "Beloved think it not strange concerning the fiery trial which is to try you, as though some strange thing happened unto you: But rejoice, inasmuch as ye are partakers of Christ's sufferings; that when his glory shall be revealed, ye may be glad also with exceeding joy. I Peter 4:12-13.

Dreamers have mandated earnestness from, and toward, God. Dreamers' enemies are the devil and his cohorts. Satan's trademark condones treating people like garbage and dumping them in pits. Consequently, he intends on hurting and killing God's people, along with dreams.

Some perceive dreamers' traits and values as high-mindedness. These perceptions cause jealousy and hate toward them. Still, **the following traits are necessary for dream attainment:**

Fully Embrace God's Word. "So shall my word be that goeth forth out of my mouth: it shall not return unto me void, but it shall accomplish that which I please, and it shall prosper *in the thing* whereto I sent it." Isaiah 55:11.

Dreamers live and vocalize personal relationships with God. Christian bodies are Holy Ghost temples and treated as such. Christian dreamers' lifestyle tells friends and foes whether there is a personal relationship with God, or not. Christians are righteous lights living in a crooked and perverse generation.

Appointed Once. Riches, power, and man-made accolades, do not save souls. Man-made ploys are not enough. Individuals who have all things, except Jesus, lose their souls forever. "…it is appointed unto men once to die, but after this the judgment…Christ was once offered to bear the sins of many; and unto them that look for him shall he appear the second time without sin unto salvation." Hebrews 9:27-28.

Aspiration Number One. Desire and aim to be like Jesus. If most, or all, investments are made in worldliness, what is available for godliness? God wants hot or cold. Otherwise, "I know thy works, that thou art neither cold nor hot: I would thou wert cold or hot. So then because thou art lukewarm, and neither cold nor hot, I will spue thee out of my mouth."

Revelation 3:15-16. What does God want you to do in life? Where does He want you to spend eternity? Where are you preparing to spend eternity? Will your lifestyle take you to heaven? If not, change is needed instantly. So-called "earthly role models" do not own heaven or hell. But, with your consent, they may have input where you live eternally. Why? What you do and who you spend time with matters. Jesus-centered environments are wholesome. In godly environments, growth and fulfillment for God's plans evolve and work. Ungodly people and avenues pursue worldly matters. Departure from God means figuring things out for self. Humans were made to worship God. Relationship with God is essential for earthly living and acquiring heavenly eternity.

Pursue God. From the beginning, godless pursuits are doomed. God created you. God loves you. He loves helping you. He wants you to prosper. He hopes you give Him a permanent place in your heart and live with Him in heaven. "Beloved, I wish above all things that thou mayest prosper and be in good health, even as thy soul prospereth." III John 2.

Serving Satan is life-threatening – eternal liability and loss. Investment in Satan and his work is defeatism. Come to Jesus, now, while you have opportunity. Don't wait. Now! Come now! Jesus is calling. "Behold, I stand at the door, and knock: if any man hear my voice, and open the door, I will come in to him, and will sup with him, and he with me." Revelation 3:20. "Today, if ye hear my voice, harden not your hearts." Hebrews 4:8. "But as the days of No-é *were*, so shall also be the coming of the Son of man be. For as in the days that were before the flood they were eating and drinking, marrying and giving in marriage, until the day that No-é entered into the ark, and knew not until the flood came, and took them all away; so shall also the coming of the Son of man be." St. Matthew 24:37-39.

If Jesus comes this second, where would your eternal home be? Heaven or hell? Immediate action is cognizance.

Ask self: If I am not ready, what should I do to ready myself for heaven? "If we confess our sins, he is faithful and just to forgive us *our* sins, and to cleanse us from all unrighteousness." I John 9. Arrivals to heaven, or hell, are personal decisions, not accidents. Make heavenly reservations now!

Adversity. Dreamers hold fast to salvation crowns. In spite of hard trials, God's embrace lifts spirits. God's embrace gives strength and courage. Faint not because eternal life can be yours, if you choose. "Henceforth there is laid up for me a crown of righteousness, which the Lord, the righteous judge, shall give me at that day: and not to me only, but unto all them also that love his appearing." II Timothy 4:8. "Fear none of those things which thou shalt suffer: behold, the devil shall cast *some* of you into prison, that ye may be tried; and ye shall have tribulation ten days: be thou faithful unto death, and I will give thee a crown of life: Revelation 2:10. Even though trials come before, during, and after dream fulfilment, obeying God's Word is proactive, interactive, and assures eternal life. Contrastingly, nondreamers act only when events force them. Diverters' opposition tactics toward dreamers hurt and oftentimes kill dreamers and dreams. "The thought of foolishness *is* sin: and the scorner *is* an abomination to men. *If* thou faint in the day of adversity, thy strength *is* small." Proverbs 24:9-10.

Banishment Intentions. God is faithful. When opposition tactics stare dreamers in the eyes, God provides wisdom and understanding to keep moving for His plans. "He...preserveth the way of his saints." Proverbs 2:8.

Clearly, some people are not who they appear to be – nice outward, but mean-spirited inside. "Because with lies ye have made the heart of the righteous sad, whom I have not made sad; and strengthened the hands of the wicked, that he should not return from his wicked way, by promising him life: Therefore ye shall see no more vanity...for I will deliver my people out of your hand: and ye shall know that I *am* the Lord." Ezekiel 13:22-23. "Thus saith the Lord concerning the prophets that make my people err, that bite with their teeth, and cry, Peace; and he that putteth not into their mouths, they even prepare war against him. Therefore night *shall be* unto you, that ye shall not have a vision; and it shall be dark unto you, that ye shall not divine; and the sun shall go down over the prophets, and the day shall be dark over them." Micah 3:5-6. In essence, counterfeiters' refusal to publicly announce, or acknowledge, their crookedness at podiums saying, "I am an antichrist, stumblingblock, or pew villain, is deceitful and despicable. Generally, pew villains (nondreamers) cause enormous sufferings. Indeed, they try to hide some dirty deeds. The truth comes out. Are crooks proud of wickedness? Notice fruits. Many pew villains, expediting problems and bribes, are hired peace breakers. Antichrists reject God's Word. Dreamers are praying and watching. "… if thou wilt receive my words, and hide my commandments with thee… if thou criest after knowledge, *and* lifteth up thy voice for understanding; if thou seekest her as silver, and searchest for her as *for* hid treasures; then shalt thou understand the fear of the Lord, and find the knowledge of God. For the Lord giveth wisdom: out of his mouth *cometh* knowledge and understanding. He layeth up sound wisdom for the righteous: *he is* a buckler for them that walk uprightly. He keepeth the paths of judgment, and preserveth the way of his saints. Then shalt thou understand righteousness, and judgment, and equity; *yea*, every good path. When wisdom entereth into thine heart, and knowledge is pleasant unto thy soul; discretion shall preserve thee, understanding shall keep thee. To deliver thee from the way of the evil *man*, from the man that speaketh forward things; who leave the paths of uprightness, to walk in the ways of darkness; who rejoice to do evil *and* delight to rejoice in the forwardness of the wicked; whose ways *are* crooked, and *they* forward in their paths…To deliver thee from the…stranger *which* flattereth with…words…forgetteth the covenant of…God. For her house inclineth unto death, and her paths unto the dead. None that go unto her return again, neither take they holds of the paths of life. That thou mayest walk in the way of good *men*, and keep the paths of the righteous. For the upright shall dwell in the land, and the perfect shall remain in it. But the wicked shall be cut off from the earth, and the transgressors shall be rooted out of it." Proverbs 2:1, 3-22. Do not be hesitant, or afraid, to avoid confusion mongers and falsehood.

Nondreamers attempt to convict, evict, and exterminate the righteous; but "…the upright shall dwell in the land, and the perfect shall remain in it. But the wicked shall be cut off from the earth, and the transgressors shall be rooted out of it." Proverbs 2:21-22. "Then shalt thou delight thyself in the Lord; and I will cause thee to ride upon the high places of the earth, and feed thee with the heritage of Jacob thy father: for the mouth of the Lord hath spoken *it*." Isaiah 58:14. Insults (opposition tactics) are meant to steal, kill, and destroy. God keeps Satan from eradicating His people.

Be Saved. Through the ages, man tries to outdo God. God's greatness and wondrous works are sometimes incomprehensible but not duplicable. "Thus saith the Lord to his anointed...whose right hand I have holden, to subdue nations before him; and I will loose the loins of kings, to open before him the two leaved gates; and the gates shall not be shut; I will go before thee; and make the crooked places straight...thus saith the Lord that created the heavens; God himself that formed the earth and made it; he hath established it, he created it not in vain, he formed it to be inhabited: I *am* the Lord; and *there is* none else. I have not spoken in secret, in a dark place of the earth...I the Lord speak righteousness, I declare things that are right. Assemble yourselves and come...they have no knowledge that set up the wood of their graven image, and pray unto a god *that cannot* save...*there is* no god else beside me; a just God and a Saviour; *there* is none beside me. Look unto me, and be ye saved, all the ends of the earth: for I *am* God, and *there* is none else. I have sworn by myself, the word is gone out of my mouth *in* righteousness, and shall not return, That unto me every knee shall bow, every tongue shall swear. Surely, shall *one* say, in the Lord have I righteousness and strength: *even* to him shall *men* come; and all that are incensed against him shall be ashamed." Isaiah 45:1-2, 18-24.

Big-Mouthed Hypocrites Lack Integrity. Sinfully, hypocrites start and nurture problems. Without dealing with, or taking responsibility for self, hypocrites (nondreamers) blame others for life's discomforts. They lie on, and mistreat, family members, associates, as well as others persons, who come in contact with them. "And he that sat upon the throne said, Behold, I make all things new. And he said unto me, Write: for these words are true and faithful. And he said unto me...I am Alpha and Ōmeg'a, the beginning and the end. I will give unto him that is athirst of the fountain of the water of life freely. He that overcometh shall inherit all things; and I will be his God, and he shall be my son. But the fearful, and unbelieving, and the abominable, and murderers, and whoremongers, and sorcerers, and idolaters, and all liars, shall have their part in the lake which burneth with fire and brimstone: which is the second death." Revelation 21:5-8. "And death and hell were cast into the lake of fire. This is the second death. And whosoever was not found written in the book of life was cast into the lake of fire." Revelation 20:14-15.

Dreamers create peaceful-oriented environments; attending their business. On the other hand, nondreamers meddle, creating pandemonium everywhere they go contemplating tearing dreamers apart and throwing them in despair pits. Because of covetous nondreamers' opposition tactics, untruths are laid to dreamers' charge. Before self is satisfied, self-dissatisfaction issues must be acknowledged and addressed appropriately. When God is not sought for help, jealousy overtakes nondreamers, thus lashing out at dreamers maliciously. Heart matters can be hard to face. Denial is inappropriate and unrealistic. Wisely, and circumspectly, note who people are. Living in denial is catastrophic and imprudent. When you discern, and/or see, some family members, associates, acquaintances, or so-called friends, are enemies, accept it. Discreetly, manage relationships and affairs appropriately and realistically. Realize this fact, some relationships are unwise, unmanageable, and worthless. Pursuits should be beneficial. Denial may last for a "minute", then reality takes over. Deceivers are cold-hearted connivers, fictitious handlers, who sometimes make it difficult for honest folks to believe the wickedness perpetrated. The Bible teaches us not to be deceived. Satan and his troops are deceiving cohorts. Prayer, fasting, and vigilance are required. Prudently and early, dreamers recognize mean-spirited, deceitfulness. Foolishly, some family members, associates, acquaintances, and so-called friends, assume they are in better positions to harm dreamers. Misleading appearances and dramas confuse unsuspecting souls swaying opinions in wrong directions and blame toward innocent parties. Nondreamers are notorious for fake, wrongful, despicable chaos. Consciously, "so-calls" are met with prudent interactions like casualness and skepticism, never intimacy or comradery. Even when so-called friends try to hide "true selves", wickedness manages to seep out showing their mischief. Beware! Be leery of grins, flattery, and peculiar circumstances. These constant disguises are prevalent among ravening wolves. Test circumstances and occasions by the Spirit. "Beware of false prophets, which come to you in sheep's clothing, but inwardly they are raving wolves. Ye shall know them by their fruits. Do men gather grapes of thorns, or figs of thistles? Even so every good tree bringeth forth good fruit; but a corrupt tree bringeth forth evil fruit." St. Matthew 7:15-17…for *the Lord seeth* not as man seeth; for man looketh on the outward appearance, but the Lord looketh on the heart…" I Samuel 16:7. "Again there was a day when the sons of God came to present themselves before the Lord, and Satan came also among them to present himself before the Lord. And the Lord said unto Satan, From whence comest thou? And Satan answered the Lord, and said, From going to and fro in the earth, and from walking up and down in it." Job 2:1-2. "Be sober, be vigilant; because your adversary the devil, as a roaring lion, walketh about, seeking whom he may devour…" I Peter 5:8. "Ye are of your father the devil, and the lusts of your father ye will do: He was a murderer from the beginning, and abode not in the truth; because there is no truth in him. When he speaketh a lie, he speaketh of his own: for he is a liar, and the father of it." St. John 8:44.

"Whether evil comes from family member(s) or non-family foe(s), the results are the same – unfairness, devastation, and pain."

-GAILLEE SOLOMON

Remember, Jesus is our Friend and is always here for good. On the other hand, Satan is an adversary. Satan is there for bad. Good and bad differ. Mankind makes his choice whether good or bad. Void of respect, understanding, and discretion, pew villains creep into congregations bringing, and fostering, chaos. "An hypocrite with *his* mouth destroyeth his neighbor but through knowledge shall the just be delivered." Proverbs 11:9.

Dreamers maintain alertness of nondreamers' opposition tactics. "Behold, I send you forth as sheep in the midst of wolves: be ye therefore wise as serpents, and harmless as doves." St. Matthew 10:16. Nondreamers' goals defame and kill dreams. Nondreamers are reckless, dream, terminators.

For sustainability and survival, dreamers depend on God. He never lies or lets us down. "The integrity of the upright shall guide them: but the perverseness of transgressors shall destroy them. The righteousness of the perfect shall direct his way: but the wicked shall fall by his own wickedness. The righteousness of the upright shall deliver them: but transgressors shall be taken in *their own* naughtiness. The righteous is delivered out of trouble, and the wicked cometh in his stead. He that is void of wisdom despiseth his neighbor: but a man of understanding holdeth his peace. As righteousness *tendeth* to life: so he that pursueth evil *pursueth it* to his own death. The desire of the righteous *is* only good: *but* the expectation of the wicked *is* wrath. The liberal soul shall be made fat: and he that watereth shall be watered also himself. He that diligently seeketh good procureth favor: but he that seeketh mischief, it shall come unto him. He that trusteth in his riches shall fall: but the righteous shall flourish as a branch. He that troubleth his own house shall inherit the wind: and the fool *shall be* servant to the wise of heart. The fruit of the righteous *is* a tree of life; and he that winneth souls *is* wise. Behold, the righteous shall be recompensed in the earth: much more the wicked and the sinner." Proverbs 11:3, 5-6, 8, 12, 19, 23, 25, 27-31.

Repent and confess. "If we say that we have fellowship with him, and walk in darkness, we lie, and do not the truth. If we confess our sins, he is faithful and just to forgive us *our* sins, and to cleanse us from all unrighteousness." I John 1:6, 9. Compensation, for actions, whether positive or negative, comes. Making, and maintaining, righteousness with God is daily devotion. Praise and worship pleases Him. God loves our praise for His goodness and awesomeness.

Trust in God. Trusting, in man, houses, and land, is misguidance. Worldly goods are temporary. Worship God. He is eternal. "…he looked for a city which hath foundations, whose builder and maker *is* God." Hebrews 11:10. "Thus saith the Lord; Cursed be the man that trusteth in man, and maketh flesh his arm, and whose heart departeth from the Lord. Blessed is the man that trusteth in the Lord, and whose hope the Lord is." Jeremiah 17:5, 7. "Put not your trust in princes, *nor* in the son of man, in whom *there is* no help." Psalm 146:3.

Accountability. Mankind must answer to God. He is The Creator, CEO – Mind - of the Universe. "In the beginning God created the heaven and the earth. And God said, Let us make man in our image, after our likeness: and let them have dominion over the fish of the sea…and over all the earth…So God created man in his own image, in the image of God created he him; male and female created he them." Genesis 1:26-27. "…O man, who art thou that repliest against God? Shall the thing formed say to him that formed *it*, why has thou made me thus? Romans 9:20.

Since individuals are God's handiwork, why do some people take audacities to show favoritism? Hating His creation means hating The Creator. For His glory, God gives, and changes, lives.

Souls are priceless. You have a chance for redemption; but the devil does not. God is Saviour and enriches the whole man. Satan, decapitates man, poisoning everything he touches.

Perversely, minimization and abolishment of, Jesus' role, in societies and lives, is growing. Senselessly, Bibles, righteous living, pictures, nativity scenes, fairness, and godly expressions, are discouraged. In some cases, Jesus association, is punished; while Jesus disassociation is rewarded. Satan seeks to drown Jesus callers in pools of fear, embarrassment, and opposition tactics.

Dreamers surrender to Jesus. Nondreamers refuse godly instruction swimming in devilish pools. Sadly, many individuals think they can tell God what to do. Intellect and advancement does not erase God's authority position. Can never happen!

Affections in Wrong Places. "But, I know you, that ye have not the love of God in you. I am come in my Father's name, and ye receive me not: if another shall come in his own name, him ye will receive. How can ye believe, which receive honour one of another, and seek not the honour that *cometh* from God only?" St. John 5:42-44.

God deserves and desires our undivided attention. God is Jealous. When all time allocations are spread among earthly personalities and endeavors, only short ends, or no ends, are left for God. God deserves our firstfruits. He is displeased with leftovers. Give God much time. He died for mankind. He was crucified for us. If it was not for God's provisions, there would not be any fruits. Without God, mankind cannot survive. Everybody needs God.

"If ye be risen with Christ, seek those things which are above, where Christ sitteth on the right hand of God. Set your affection on things above, not on things on the earth. For ye are dead, and your life is hid with Christ in God. When Christ, *who, is* our life, shall appear, then shall ye also appear with him in glory. Mortify your members which are upon the earth; fornication, uncleanness, inordinate affection, evil, concupiscence, and covetousness, which is idolatry; for which things' sake the wrath of God cometh on the children of disobedience: In which ye also walked sometime, when ye lived in them. But now ye also put off all these; anger, wrath, malice, blasphemy, filthy communication out of your mouth. Lie not one to another, seeing that ye have put off the old man with his deeds..." Colossians 3:1-9.

Profound concern is extended to those minding temporalities, but deny God. God is mankind's Creator. Our Creator deserves acknowledgment, both public and private.

Deservingly, or undeservingly, compliments are given among peoples. But, it seems harder and harder for people to call God's name or express His blessings. When He saves lives from car accidents, drownings, falls, earthquakes, tornadoes, volcanoes, or other dilemmas, why is timidity shutting mouths??? Publicly, God's Works should be exalted. Unless God permits, one breath is not taken. Praise the Lord plenty and often.

People or things cannot save souls. God gives salvation. When mismanaged, riches and other temporalities take souls from heaven, while sending souls to eternal heat. Because people forget God, riches are mishandled. Schedules are consumed with worldly pleasures, while neglecting the poor. Riches are consumed on worldly desires; therefore, no time is spent on God's Word, Work, or Soul-Saving!

Sadly, some nondreamers are unprepared; looking up one day and it is time to leave this earth. Preparations are unmade to meet the Lord in peace. Getting right with God now is important. Rescuing souls from torment eternity is important. Telling others about Jesus is important. He is knocking at your heart's door to save your soul. He loves you unconditionally.

Alertness. Dreamers are not ignoring their enemies. These honorable warriors observe and anticipate enemy opposition tactics. On all fronts, prudence is emphasized. Treacherously, pew villains wrap falsehood in beautiful packages –– entrapping many unsuspecting, prayless, and unwatchful persons. Pew villains are unhappy so they say and do hurtful things to others. Gullibility is ideal targets. The devil roams day and night looking for imprudent, unsuspecting, souls.

Informational integrity is not on the devil's plate. Backbiters, fighters, and destroyers' docility is masked with confusion and poison. They are responsible for many pew problems and downfalls. Pew villains show wickedness to their targets, but seek hiding from others. Jesus is Protector and Vindicator of our faith.

Nondreamers pretend to be gentle-natured. Negatively, they are enemies whose dream killing instincts invade, injure, and destroy.

Abominations. The Lord disapproves wickedness. "Are there...treasures of wickedness in the house of the wickedness, and the scant measure *that* is abominable? Shall I count *them* pure with the wicked balances, and with the bag of deceitful weights? For the rich men thereof are full of violence, and the inhabitants thereof have spoken lies, and their tongue is deceitful in their mouth. Therefore also will I make *thee* sick in smiting thee, in making *thee* desolate because of thy sins. Thou shalt eat, but not be satisfied...thou shalt take hold, but shalt not deliver...and that which thou deliverest will I give up to the sword. Thou shalt sow, but thou shalt not reap..." Micah 6:11-15.

Sin is unhidden from God. He sees and knows every person and everything. Sin permits heartbreaks. Righteousness exalts. "Be not overcome of evil, but overcome evil with good." Romans 12:21.

Anger is an oven. But, in order to succeed, coolness prevails. In the Name of Jesus, rebuke the devil. "Be ye angry, and sin not: let not the sun go down on your wrath. Neither give place to the devil." Ephesians 4:26-27. Anger is outward showings of inward pain. Jesus can eliminate inward and outward pains. "But he *was* wounded for our transgressions, *he was* bruised for our iniquities: the chastisement of our peace *was* upon him; and with his stripes we are healed." Isaiah 53:5.

Ask God...anything...anytime...anywhere. He has all answers. His motives are righteous. "If ye abide in me, and my words abide in you, ye shall ask what ye will, and it shall be done unto you." St. John 15:7.

God is satisfaction, not people, money, gimmicks, or fame. Without God, life is void of fulfillment. There are no substitutions for God. No – body or no – thing can fill God's place, in hearts, for Him.

Avoidance/Withdrawal is sometimes necessary. Dream snatchers create chaos in their lives and others' lives. They hate dreamers and positivity, but love negativity. "Be not deceived: evil communications corrupt good manners." I Corinthians 15:33.

Avoidance is prudent. Since chaos stirrers are recognized, protective measures are taken accordingly. Otherwise, walking with the Lord may be weakened – threatened. Nondreamers' opposition tactics create unfair, uncanny, predicaments. Pew villains are nondreamers. Opposition tactics are sinful, division-prone, clicks. Chaos stirrers, complain, lie, slander, and support confusion. Sinister operators' opposition tactics are time-consuming, detrimental, wicked occupations. "Now I beseech you, brethren, mark them which cause divisions and offences contrary to the doctrine which ye have learned; and avoid them." Romans 16:17. The Bible teaches us how to handle evil workers. "...beware of evil workers..." Philippians 3:2.

"Keep thee far from a false matter; and the innocent and righteous slay them not: for I will not justify the wicked." Exodus 23:7. "For the wrath of

God is revealed from heaven against all ungodliness and unrighteousness of men, who hold the truth in unrighteousness..." Romans 1:18.

"But the Lord is faithful, who shall stablish you, and keep *you* from evil. And the Lord direct your hearts into the love of God, and into the patient waiting for Christ. Now we command you, brethren, in the name of our Lord Jesus, that ye withdraw yourselves from every brother that walketh disorderly, and not after the tradition which he received of us." II Thessalonians 3:3, 5-6. Dreamers follow God's tradition, because His tradition is PERFECT, RIGHT, and EVERLASTING.

Babes. Who keeps promises? God. Who breaks promises? Satan and mankind. "Let us therefore fear, lest, a promise being left *us* of entering into his rest, any of you should seem to come short of it. For unto us was the gospel preached, as well as unto them: but the word preached did not profit them, not being mixed with faith in them that heard *it*. For we which have believed do enter into rest..." Hebrews 4:1-3.

Undefeated dreamers have purpose and commitment. "For when for the time ye ought to be teachers, ye have need that one teach you again which *be* the first principles of the oracles of God; and are become such as have need of milk, and not of strong meat. For everyone that useth milk *is* unskillful in the word of righteousness: for he is a babe. But strong meat belongeth to them that are of full age *even* those who by reason of use have their senses exercised to discern both good and evil." Hebrews 5:12-14.

Dreamers have different habits from nondreamers. Dreamers enjoy excellence but despise mediocrity. Nondreamers consume mediocrity. They are settlers/participants satisfied with pew gangster behaviors.

When possible, efforts are made to mentor nondreamers. Godly lifestyles are indication of devotion. Godly wisdom merges beliefs and works; that is, interactive, intergrade, and proactive. Belief produces action. Saying, but not doing, defies plausibility. Speaking and living truth pairs. Stand-alone yields incompletion.

God owns heaven and earth. His people are godly soul-saving operators (believers). "Take heed, brethren, lest there be in any of you an evil heart of unbelief, in departing from the living God. But exhort one another daily; while it is called To day; lest any of you be hardened through the deceitfulness of sin." Hebrews 3:12-13.

Beliefs. "In the beginning was the Word, and the Word was with God, and the Word was God. He came unto his own, and his own received him not. But as many as received him, to them gave he power to become the sons of God, *even* to them that believe on his name: which were born, not of blood, nor of the will of the flesh, nor of the will of man, but of God." St. John 1:1, 11-13.

Your conviction system determines conduct. Bold Eagle-tis-ti-cal Dreamers (strong people of God) are not surprised, by mistreatment, but undeterred.

Body. The body is the Holy Ghost temple. Sin defiles. When sin is committed, God-given consciousness relays warning to stop, confess, and repent. Sin approval conflicts with repentance. Scripture says, "Flee fornication. Every sin that a man doeth is without the body; but he that commiteth fornication sinneth against his own body. What? know ye not that your body is the temple of the Holy Ghost *which is* in you, which ye have of God, and ye are not your own? For ye are bought with a price: therefore glorify God in your body, and in your spirit, which are God's." I Corinthians 6:18-20.

Body language, speech, and fruits, show you love Jesus. He says, "If you love me, keep my commandments." St. John 14:15. Others should realize you love Him.

Boldly Speaking the Gospel. Jesus' ambassadors have responsibilities for living righteously, preaching, and teaching to souls so preparations are made for heavenly homes. Satan imparts hindrances; but, boldness subjugates blockages. By obeying and promoting righteousness, dreamers take God's Word seriously. Preaching and teaching God's Word alone amounts to unfinished business. Unfinished business, with God, keeps souls from eternal peace. Dreamers live God's teachings. Dreamers start and finish business. "...even after that we had suffered before, and were shamefully entreated...we were bold in our God to speak unto you the gospel of God with much contention. For our exhortation *was* not of deceit, nor of uncleanness, nor in guile: But as we were allowed of God to be put in trust with the gospel, even so we speak; not as pleasing men, but God, which trieth our hearts…neither at any time used we flattering words… nor a cloke of covetousness; God *is* witness: Nor of men sought we glory… not *yet* of others, when we might have been burdensome, as the apostles of Christ…That ye would walk worthy of God, who hath called you unto his kingdom and glory. For what *is* our hope, or joy, or crown of rejoicing? *Are* not even ye in the presence of our Lord Jesus Christ at his coming?" I Thessalonians 2:2-6, 12, 19.

Breaks are coping mechanisms. Dream fulfillment is work - action. For refreshment and encouragement, dreamers use rejuvenation intermissions. Relaxations are beneficial, emotional, outlets.

Cain and Abel Derivatives. Unmistakably, God calls and chooses ambassadors. In the womb, some are called and chosen. God's distinction mark shows. Supporters and nonsupporters sense divine differences. Reactions, toward dreamers, are different from reactions toward non-dreamers. Some positive; but some negative. God haters are not lovers of His chosen. Righteous leaders – dreamers - pray for divine missions and proper navigations.

Obviously, dreamers are targets. Joseph's brothers were contemplating murder against him. Cain's work was righteous, therefore problems with his brother arises. Many times, family members' fierce oppositions encompass growth or dream death. Jealousy fogs. Nondreamers go to extraordinary lengths hindering some, but killing others. Lies, thefts, and confusion, are plotted against dreamers, hoping they quit – give up – stop moving. Naturally, these intentional, wicked Cain mentalities perpetuate negativity. Jealous minds are nourished and processed with babbling and confusion. Instead of physical slaying, babbling mouths are used as firing squads. Misrepresentations are planted among family members, church leaders, church members, community leaders, coworkers, etc. God's Son, Jesus Christ, was hated and crucified. Satan uses dishonest, jealous, people for promoting confusion and wickedness toward God's chosen. After all, scammers find malicious audiences. "For God is not *the author* of confusion, but of peace, as in all churches of the saints." I Corinthians 14:33.

Pew villains disrespect God's house. Instrumentally, bandits approve and channel disorder, but disapprove chaos detoxification on church pews as well as other surroundings.

For dreamers, God is priority. Focus and keenness stems from godly priorities. Practice selflessness. Nondreamers' mediocrity, naivety, selfishness, etc., stress resources. For them, Christ comes second or maybe somewhere on their list. Christians' lives should display God's prioritizations.

Dreamers, believe and live in Him - incomplete without Him. On the other hand, nondreamers (pew villains) trust riches and man. Wrapped in smokescreens; such as, deceit, jealousy, and traditionalism, they are unequipped to make God priority in all life's areas. Dreamers discern so-called hidden, ungodly, acts recognizing how wicked systems work.

Disappointingly, pew villains' selfishness, deceit, and personal gratification, entail every life facet. Psychologically, entanglement with tormentors leads to beguilement. "...lest any man should beguile you with enticing words." Colossians 2:4. "Beware lest any man spoil you through philosophy and vain deceit, after the tradition of men, after the rudiments of the world, and not after Christ." Colossians 2:8.

When used righteously, persuasion can be a powerful mechanism for soul saving. Otherwise souls are misguided and lost to eternal damnation – fire and brimstone. Reiteration, of hell's fire and brimstone, is warning to unpreparedness. As in the days of No'e, many will be caught off guard sinning. For the unprepared, Jesus is coming as a thief in the night. Now is the time to work out your salvation with fear and trembling. Are you ready to meet God? In No'e's days, he preached 120 years. Yet, only eight souls were saved from the flood. "Having a good conscience; that, whereas they speak evil of you, as of evildoers, they may be ashamed that falsely accuse your good conversation in Christ. For *it is* better, if the will of God be so, that ye suffer for well doing, than for evil doing. For Christ also hath once suffered for sins, the just for the unjust, that he might bring us to God, being put to death in the flesh, but quickened by the spirit...when once the longsuffering of God waited in the days of Noah, while the ark was a preparing, wherein few, that is, eight souls were saved by water. I Peter 3:16-18, 20.

Now is the time to get right and stay right with God. "For this is the message that ye heard from the beginning, that we should love one another. Not as Cain, *who* was of that wicked one, and slew his brother. And wherefore slew he him? Because his own works were evil, and his brother's righteous. Marvel not, my brethren, if the world hate you." I John 3:11-13. "Ye have not chosen me, but I have chosen you, and ordained you…If the world hate you, ye know that it hated me before *it hated* you. If ye were of the world, the world would love his own: but because ye are not of the world, but I have chosen you out of the world, therefore the world hateth you. Remember the word that I said unto you, The servant is not greater than his lord. If they have persecuted me, they will also persecute you; if they have kept my saying, they will keep yours also. But all these things will they do unto you for my name's sake, because they know not him that sent me. St. John 15:16, 18-21.

Sorrowfully, Satan dispenses foolishness and wickedness among nondreamers. In turn, these groups wreak mayhem on church pews and everywhere they go. Only through fasting and prayer, dreamers move forward in pursuit of God's plans and purposes. "For unto you it is given in the behalf of Christ, not only to believe on him, but also to suffer for his sake…" Philippians 1:29.

Calendar. "Many are the afflictions of the righteous: but the Lord delivereth him out of them all." Psalm 34:19. "For we must all appear before the judgment seat of Christ; that every one may receive the things *done* in *his* body, according to that he hath done, whether *it be* good or bad." II Corinthians 5:10.

Right, and wrong, doings may return in unexpected ways, from unexpected people, and in unexpected settings. Inevitably, reaping times' calendar includes dates, times, places, and recompenses whether good or bad. Planting, good seeds, ensures godly results. Truly, no one is above God's Word. Show mercy. Even merciless souls need mercy. Build a large mercy account. Too many souls are salvation bankrupt; because, only inconsideration and respect of persons are paid into their accounts. Turning to God is the solution, way of escape.

Cause Without. Unscrupulously, dreamers are hated without cause, and persecuted because of jealousy. Groundless charges are made; but proof is unavailable. Nondreamers' irresponsible, loose missile, mouths boost persecutions – unfairness. Particularly, this book points out how Joseph experienced family jealousy, murder contemplation, and the slanderous lie that caused his imprisonment. Joseph was not guilty. Some prisoners are "framed" – not guilty. "They that hate me without a cause are more than the hairs of mine head: they would destroy me, being mine enemies wrongfully, are mighty: then I restored that which I took not away." Psalm 69:4." Mine enemies chased me sore, like a bird, without cause." Lamentations 3:52. "They compassed me about also with words of hatred; and fought against me without a cause." Psalm 109:3.

"If I had not done among them the works which none other man did, they had not had sin: but now have they both seen and hated both me and my Father. But *this cometh to pass*, that the word might be fulfilled that is written in their law, They hated me without a cause." St. John 15:24-25.

Eagle-tis-ti-cal dreamers have extraordinary hopes and strong visions, soaring in excellency halls. Oppositely, nondreamers scratch in mediocrity yards which explains why they spend time committing ungodly acts against dreamers without cause. Eagle-tis-ti-cal dreamers' mentalities (value traits) and mediocre mentalities (opposition tactics) clash. Nondreamers tend to be slothful, jealous, unwilling workers, and evil doers, purposely persecuting dreamers. Wasted time, misused energies, and efforts, epitomize evil commitments. What a tragedy! Debacle!

Cheerful Givers realize investment in God's Kingdom assures bountiful blessings. "Every man according as he purposeth in his heart, *so let him give*; not grudgingly, or of necessity: for God loveth a cheerful giver." II Corinthians 9:7. "Whoso stoppeth his ears to the cry of the poor, he also shall cry himself, but shall not be heard." Proverbs 21:13.

Dreamers give Jesus first fruits. Cheerless givers offer graven images and leftovers. They hate giving; but make false pretenses. False pretenses are lies. The Bible teaches against falsification. Pretenders prohibit growth. Miserably, evil status quos' maintenance is encouraged. Righteousness stands tests. Itching ears fight genuineness. Mankind does not possess capability to outthink or outgive God. He is Epic. He is Victory. Dreamers enjoy living right and participating in giving opportunities.

Skirmishes, between right and wrong, are valid. Paths lead to different places. Dreamers follow righteousness. Heaven's path is narrow and fulfilling. Sin is hell's path. You have to make your choice.

(*Eagle-tis-ti-cal*) **Dreamers** are Christian, God, lovers and are bold warriors in His Army. Scripture says, "I charge *thee* therefore before God, and the Lord Jesus Christ, who shall judge the quick and the dead at his appearing and his kingdom; preach the word; be instant in season, out of season; reprove, rebuke, exhort with all longsuffering and doctrine. For the time will come when they will not endure sound doctrine; but after their own lust shall they heap to themselves teachers, having itching ears; and they shall turn away *their* ears from the truth, and shall be turned into fables. But watch thou in all things, endure afflictions, do the work of an evangelist, make full proof of thy ministry." II Timothy 4:1-5. Dreamers speak and move on God's commands. Fortunately, dreamers' advocacies; namely, humanitarianism, and animalism, capitalize on mercies.

Wisely, dreamers use their minds more than their mouths. Never stop moving; nor, succumb to mediocrity. Less talk, more action equals more dream fulfillment. "…be strong in the grace that is in Christ Jesus. Thou therefore endure hardness, as a good solider of Jesus Christ. No man that warreth entangleth himself with the affairs of *this* life; that he may please him who hath chosen him to be a solider." II Timothy 2:1, 3-4.

Lean on God because, "For with God nothing shall be impossible." St. Luke 1:37. "…The things which are impossible with men are possible with God." St. Luke 18:27.

God exalts dreamers, otherwise, many may give up. Without God's Strength, dreamers would not have knowledge or capacity to answer, or carry out, His Call. Purposely, nondreamers' design opposition tactics for sabotages.

Christ Is Faithful. Spectacles, standout, and up, speaking for Christ. Christian, Eagle-tis-ti-cal, dreamers face persecutions and hate, yet remain unashamed of The One Who made the human race in His Image. "Let a man so account of us, as of the ministers of Christ, and stewards of the mysteries of God…it is required in stewards, that a man be found faithful. For I think that God hath set forth us the apostles last, as it were appointed to death: for we are made a spectacle unto the world, and to angels and to men. We *are* fools for Christ's sake, but *ye* are wise in Christ; we *are* weak, but *ye* are strong; *ye* are honourable, but we *are* despised. Being defamed, we intreat: we are made as the filth of the world, and are the offscouring of all things until this day. I write not these things to shame you, but as my beloved sons I warn *you*. For the kingdom of God *is* not in word, but in power." I Corinthians 4:1-2, 9-10, 13-14, 20. "And my speech and my preaching *was* not with enticing words of man's wisdom, but demonstration of the Spirit and of power: That your faith should not stand in the wisdom of men, but in the power of God." I Corinthians 2:4-5. "For I am not ashamed of the gospel of Christ for it is the power of God unto salvation to everyone that believeth…" Romans 1:16.

Joseph is a bold dreamer. His brothers' inhospitableness is unconscionable. Their wrongful actions say "dreamers are spectacles and outcasts." In spite of all their opposition tactics, Joseph realizes his dreams and helps his family. He did not return evil for evil. Dreamers soar in God. God is Keeper of our souls and heavenly home. "O give thanks unto the Lord; call upon his name: make known his deeds among the people…Touch not mine anointed, and do my prophets no harm." Psalm 105:1, 15.

Christ Suffered. Dreamers suffer. Dreamers expect nondreamers' opposition tactics. "Forasmuch then as Christ hath suffered for us in the flesh, arm yourselves likewise with the same mind: for he that hath suffered in the flesh hath ceased from sin: That he no longer should live the rest of *his* time in the flesh to the lusts of men, but to the will of God." I Peter 4:1-2. "For such an high priest became us, *who* is holy, harmless, undefiled, separate from sinners, and made higher than the heavens; who needeth not daily, as those high priests, to offer up sacrifice, first for his own sins, and then for the people's: for this he did once, when he offered up himself." Hebrews 7:26-27.

Dreamers live to please Jesus. Nondreamers live to please men-pleasers. "…ye are they which justify yourselves before men; but God knoweth your hearts: for that which is highly esteemed among men is abomination in the sight of God." St. Luke 16:15.

Clarity Hearing. Spiritual intimacy (personal relationship with God) lets us hear Him clearly. Dreamers are willing to do what He says no matter what men-pleasers, oppositionists, and obstructionists say or do. God is The Just Judge. Unfortunately, nondreamers are dutiful, church-trained, flip-floppers, deceiving some worshippers. Duties alone (works) are insufficient for eternal life acquisition.

Jesus' way is straight, right, leading to heaven. There is one way to heaven. Hell also has one way. Repetitively, living according to God's Word gets you to heaven; whereas, living unrighteous takes you to hell. Make sure you purchase the right ticket. Tickets are nontransferable and nonrefundable. Choose wisely. Before it is too late, Come to Jesus now before it is too late. Dreamers do God's Will; whereas, nondreamers do Satan's will. Appearances fall short. **Only living according to God's Word gets you to heaven.**

Color. "So God created man in his *own* image, in the image of God created he him; male and female created he them. And God blessed them, and God said unto them, Be fruitful and multiply, and replenish the earth, and subdue it: and have dominion over the fish of the sea, and over the fowl of the air, and over every living thing that moveth upon the earth. And God saw that everything that he had made, and, behold, *it was* very good…" Genesis 1:27-28, 31. *Eagle-tis-ti-cal* **dreamers** treat each person justly, not blinded with any form of injustice.

God's Word is Truth-uncompromised, unchanging, everlasting. Respectively, man is made in God' image. God's Word teaches and shows His love and how mankind is to love one another. God's love supersedes manmade correctness, worldly love principles, and so-called justice criteria. Respecter of persons is unfair and unjust. Injustice deprives people, while superficially elevating others. God is displeased. God is fair to everybody. People who love God treat people fairly. There are no exceptions. There are no in-betweens.

<u>Right</u> stands tall; but sometimes right stands alone. But, that is okay because righteousness is bold and strong. Righteousness has legs; whereas, unrighteousness is propped up with lies and injustice. Wrongness is squeamish and need many props; namely, liars, manipulators, slanders, thieves, etc. Props are unsustainable; because recompenses shatter false security.

Right does win. Wrong loses. "And we have seen and do testify that the Father sent the Son to be the Saviour of the world. Whosoever shall confess that Jesus is the Son of God, God dwelleth in him, and he in God. And we have known and believed the love that God hath to us. God is love; and he that dwelleth in love dwelleth in God, and God in him. Herein is our love made perfect, that we may have boldness in the day of judgment: because as he is, so are we in this world. There is no fear in love; but perfect love casteth out fear: because fear hath torment. He that feareth is not made perfect in love. We love him, because he first loved us. If a man say, I love God, and hateth his brother, he is a liar: for he that loveth not his brother whom he hath seen, how can he love God whom he hath not seen? And this commandment have we from him, That he who loveth God, love his brother also." I John 4:14-21.

God's creation includes different genders, colors, heights, and weights. God does not make mistakes. Tragically, self-appointed "respecter of persons" proliferate unfairness, neglect, and suffering. Hate and belittlement are sins. God is not pleased. God loves His creation. God is satisfied with how He create mankind in His image. God is no respecter of persons.

God-lovers are not bigots. Partiality, hate, and discord are wicked behaviors. "He that saith he is in the light, and hateth his brother, is in darkness even until now." I John 2:9. "For this is the message that ye heard from the beginning, that we should love one another. Not as Cain, *who* was of that wicked one, and slew his brother. And wherefore slew he him? Because his own works were evil, and his brother's righteous. Marvel not, my brethren, if the world hate you. We know that we have passed from death unto life, because we love the brethren. He that loveth not *his* brother abideth in death. Whosoever hateth his brother is a murderer: and ye know that no murderer hath eternal life abiding in him. Hereby perceive we the love *of* God, because he laid down his life for us: and we ought to lay down *our* lives for the brethren. But whoso hath this world's good, and seeth his brother have need, and shutteth up his bowels *of compassion* from him, how dwelleth the love of God in him?...let us not love in word, neither in tongue; but in deed and in truth. And whatsoever we ask we receive of him, because we keep his commandments, and do those things that are pleasing in his sight." I John 3:11-18, 22.

Commitment is powerful, and irreplaceable, for attaining happiness and dream fulfillment. Personal relationship with Jesus yields peace of mind.

Sensibly, dreamers cannot afford embracing nondreamers, troublemakers, or naysayers', philosophies. Troublemakers and their cronies' bellies are full of condemnation. Usually, their behavior stems from their personal negative, unaddressed, problems; so they seek solace by attempting to cause problems in dreamers' lives. Justification for deviant actions is reprehensible. Recompense is assured. Jesus is with us every moment; although human companionship is sometimes scarce.

Competition, misguidance, is forestry. Competition is emotional and, comprises many levels. Wisely, for assertion purposes, dreamers sometime use passive aggression. Often, nondreamers, overthink, overdo, and use wickedness and physical aggression against Eagle-tis-ti-cal dreamers.

Understanding healthy, camaraderie means all trees – in the forest – do not need cutting. All need pruning. With pruning and growth, good trees become better. Pruning helps; whereas, cutting ends many lives altogether. The same principle applies to people. Some nondreamers become dreamers. "Another parable put he forth unto them, saying, "The kingdom of heaven is likened unto a man which sowed good seed in his field: But while men slept, his enemy came and sowed tares among the wheat, and went his way. But when the blade was sprung up, and brought forth fruit, then appeared the tares also. So the servants of the householder came and said unto him, Sir, didst not thy sow good seed in thy field? From whence then hath it tares? He said unto them, An enemy hath done this. The servants said unto him, Wilt thou then unto thee that we go and gather them up? But he said Nay; lest while ye gather up the tares, ye root up also the wheat with them. Let both grow together until the harvest: and in the time of harvest I will say to the reapers, Gather ye together first the tares, and bind them in bundles to burn them: but gather the wheat into my barn." St. Matthew 13:24-30. "And *that* they may recover themselves out of the snare of the devil, who are taken captive by him at his will." II Timothy 2:26.

Seemingly, horrors and mine fields in church? Yes! Wheat and tares in church? Yes! Wake up! "Ever learning, and never able to come to the knowledge of the truth." II Timothy 3:7.

Keep in mind, the devil (enemy) uses church-goers (pew villain bullies), dehumanization, and unfairness, for tyrannical suffering harbors. Dehumanization ignites inequality. When God's creation (humans) are viewed, and treated inhumanely, unfair measures are taken against them.

Sadly, bullies' (clicks and outcasts) numbers are rising; because enormous energies are infused with futility. Dreamers stand for equality - righteousness; whereas, nondreamers pitch inequality as worthy and right. Inequality is unrighteousness. Unrighteousness is against Bible teachings.

Wisdom have humane perspectives. The devil wants you to think mistreatments are okay. Positivity (wheat) and negativity (tares) grow together; but God separates – justly. "For God is not *the author* of confusion, but of peace, as in all churches of the saints." I Corinthians 14:33.

Confess and Forsake. "He that covereth his sins shall not prosper: but whoso confesseth and forsaketh them shall have mercy." Proverbs 28:13. "THUS saith the Lord, Keep ye judgment, and do justice: for my salvation *is* near to come, and my righteousness to be revealed. Blessed *is* the man *that* doeth this, and the son of man *that* layeth hold on it; that keepeth the sabbath from polluting it, and keepeth his hand from doing any evil." Isaiah 56:1-2. Humans have common denominators. Unfortunately, many people defy the human race's commonalities. Thankfully, no one can change God's Word or His creation.

God's Word remains the same forever; but, man's minds and hearts err. Disregarding God's commandments paves the way to everlasting torment.

Sadly, many people boast on man. Without giving God credit, they claim people and/or circumstances save lives and help them in distress. When God permits, man breathes.

Give God praise and worship. God created man and works through him. Humans need God. He is our Helper. "In the beginning God created the heaven and the earth." Genesis 1:1. Boast, in God. Boast, about God. "Thou art my King, O God...In God we boast all the day long, and praise thy name for ever...Psalm 44:4, 8. "JUDGE me, O God, and plead my cause against an ungodly nation: O deliver me from the deceitful and unjust man." Psalm 43:1. "I will bless the Lord at all times: his praise *shall* continually *be* in my mouth. O magnify the Lord with me, and let us exalt his name together. I sought the Lord, and he heard me, and delivered me from all my fears." Psalm 34: 1, 3-4.

Confession publicizes acknowledgement and commitment to live in godly fashion. Does your life harmonize with your profession and confession? If you are blending with worldliness, rather than living for God, press re-start. Draw lines, and build partitions, so worldly people realize differences in godly and ungodly living. "I know thy works, that thou art neither cold nor hot: I would thou wert cold or hot. So then because thou art lukewarm, and neither cold nor hot, I will spue thee out of my mouth." Revelation 3:15-16. Make sure your body does what your mouth confesses; otherwise confusion is imminent.

Public acknowledgement is part of living for Jesus. Secretly knowing Jesus is impossible. His presence is too powerful for concealment. Knowing Jesus and not being afraid, to openly confess Him, is expected and righteous. Profession and confession are requirements. "Nevertheless among the chief rulers also many believed on him; but because of the Pharisees they did not confess *him*, lest they should be put out of the synagogue. For they loved the praise of men more than the praise of God." St. John 12:42-43.

Consequences. Dreamers – leaders - stay in step with righteousness. Reciprocity can be positive, or negative, depending on deeds done. "And whosoever shall offend one of *these* little ones that believe in me, it is better for him that a millstone were hanged about his neck, and he were cast into the sea." St. Mark 9:42.

There are costs for, actions and, inactions. Murmuring, and complaining, is ungodly. Rending only lip service is inaction. *Rarely are talkers doers.* Nondreamers/nonleaders stay in step with designated audiences, whether right or wrong. In cesspool circles, moral values are ignored. Nondreamers blame their leaders for all ills; but when asked for their suggestions or recommendations only murmurings and complaints are given. Unfortunately, nondreamers think demonizing dreamers make them look good and strong. Demonizing dreamers shows jealousy and weakness displaying inhumane tendencies. Sadly, nondreamers are enemies of goodwill. Goodwill's enemies fight positive changes, but endorse reprehensible behaviors; such as, unfairness, negativity, and cruelty. Oftentimes, nondreamers put their own safety at risk hoping to decimate bold, godly, leaders – Bold Eagle-tis-ti-cal Christians. Regrettably, nondreamers waste valuable time, money, and resources, on lip services and inapt complaints. In spite of stupidities, dreamers lead and soar in excellency halls.

Contrasting Eternal Homes. Righteous, and unrighteous, lifestyles determine eternal outcomes. Clearly, **God is always right!** In order to go to heaven, you must choose Jesus Christ. The other alternative leads to endless problems.

Notably, Noah is a righteous man. He and his household is saved from the flood. Everyone else perishes. " And the Lord said unto Noah, Come thou and all thy house into the ark; for thee have I seen righteous before me in this generation...they that went in, went in male and female of all flesh, as God had commanded him: and the Lord shut him in...the flood was forty days upon the earth; and the waters increased, and bare up the ark, and it was lift up above the earth...the waters prevailed, and were increased greatly upon the earth; and the ark went upon the face of the waters...the waters prevailed exceedingly upon the earth...all the high hills, that were under the whole heaven, were covered...all flesh died that moved upon the earth, both of fowl, and of cattle, and of beast, and of every creeping thing that creepeth upon the earth, and every man... in whose nostrils was the breath of life, of all that was in the dry land, died...every living substance was destroyed which was upon the face of the ground, both man, and cattle, and the creeping things, and the fowl of the heaven; and they were destroyed from the earth: and Noah only remained alive, and they that were with him in the ark." Genesis 7:1, 16-19, 21-23.

People ignoring God, and not changing their evil ways, what is their fate? The Bible teaches what He wants for mankind. "Then said Jesus unto them...Verily, verily, I say unto you, I am the door of the sheep. All that ever came before me are thieves and robbers: but the sheep did not hear them. I am the door: by me if any man enter in, he shall be saved, and shall go in and out, and find pasture...I am come that they might have life, and that they might have *it* more abundantly. I am the good shepherd: the good shepherd giveth his life for the sheep" St. John 10:7-11.

Satan is wrong. Convincingly, con artists sit on church pews putting worldly spins on righteous-intentioned endeavors. Alertness on, and off, church pews is wisdom. The Bibles teaches, "...be...wise as serpents, and harmless as doves." St. Matthew 10:16. "The thief cometh not, but for to steal, and to kill, and to destroy: I am come that they might have life, and that they might have *it* more abundantly." St. John 10:10. "But he that is an hireling, and not the shepherd, whose own the sheep are not, seeth the wolf coming, and leaveth the sheep, and fleeth: and the wolf catcheth them, and scattereth the sheep. The hireling fleeth, because he is an hireling, and careth not for the sheep." St. John 10:12-13.

What is your choice? "And thou say in thine heart, My power and the might of *mine* hand hath gotten me this wealth. But thou shalt remember the Lord thy God: for *it is* he that giveth thee power to get wealth, that he may establish his covenant...And it shall be, if thou do at all forget the Lord thy God, and walk after other gods, and serve them, and worship them, I testify against you this day that ye shall surely perish... because ye would not be obedient unto the voice of the Lord your God." Deuteronomy 8:17-20. "...if it seem evil unto you to serve the Lord, choose you this day whom ye will serve...whether the gods which your fathers served that *were* on the other side of the flood…but as for me and my house, we will serve the Lord." Joshua 24:15.

The Creator. God created heaven and earth. "…I am Alpha and Omeg'a, the beginning and the end. I will give unto him that is athrist of the fountain of the water of life freely. He that overcometh shall inherit all things; and I will be his God, and he shall be my son. But the fearful, and unbelieving, and the abominable, and murderers, and whoremongers, and sorcerers, and idolaters, and all liars, shall have their part in the lake which burneth with fire and brimstone: which is the second death." Revelation 21:6-8.

Credit Is Given for Deeds – Good or Bad. Jesus spent his earthly time helping people. Jesus' followers have a calling to lead souls to heaven. Jesus is coming back! Are you ready? "…in every nation he that feareth him and worketh righteousness, is accepted by him. How God anointed Jesus of Nazareth with the Holy Ghost and with power: who went about doing good, and healing all that were oppressed of the devil; for God was with him. Acts 10:35, 38. "Marvel not at this: for the hour is coming, in the which all that are in the graves shall hear his voice, and shall come forth; and they that have done good, unto the resurrection of life; and they that have done evil, unto the resurrection of damnation." St. John 5:28-29. "…many of them that sleep in the dust of the earth shall awake, some to everlasting life, and some to shame *and* everlasting contempt. And they that be wise shall shine as the brightness of the firmament; and they that turn many to righteousness as the stars for ever and ever." Daniel 12:2-3.

Crown. Eternal life, with God, is top award and most precious, gift prepared for mankind. Living for Jesus Christ is the highpoint. Dreamers examine attitudes and actions. Righteous living, faith, and prayer, are keys for crown achievement - heaven homegoing. "All the while my breath *is* in me, and the spirit of God *is* in my nostrils; my lips shall not speak wickedness, nor my tongue utter deceit…till I die I will not remove mine integrity from me. My righteousness I hold fast, and will not let it go. Let mine enemy be as the wicked, and he that riseth up against me as the unrighteous. For what *is* the hope of the hypocrite, though he hath gained, when

God taketh away his soul?" Job 27:3-4, 6-8. "Fear none of those things which thou shalt suffer...be thou faithful until death, and I will give thee a crown of life." Revelation 2:10.

Deterrence. Eagle-tis-ti-cal dreamers watch and pray. Nondreamers' opposition tactics are designed to kill dreams. Adherence, to godly precautions and warnings, keeps dreams alive. Christian, Eagle-tis-ti-cal, dreamers live godly lifestyles. "...mark them which cause divisions and offences contrary to the doctrine which ye have learned; and avoid them. For they that are such serve not our Lord Jesus Christ, but their own belly; and by good words and fair speeches deceive the hearts of the simple... I would have you wise unto that which is good, and simple concerning evil. And the God of peace shall bruise Satan under your feet..." Romans 16:17-20. "For such *are* false apostles, deceitful workers, transforming themselves into the apostles of Christ. And no marvel; for Satan himself is transformed into an angel of light. Therefore *it is* no great thing if his ministers also be transformed as the ministers of righteousness; whose end shall be according to their works." II Corinthians 11:13-15. "Submit yourselves therefore to God. Resist the devil, and he will flee from you." James 7:7.

Denial. Deny ungodly lusts. "For the grace of God that bringeth salvation hath appeared to all men, teaching us that, denying ungodliness and worldly lusts, we should live soberly, righteously, and godly, in this present world; looking for that blessed hope, and the glorious appearing of the great God and our Saviour Jesus Christ..." Titus 2:11-13.

Dependence on God. "Casting all your care upon him; for he careth for you." I Peter 5:7. For avoidance of dream derailments, God's supernatural power is sufficient and available.

Behind veils of secrecy, snares are plotted for the righteous. God provides a way of escape. "There hath no temptation taken you but such as is common to man: but God *is* faithful, who will not suffer you to be tempted above that ye are able; but will with the temptation also make a way to escape, that ye may be able to bear it." I Corinthians 10:13. God sees and knows all.

Discernment – Gift of knowing. "Whoso keepeth the commandment shall feel no evil thing: and a wise man's heart discerneth both time and judgment. Because to every purpose there is time and judgment..." Ecclesiastes 8:5-6. To human eyes, some enemies are visible; but, some are not. Discernment informs eyes, ears, feelings, and intellect. Is Satan your friend? No! Are some of your friends really enemies? Yes! Stay prayful, vigilant, and focused.

Discretion. Appropriate behavior fosters dream materialization. Dreamers acquire knowledge; then act. "The heart of the prudent getteth knowledge; and the ear of the wise seeketh knowledge." Proverbs 18:15.

Doing Jesus' Will. Jesus went about doing good; although He had accusers, persecutors, and conspirators, seeking to slay him. Jesus' followers do His will. Jesus' followers help, give, and keep moving in righteousness. "Fear thou not, for I *am* with thee; be not dismayed, for I *am* thy God: I will strengthen thee; yea, I will help thee; yea, I will uphold thee with the right hand of my righteousness." Isaiah 41:10.

God's Work requires finance, time, and resources – faithful stewardship. Cheerfully, Eagle-tis-ti-cal dreamers give to God's Work. "Then Jesus answered and said unto them, Verily, verily, I say unto you, The son can do nothing of himself, but what he seeth the Father do: for what things soever he doeth, these also doeth the Son likewise. For as the Father raiseth up the dead, and quickeneth *them*; even so the Son quickeneth whom he will. Verily, verily, I say unto you, He that heareth my word and believeth on him that sent me, hath everlasting life, and shall not come into condemnation; but is passed from death unto life. For as the Father hath life in himself; so hath he given to the Son to have life in himself...And hath given him authority to execute judgment, because he is the Son of man. I can of mine own self do nothing: as I hear, I judge: and my judgment is just; because I seek not mine own will, but the will of the Father which hath sent me. How can ye believe, which receive honour one of another, and seek not the honour that *cometh* from God only? Do not think that I will accuse you to the Father: there is *one* that accuseth you, *even* Moses, in whom ye trust. For had ye believed Moses, ye would have believed me: for he wrote of me. But if he believe not his writings, how shall ye believe my words?" St. John 5:19, 21, 24, 26-27, 30, 44-47.

"But Jesus answered them, My Father worketh hitherto, and I work." St. John 5:17. Eagle-tis-ti-cal Christian dreamers live for Jesus and do His Work. Eagle-tis-ti-cal, Jesus-loving, dreamers realize Jesus' importance in every life cell and cycle. God's presence is vital in every facet and decision. Taking advice, from God, is life-sustaining. Confidence in Him is the roadway to happiness and success. Obeying God and being with Him is the best decision in life. No one, or nothing, can take the place of God. Affirmatively, God's place, in human beings' lives, is supreme. God has all answers. He is our Helper, in pleasant places as well as, in troublesome valleys. God knows everything and everybody. God-living offers holistic care. God does awesome things daily. "And the Lord said unto Gideon, The people *are* yet *too* many; bring them down unto the water, and I will try them for thee there: and it shall be, *that* of whom I say unto thee, This shall go with thee; and of whomsoever I say unto thee, This shall not go with thee, the same shall not go." Judges 7:4. God's needed presence in human beings' lives cannot be underestimated or overstated. Heaven is real. Anyone with common sense does not want to make hell home. Jesus gave his life so humans can spend eternity, in heaven, with Him. When preparations are unmade to go to heaven, Hade is the only other alternative. "And when I saw him, I fell at his feet as dead. And he laid his right hand upon me, saying unto me, Fear not; I am the first and the last: I *am* he that liveth, and was dead; and, behold, I am alive forevermore, Amen; and have the keys of hell and of death. Write the things which thou hast seen, and the things which are, and the things which shall be hereafter..." Revelation 1:17-19.

Drawing Souls. Christian Eagle-tis-ti-cal dreamers' mission includes guiding souls to Christ. On the other hand, nondreamers wreak chaos on church pews causing stumblingblocks and possibly some soul losses. Satan works through cohorts wherever he finds them.

Separation is the same as "respect of persons." Man-made innuendos and partitions create friction among peoples. Peoples are made in God's image.

Wickedly, and conveniently, factions are mesmerized with worldly tempo-ralities and do not abide by God's Word seeming to forget recompenses, vengeance, and accountability. Who dares belittling God's creation??? Arrogance cost many souls to end up in that eternal wrong, hot, place!

Consumption in one's self meaningless chatter, tasks, and endeav-ors, dumbs down. Minds and talents are wasted because nondreamers' personal, ill-fated aspirations leave God out. Leaving God out is impru-dent, irresponsible. Dreamers put God first asking Him for guidance. Nondreamers are intolerant of faithful stewards and are responsible for much chaos, not only on church pews, but all environments. Nondreamers deceive. Seemingly innocent approaches are not innocent at all; but full of wickedness. Beware of dream snatchers! Useless drama and mind waste amounts to time and resources' loss. Chaos-intenders (nondreamers) capi-talize on weak-mindedness. Psychologically speaking, consider minds as battlegrounds. Battlegrounds are full of uncertainties, dangers, and sor-rows. Knowing Jesus personally, consoles and guards hearts. Jesus pro-vides true happiness and safety. Satan deceives by giving false hopes and imaginations. Jesus is the Only One Who provides true happiness.

Righteous consumption devoid pew chaos, idleness, wicked separa-tions, and other nondreaming tactics.

Dreamer Ethics. Live for God. Give Him mind, body and soul. Godly ambassadors edify Helping others, particularly, the poor, is righ-teousness and humane.

Eagle-tis-ti-cal dreamers know God, having personal relationships with Him. Dreamers acknowledge God's Might and seek His approval. What should Christians do daily? Practice righteousness. Righteousness exalts. "Righteousness exalteth a nation: but sin *is* a reproach to any peo-ple." Proverbs 14:34.

Living, preaching, and teaching what "thus saith the Lord" is dream-ers' lifestyle. Personal relationship with God is journey from earth to heaven.

Sin reaps deficiency and debasement. "Hear, ye *that are* far off, what I have done; and ye, *that are* near, acknowledge my might. The sinners…

are afraid; fearfulness hath surprised the hypocrites. Who among us shall dwell with the devouring fire? who among us shall dwell with everlasting burnings? He that walketh righteously, and speaketh uprightly; he that depiseth the gain of oppressions, that shaketh his hands from holding of bribes, that stoppeth his ears from hearing of blood, and shutteth his eyes from seeing evil; He shall dwell on high: his place of defence *shall be* the munitions of rocks: bread shall be given him; his waters *shall be* sure. Thine eyes shall see the king in his beauty: they shall behold the land that is very far off." Isaiah 33:13-17.

Dreamers upgrade. Nondreamers' sequestration, mediocrity, and dumb-downs are heartbreaking and regressive. Publicly and boldly, Joseph voices his dreams to his brothers. Dreamers' farsightedness display hope. Undoubtedly, God created heaven and earth. Anyone saying humans or forces created the universe speaks untruthfulness. The Holy Bible is Truth. Beliefs, not backed up by The Holy Bible, is untruth.

Edification. Persuasively, positive role modeling radiates from goodwill-building dreamers. In contrast, nondreamers destroy goodness, designing and designating ill-wills. Ill-will includes opposition tactics; such as, reputation assassination, lying, stealing, and disseminating hate.

Pew nondreamers formulate immobilization strategies. Through fasting and prayer, deviant ploys can be overcome. Pew villains are intrusive, reckless, bullies. Destroyers emphasize "faking" and "saving face" rather than truthfulness. While core problems are unattended, preoccupation with destructive outlets and mediocrities is nursed. Nondreamers' life concepts are disorienting and chaotic.

Nondreamers stalk dreamers. Because of unaddressed personal reasons, they choose not to be dreamers. Instead, they choose congregation and community harassment. When dreamers fast and pray, nondreamer opposition tactics are thwarted.

Secularism is a stronghold. Inevitably, building others up is a state of mind. Since some grown-ups are still children, deceit is used prevalently. "That we *henceforth* be no more children, tossed to and fro, and carried about with every wind of doctrine, by the sleight of men, *and* cunning craftiness, whereby they lie in wait to deceive; but speaking the truth in love, may grow up into him in all things, which is the head, *even* Christ...be renewed in the spirit of your mind. And that ye put on the new man, which after God is created in righteousness and true holiness. Wherefore putting away lying, speak every man truth with his neighbor: for we are members one of another. Neither give place to the devil. Let him that stole steal no more: but rather let him labour, with *his* hands the thing which is good, that he may have to give to him that needeth." Ephesians 4:14-15, 23-25, 27-28.

Pew violence is unfavorable, stifling, annulling edification. Uplift spirits. "Let no corrupt communication proceed out of your mouth, but that which is good to the use of edifying, that it may minister grace to the hearers. Let all bitterness, and...evil speaking...be put away from you...And be ye kind one to another, tenderhearted, forgiving one another, even as God for Christ's sake hath forgiven you." Ephesians 4:29, 31-32.

Eloquence. The Lord calls, and sends, who He pleases to do His Work. Men-pleasers abuse, denounce, and scoff at His ambassadors. But God comes to see about His people. "...the Lord said, I have surely seen the affliction of my people...and have heard their cry by reason of their taskmasters; for I know their sorrows; and I am come down to deliver them...and to bring them up out of that land unto a good land and a large, unto a land flowing with milk and honey...Now therefore, behold, the cry of the children...is come unto me: and I have also seen the oppression... Come now therefore, and I will send thee...that thou mayest bring forth my people..." Exodus 3:7-10.

When God calls His ambassadors, His equipment and qualifications are sufficient. He is with us always; but sometimes we say to God, "Who *am* I, that I should go...and that I should bring forth...out? And He said, Certainly I will be with thee; and this *shall be* a token unto thee, that I have sent thee: When thou hast brought forth...ye shall serve God..." Exodus 3:11-12.

God gives signs and performs wonders. He touches our mouths. Publicly acknowledging God is part of our Christian walk. When God calls us to do His Work, the devil tells us we are not good enough. Satan seeks to suppress, and marginalize, God's ambassadors. Satan hates ambassadors who brag on God. God's people are good enough. He chooses and calls His workers. Work is plentiful in His vineyard. Souls are at stake.

Clearly, Satan is dissatisfied with God and His followers. Even though Satan's opposition tactics are brutal, God avenges His own. Satan wants dreamers to give up and quit living and ministering for Jesus. Dreamers, stay focused and do not stop doing God's Will.

"And Moses said unto the Lord, O my Lord, I *am* not eloquent, neither heretofore, nor since thou hast spoken unto thy servant: but I *am* slow of speech, and of a slow tongue. And the Lord said unto him, Who hath made man's mouth? Or who maketh the dumb, or deaf, or the seeing, or the blind? Have not I the Lord? Now therefore go, and I will be with thy mouth, and teach thee what thou shalt say. And he said, O my Lord, send, I pray thee, by the hand *of him whom* thou wilt send…the anger of the Lord was kindled against Moses, and he said, *Is* not Aaron the Levite thy brother? I know…he can speak well…And thou shalt speak unto him, and put words in his mouth: and I will be with thy mouth, and will teach you what he shall do. And he shall be thy spokesman unto the people: and he shall be, *even* he shall be to thee instead of a mouth, thou shalt be to him instead of God." Exodus 4:10-16.

God is powerful! He calls whom He pleases, when He pleases, and how He pleases. He does things His way. God's eloquence is perfection. Men-pleasers' standards are worldliness. Many worldly standards are indecent, immoral, and unethical. God's Word teaches righteousness. Satan plots evil scams. Listening to Jesus is safety and trustworthiness. Listening, to the devil, is irresponsible and destructive behavior. The devil is a counterfeiting liar.

When God calls us to His Work, excuses are unnecessary. God advises and equips dreamers with boldness, speech, helper(s), education, supplies, resources, etc. Obey God rather than men-pleasers. He does not do things half-heartedly. Neither should we. He is Completion – Wholeness.

Endorsements. Dreamers live for God's approval and glorification. Seeking man's walks, and walls, of fames, are fruitless. In order to receive man's backing, expectations of saying and doing what He commands whole-heartedly, is prerequisite.

When protocols are inconsistent with God's Word, dreamers reject them; but, nondreamers do not. Satan purchases souls for millions of dollars, along with so-called opportunities. Selling self to the devil betrays self. He is enlist millions of clients doomed for **eternal, hot, accommodations.**

Names written in the Lamb's

Book of Life counts. All other books matter nothing. God's promises are reliable. Men's enticements are temporal and unreliable. On all fronts, God offers the best anyone could possibly receive. Spending eternity in heaven is unfathomably wonderful. Souls are priceless. Acceptance of temporalities - monies, diamonds, and opportunities - is a cheap price to place on your eternal life. Worldly pleasures may seem gainful and joyous for a season; but heaven is eternal. Of course, it is your choice whether you accept a few worldly items in exchange for your soul. Forgetting God is the worst decision anyone could possibly make.

Dreamers put God first. God made and owns heaven and earth. He created prosperity. There is no need to commit sin; namely, wealth acquisition. Trust God. Live for Him. He loves you unconditionally. When we stand before God, if your names are written in His book, you are saved. Otherwise..."Hearken unto me, ye that know righteousness, the people in whose heart *is* my law; fear ye not the reproach of men, neither be ye afraid of their revilings. For the moth shall eat them up like a garment, and the worm shall eat them like wool: but my righteousness shall be for ever, and my salvation from generation to generation. Awake, awake, put on strength, O arm of the Lord; awake, as in the ancient days, in generations of old..." Isaiah 51:7-9.

Entertainer. God's entertainment is flawless. When He uses humor, it is funny – not forced false laughter. Jesus living involves physical and emotional behaviors. Sinful living, demeans, stressing the body and psyche.

Phases of life differ – laughter and sorrow. In each phase, God is present. Interaction between God and man is serious; but, at times, amusing.

Why? He satisfies *all* dimensions of life. His mind, soul, and body therapies are heavenly. "To every *thing there is* a season, and a time to every purpose under the heaven…A time to weep, and a time to laugh; a time to mourn, and a time to dance…He hath made every *thing* beautiful in his time: also he hath set the world in their heart, so that no man can find out the work that God maketh from the beginning to the end. I know that, whatsoever God doeth, it shall be for ever: nothing can be put to it, nor any thing taken from it: and God doeth *it*, that *men* should fear before him. I said in mine heart, God shall judge the righteous and the wicked: for *there is* a time there for every purpose and for every work." Ecclesiastes 3:1, 4, 11, 14, 17.

Eternity. God provides everlasting gifts; namely, salvation and eternal life. Individuals make choices whether to receive or reject His gifts. "THESE words spake Jesus, and lifted up his eyes to heaven, and said, Father, the hour is come; glorify thy son, that thy Son also may glorify thee…should give eternal life to as many as thou hast given him. And this is life eternal, that they might know thee the only true God, and Jesus Christ, whom thou hast sent. I have glorified thee on the earth: I have finished the work which thou gavest me to do. And now, O Father, glorify thou me with thine own self with the glory which I had with thee before the world was. I have given them thy word; and the world hath hated them, because they are not of the world, even as I am not of the world. I pray not that thou shouldest take them out of the world, but that thou shouldest keep them from the evil. Sanctify them through thy truth: thy word is truth. As thou hast sent me into the world, even so have I also sent them into the world." St. John 17:1-5, 14-15, 17-18.

Choose carefully. Heaven, or hell, is final destination. Emphatically, final destinations are permanent. Heaven is epitome of peace everlasting. The requirement for heaven eternity is keeping God's commandments. "…as for me and my house we shall serve the Lord." Joshua 24:15. Keeping not God's commandments purchase tickets to eternal torment. If worldliness sinks your heavenly ship, hell awaits.

Ethical Living. Dreamers' live moral lives not bowing to graven images. The devil has plenty temporal snares; but wise people do not depart from God's Word. "Depart from me, ye evildoers: for I will keep the commandments of my God." Psalm 119:115. "Depart from me, all ye workers of iniquity; for the Lord hath heard the voice of my weeping." Psalm 6:8. "And then will I profess unto them, I never knew you: depart from me, ye that work iniquity." St. Matthew 7:23.

Expound. Psychologically, balance and discipline show restraint sense. Bible teaching, in its entirety, is right and important. Temperance shows wisdom.

Even if adultery or other sins are not committed, stealing and lying is wrong. Bragging on commandments kept, but unwilling to discuss the ones not kept, is hypocritical. Hypocrisy negatively affects audiences; because your behaviors are known. Lifestyle contradicts teachings. Lies and cover-ups are unworkable and adversarial. Sinfulness deserves repentance, not cover-ups. **All sin is wrong.**

To nondreamers, fabrication of the truth is mainstream practice. Any form of sin is wrong. Just because sin is widespread does not make it right. Itching ears' intention is to cloud motives. Clearness is unexpected for pew problem-makers. Their lifestyle calls for hopelessness and grief sessions. Each recruit is enlisted for corrupt communications and opposition tactics against dreamers. Technically, unless righteous dreamers are steadfast, pew leeches mushroom. "He that walketh uprightly walketh surely: but he that perverteth his ways shall be known. He that winketh with the eye causeth sorrow: but a prating fool shall fall." Proverbs 10:9-10. Precisely, deeds are noted in The Book of Life and consequences are assured.

Investment, in worldliness, is unsatisfactory. "For what is a man profited, if he shall gain the whole world, and lose his own soul? or what shall a man give in exchange for his soul?" St. Matthew 16:26. "For we brought nothing into *this* world, *and it is* certain we can carry nothing out." I Timothy 6:7. Many desert God for people and – temporal - worldly goods. Attention to things above spells heavenly asset maximization which is fruitful and lasting.

God strengthens and gives opportunities. Rationally, there is no reason to leave God. Trust in God not in man. "For the word of the Lord *is* right; and all his works *are done* in truth. He loveth righteousness and judgment: the earth is full of the goodness of the Lord. Let all the earth fear the Lord: let all the inhabitants of the world stand in awe of him. The Lord bringeth the counsel of the heathen to nought: he maketh the devices of the people of none effect. There is no king saved by the multitude of an host: a mighty man is not delivered by much strength. An horse *is* a vain thing for safety: neither shall he deliver *any* by his great strength. Behold, the eye of the Lord *is* upon them that fear him, upon them that hope in his mercy. To deliver their soul from death, and to keep them alive in famine. Our soul waiteth for the Lord: he *is* our help and our shield." Psalm 33:4-5, 8, 10, 16-20.

Fairness. God made man in His image. He is not respecter of persons.

Dreamers are even-handed. Love is a part of the equality equation. "Shalt thou reign, because thou closest *thyself* in cedar? Did not thy father eat and drink, and do judgment and justice *and* then *it was* well with him? He judged the cause of the poor and needy; then *it was* well with *him: was* not this to know me, saith the Lord? But thine eyes and thine heart is not but for thy covetousness, and for to shed innocent blood, and for oppression, and for violence, to do *it*. I spake unto thee in thou prosperity; *but* thou saidst, I will not hear. This *hath been* thy manner from thy youth, that thy obeyedst not my voice. The wind shall eat up all thy pastors, and thy lovers shall be in captivity: surely then shalt thou be ashamed and confounded for all thy wickedness." Jeremiah 22:15-17, 21, 22. "He that hath pity upon the poor lendeth unto the Lord; and that which he hath given will he pay him again." Proverbs 19:17.

Unfortunately, many millionaires become rich because of sleight balances. Oftentimes, riches (ill-gotten gains) are handed-down spoils. "Privileged" history shows much injustice. Injustices carry negative impacts. Needy persons are starved, worked to death, and murdered. Perpetuators gain improperly causing suffering and harm to innocent, poor, needy, souls. Free labor lines pockets. What happens to souls performing free labor? Free labor is like being thrown in a pit and no one lets you out. Unlikely, perpetuators, or anyone benefitting from free labor gives a helping hand. This type injustice holds rich and poor citizens in limbo; because fairness has flown the coup. Some poor people are treated worse than animals. Slave labor hurts and kills people. Dishonest monies made from free labor lie in wealthy millionaires and billionaires' coffers. Boasting about ill-gotten gain is pathetic. Christian dreamers stand for fairness; however, nondreamers do not.

Fairness cries out haunting foundations of so-called self-made millionaires and billionaires who benefit from ill-gotten gains. Instead of softer, justice cries become louder and cannot be silenced. Unfair minds want everything for self; therefore, they are unwilling to love neighbors as themselves. Unfortunately, some people steal, kill, and destroy for wealth. Remorsefulness is far from hard-hearted, greedy, perpetuators. Evil acts are unhidden from God as they are from some men. Get right with God and stay right. Money, or any other resource, is not worth losing your soul. Individually, accountability comes at appointed times.

What does your record reflect? Are you harboring and/or nursing hatred, respect of persons, stolen properties, goods, and services? "Defend the poor and fatherless: do justice to the afflicted and needy. Deliver the poor and needy: rid them out of the hand of the wicked." Psalm 82:3-4. Do you treat everyone right or do you show respect of persons? If your life record is not reflection of God's Word, now is the time for lifestyle revision. Revise actions, according to God's Word, before it is too late. Change before final appointment. "He that overcometh shall inherit all things; and I will be his God, and he shall be my son. And there shall in no wise enter into it anything that defileth, neither *whatsoever* worketh abomination, or *maketh* a lie: but they which are written in the Lamb's book of life." Revelation 21:7, 27. "He that is unjust, let him be unjust still: and he which is filthy, let him be filthy still: and he that is righteous: let him be righteous still: and he that is holy, Let him be holy still. And, behold, I come quickly; and my reward is with me, to give every man according as his work shall be. I am Alpha and Omega, the beginning and the end, the first and the last." Revelation 22:11-13.

Hopefully, pit mongers change their hearts to God's Word. Justice pursuits are righteous and honorable. Turn from wickedness and do right. Earthly goods are left here. Bold, Eagle-tis-ti-cal dreamers, teach and preach the unadulterated gospel. Teach all of God's Word. God's Word is Whole. Teaching the Full Gospel is righteous. When the Full Gospel is not preached, much is left out, which is not good. "Thou shalt not steal." Exodus 20:15. "Every way of a man *is* right in his own eyes: but the Lord pondereth the hearts. The getting of treasures by a lying tongue *is* a vanity tossed to and fro of them that seek death. The robbery of the wicked shall destroy them; because they refuse to do judgment." Proverbs 21:2, 6, 7. The lip of truth shall be established for ever: but a lying tongue *is* but for a moment. Deceit *is* in the heart of them that imagine evil: but to the counsellors of peace is joy." Proverbs 12:19-20. "A false witness shall not be unpunished, and *he that* speaketh lies shall perish." Proverbs 19:9.

"In the way of righteousness *is* life; and *in* the pathway *thereof there is* no death." Proverbs 12:28.

Fairness Management Systems. This book focuses on Joseph's dream vocalization, opposition received for aspirations, and inevitable responsibilities. Although Joseph was innocent, he became a victim both in his family and the criminal justice system. He caused neither predicament, but in the center of both.

Apparently, many systems are intentionally unfair; specifically, some jail and imprisonment criteria. All citizens are not treated uniformly. Many overseers, and managers, are unfair and prejudiced. Automatically, biased minds are geared toward unjust implementations and outcomes causing innocent people and their families much unnecessary suffering. Truthfully, this explains why some prisoners say they are imprisoned for crimes they did not commit. Reportedly and randomly, many innocent persons are randomly grabbed up and incarcerated solely on biased grounds. Under bias, suppressive, conditions, healthy individuals, families, communities, societies, and countries, dwindle. Actually, unfairness affects everyone negatively.

Fair-minded, reputable, thinkers, believe many innocent people sit in prisons while many criminals roam in society committing crimes. These roamers are never jailed. Without serving deserved prison sentences, non-dreamers brag taking comfort seeing, and knowing, innocent citizens are blamed for crimes they did not commit. While taunting dreamers, non-dreamers hurt in various ways.

Joseph was jailed because the king's wife lied on him. "…one witness shall not testify against any person *to cause him* to die." Numbers 35:30. Stereotypical, profiling, lands innocent men and women in jail. As long as any public administrators and foundations are corrupt, results are tainted yielding unfair sentences and plights.

Just as freedom opportunities are withheld from deserving applicants, so are prison sentences withheld from many deserving criminals. Perpetrators answer to the aforementioned atrocities. Fair-minded, public administrators, are essential for public administrations; otherwise, many innocent people continue wrongful treatments. Unfair treatment is sinful and shameful. Dignitaries, duplicities, and complicities, responsible for these atrocities, will stand before God. God holds us accountable for our actions and inactions. Terribly, man does not always hold man accountable. Disregarding "justice for all" comes up again. "Be not deceived; God is not mocked: for whatsoever a man soweth, that shall he also reap." Galatians 6:7.

Having to answer for respect of person actions is serious. Those participating in, and supporting, wickedness is equally guilty as primary instigators. Immediate changes are prudent. The Bible teaches against "respect of persons."

Faith. Faith consists of hands-on experiences. Apply action to dreams, or death occurs. Faith plus action equals dream realizations. "Now faith is the substance of things hoped for, the evidence of things not seen. By faith Noah, being warned of God of things not seen as yet, moved with fear, prepared an ark to the saving of his house; by the which he condemned the world, and became heir of the righteousness which is by faith." Hebrews 11:1, 7.

Obediently, Noah heard and acted on God's Word. If he had not, what would have happened to him, his family, and other ark occupants? Faith does not encompass hate. Hate is sinful. Faith and prejudice cannot coexist. Conjunctively, faith works with words, works, and knowledge. Faith is shown by obedience to God therefore response to His commands and promises. Prudence and coordination choose heavenly wisdom and shuns earthly insight. Choose who your relationship is with, God or the devil. Simultaneously serving both is impossible. Choosing God is life. Undoubtedly, adherence to the devil causes travesties and soul loss.

Farsightedness is another word for discernment. Looking ahead (prudence) saves time. "Where *there is* no vision, the people perish…" Proverbs 29:18. Preventive care, contemplation, and settlement eliminates unnecessary problems, sufferings, and catastrophic tendencies. Dreamers embrace prudent outcomes.

Survival – spiritual, physical, and mental – is dependence on God. Any other source is nearsightedness and unreliability. Dreamers' good judgment circumvents complications. "…lest I should be exalted above measure…there was given to me a thorn in the flesh, the messenger of Satan to buffet me, lest I should be exalted above measure. For this thing I besought the Lord thrice, that it might depart from me…And he said unto me, My grace is sufficient for thee: for my strength is made perfect in weakness. Most gladly therefore will I rather glory in my infirmities, that the power of Christ may rest upon me." II Corinthians 12:7-9.

Stay focused on your dreams. Everything good, *to* you, is not good *for* you. "All things are lawful for me, but all things are not expedient: all things are lawful for me, but all things edify not." I Corinthians 10:23.

Feast. Invitation, to spend eternity in heaven, is sent. Are you going? "He that hath an ear, let him hear what the Spirit saith unto the churches; To him that overcometh will I give to eat of the tree of life, which is in the midst of the paradise of God." Revelation 2:7. Heaven's, eternal, righteous, party never ends.

Gathering Unto Him. Dreamers are warned to stand fast. The Bible teaches us not to be troubled "as that the day of Christ is at hand."

II Thessalonians 2:1. Living according to God's Word is life security. His Word envelopes mankind's whole being.

Nondreamers have faking proclivities and wears false faces. False teachings and deceivableness keeps minds and hearts in uproars. The devil tells lies and destroys lives. "Let no man deceive you by any means: for *that day shall not come*, except there come a falling away first, and that man of sin be revealed, the son of perdition; who opposeth and exalteth himself above all that is called God, or that is worshipped; so that he as God sitteth in the temple of God, shewing himself that he is God. And now ye know what withholdeth that he might be revealed in his time. And with all deceivableness of unrighteousness in them that perish; because they received not the love of the truth, that they might be saved. And for this cause God shall send them strong delusion, that they should believe a lie: that they all might be damned who believed not the truth, but had pleasure in unrighteousness." II Thessalonians 2:3-4, 6, 10-12.

Embrace God's Word. He is coming back again.

Given. The Holy Bible is Perfection. God keeps promises. Pureness and truth abides. "Put not your trust in princes, *nor* in the son of man, in whom *there is* no help." Psalm 146:3. Believe God! Not the devil! Agree with God! Disagree with the devil!

God's Is Calling. Are you answering? "Then I said, I will not make mention of him, nor speak any more in his name. But *his word* was in my heart as a burning fire shut up in my bones, and I was weary with forebearing, and I could not *stay*. But the Lord *is* with me as a mighty terrible one: therefore my persecutors shall stumble, and they shall not prevail: they shall be greatly ashamed; for they shall not prosper: *their* everlasting confusion shall never be forgotten. But, O Lord of hosts, that triest the righteous, *and* seest the reins and the heart, let me see thy vengeance on them: for unto thee have I opened my cause." Jeremiah 20:9, 11-12.

God's Eyes. Simultaneously, God sees right, left, up, and down at the same time. "For the eyes of the Lord run to and fro throughout the whole earth, to shew himself strong in the behalf of *them* whose heart *is* perfect toward him..." II Chronicles 16:9.

God is looking, although Satan convinces some people otherwise. God is attentive to detail. Scripture says, "For the eyes of the Lord *are* over the righteous, and his ears *are open* unto their prayers: but the face of the Lord *is* against them that do evil." I Peter 3:12.

Happiness is measured by God's standards, not man's contentment or prerogatives. Godly exhilaration provides life-lifts and life-changing experiences.

Heaven. Even though less people choose heaven than hell, God's fan base is bold, loyal, and marching to heaven. God's Word says, "Enter ye in at the strait gate: for wide *is* the gate, and broad *is* the way, that leadeth to destruction, and many there be which go in thereat. Because strait *is* the gate, and narrow *is* the way, which leadeth unto life, and few there be that find it." St. Matthew 7:13-14.

Apparently, many people do not seriously consider sin ramifications, fire, and brimstone. Proper Bible study is imperative and relevant.

False witnesses attempt to classify The Holy Bible as outdated. Hypocritical environments have motivation for deceit, attempting to hide sins and evil. Among dreamers, wicked schemes such as false revisionism are not nurtured or encouraged.

Dreamers welcome truth; whereas, nondreamers deride truth. Righteousness is not a joke, but a matter of eternal life. Faking leads to eternal damnation.

God's Messengers. God's messengers (apostles, prophets, evangelists, pastors, and teachers) are preaching and teaching His gospel to the entire world before He returns. The Holy Ghost is called "the Spirit of truth." The "unsaved" cannot receive the "Spirit of truth" because of spiritual blindness and refusal to believe God. Nevertheless, His messengers are charged with delivering His Word to humanity. It is your choice whether you accept, or reject, His salvation gift.

Salvation acceptance, or rejection, has Biblical consequences. When God saves souls from sin, it feels like waking up from a – sinful – sleep or trance. Deliverance is seen and felt. Evidently, as you walk with God, it becomes clearer and clearer that God has delivered you from Satan's bondage – slavery. "...like as Christ was raised up from the dead by the glory of the Father, even so we also should walk in newness of life. For if we have been planted together in the likeness of his death, we shall be also in *the likeness* of *his* resurrection: Knowing this, that our old man is crucified with *him*, that the body of sin might be destroyed, that henceforth we would not serve sin. Let not sin therefore reign in your mortal body, that ye should obey it in the lusts thereof." Romans 6:4-6, 12.

Who do you serve? God? or Satan? Choosing God, or Satan, is ongoing preparation. Righteous lifestyles make daily decisions, whether heaven is eternal home, or not. Each person is responsible for choices. "Know ye not, that to whom ye yield yourselves servants to obey, his servants ye are to whom ye obey; whether of sin unto death, or of obedience unto righteousness? But God be thanked, that ye were the servants of sin, but ye have obeyed from the heart that form of doctrine which was delivered you. Being then made free from sin, ye became the servants of righteousness...for as ye have yielded your members servants to uncleanness and to iniquity unto iniquity; even so now yield your members servants to righteousness unto holiness. For when ye were the servants of sin, ye were free from righteousness. What fruit had ye then in those things whereof ye are now ashamed? for the end of those things *is* death. But now being made free from sin, and become servants to God, ye have your fruit unto holiness, and the end everlasting life. For the wages of sin *is* death; but the gift of God *is* eternal life." Romans 6:16-23.

Simply, following and serving "mere" beauty is unwise and unsafe. Satan was strikingly beautiful. "Thine heart was lifted up because of thy beauty, thy hast corrupted thy wisdom by reason of thy brightness: I will cast thee to the ground..." Ezekiel 28:17. Some beauties are killers, swindlers, liars, and thieves. The devil uses gorgeous people and luxuries for betrayals and destructions. Sometimes, beauty taints; but, holiness gives confidence, influence, and temperance. Holy Ghost-filled saints avoid conformity. Worldliness conformism is sinful.

When Jesus was on earth with his disciples, he was challenged with many attacks. Jesus' followers are also attacked. Today, believers are confronted because we love Jesus and follow Him.

Idols are set up to confuse, manipulate, and destroy. "For there shall arise false Christs, and false prophets…insomuch that, if *it were* possible, they shall deceive the very elect." St. Matthew 24:24.

Satan offers counterfeits. Idols may be people and/or things – graven images. Destruction is in the land. Be godly, be wise, and be careful. Jesus is coming back. Get ready, and stay ready, to meet Jesus. Getting into worldly lusts is sinfulness. Holiness escorts us to heaven.

Help. Ask God for assistance. He is in every place simultaneously and can do anything but fail. "Give us help from trouble: for vain is the help of man. Through God we shall do valiantly: for he *it is that* shall tread down our enemies." Psalm 108:12-13.

Dependence on man is failure. Trust, in God, causes fear to flee – not afraid what man can do or say. Jesus delivers feet from slides and falls.

Helping the Poor. Trusting God, merciful dreamers start cutting fat "at the top." Dreamers enjoy sharing with the poor. God blesses "helps ministries." Blessing needy people is fulfilling. Poor people use programs set up specifically for the needy and disadvantaged. Intentionally, these programs help people claw out of poverty barrels, but unmerciful non-dreamers shut lids. Helping others is meaningful. Mean-spiritedness such as equal opportunity shutdowns and cruel fund eliminations for poor, suffering, people, constitutes inhumaneness.

Somehow, memories lose their grips. When some inhumane persons were poor and using helps programs, advocating food-help cutoffs, medical help eliminations, or any other help eliminations, were not considered done. But now, uncaring millionaires slice needy programs. Now, it is easy for inhumane millionaires to neglect the poor; because they no longer need the programs. Needy people are now inhumane millionaires' scapegoats.

At some life points, millionaires experienced poor, living standards and poverty perplexities. These millionaires should be the first ones to step up to their "millionaire plates" and help the poor with many slices of help. Remember, you were helped with the same programs that you now denounce and defund! Riches, biasness, negligence, bigotry, and cruelty, clog memories and shut doors for others.

Some millionaires have not known poverty; but still have an obligation to help the poor. Rich and poor people have consciences and are accountable to God. Some consciences are compassionate; others are not. Unfortunately, when some people gain all they need; shutdowns and hurting the poor become their priorities. Caring, and helping only family members, and forgetting others, is ungodly. Selfish policies, and actions, cause distress and preventable circumstances. Physical, and mental affluence relocations does not negate helping the poor responsibilities. God disapproves laughter at housing, joblessness, hunger, and hurts of suffering people. The Holy Bible teaches us how to help the poor, not mistreat the poor. "To have respect of persons *is* not good: for for a piece of bread *that* man will transgress." Proverbs 28:21. "The righteous *man* wisely considereth the house of the wicked for *their* wickedness. Whoso stoppeth his ears at the cry of the poor, he also shall cry himself, but shall not be heard." Proverbs 21:12-13.

In life, sometimes, abhorred people (which are used as scapegoats) are loving and helpful; because the love of God is in their hearts. Dreamers love their enemies. God holds us accountable for our actions – how we treat each other. God is looking at our hearts. God avenges His People. He sees every poor and every rich person. He is no respecter of persons. With God, each individual receives fair treatment. "But whoso hath this world's good, and seeth his brother have need, and shutteth up his bowels of *compassion* from him, how dwelleth the love of God in him? My little children, let us not love in word, neither in tongue; but in deed and in truth. And hereby we know that we are of the truth, and shall assure our hearts before him." I John 3:17-19.

Hypocrisy says you care, without showing care. Unfortunately, as soon as many people become rich, roots are forgotten (purposely dissolved). For the rest of their lives, running from the inner man and trying to forget prior poverty is the new game plan. What a preposterous lifestyle lie! Our past is part of our lives. Lying does not erase greed, covetousness, or hyprocisy. Good, faithful, stewards help the poor.

HIGH on JESUS. His High Stays High. His High is authentic (eternal). "I sought in my heart to give myself unto wine, yet acquainting mine heart with wisdom; and to lay hold on folly, till I might see what *was* that good for the sons of men, which they should do under the heaven all the days of their life. I made me great works; I builded me houses; I planted me vineyards…And whatsoever mine eyes desired I kept not from them, I withheld not my heart from any joy; for my heart rejoiced in all my labour: and this was my portion of all my labour. Then I looked on all the works that my hands had wrought, and on the labour that I had labored to do: and, behold, all *was* vanity and vexation of spirit, and *there was* no profit under the sun. And I turned myself to behold wisdom, and madness, and folly: for what *can* the man *do* that cometh after the king?…Then I saw that wisdom excelleth folly, as far as light excelleth darkness." Ecclesiastes 2:3-4, 10-13.

Holy Bible. Looking through God's Word - lenses - what do you see? Perfection. God's Word is Credibility and Finality.

Sinners watch Christians who claim to know God. Understandably, sinners wonder why many people who claim to know Him live the same as people who do not claim to know God.

Bible study is thorough workout for mind, soul, and body. Holy Bible - spiritual education - is truth directly from our Creator and linkage to heaven. "…work out your own salvation with fear and trembling." Philippians 2:12. "Study to shew thyself approved unto God, a workman that needeth not to be ashamed, rightly dividing the word of truth." II Timothy 2:15. "All scripture *is* given by inspiration of God, and *is* profitable for doctrine, for reproof, for correction, for instruction in righteous: That the man of God may be perfect, thoroughly furnished unto all good works." II Timothy 3:16-17.

Achievement, of earthly degrees, is superb, but temporal. Study, commitment, and concentration is required for spiritual and secular studies. Heavenly homegoing is the ultimate prize. If you attain every degree possible, but go to eternal heat, what is accomplished?

"Perverse disputings of men of corrupt minds, and destitute of the truth, supposing that gain is godliness: from such withdraw thyself. But godliness with contentment is great gain." I Timothy 6:5-6.

Include God in all decision-making. His input and output are fair, correct, and lasting. God knows what is best. "...Naked came I out of my mother's womb, and naked shall I return...the Lord gave, and the Lord hath taken away; blessed be the name of the Lord." Job 1:21.

Spiritual, and secular, educations have opportunities. Truly, times are perilous. Wisdom is needed. God gives wisdom abundantly. Partnership with The Holy Bible and righteous lifestyle yield joy and eternality. Hope is found in God. Wrongness is subjection to unhappiness. Hopelessness is found in Satan.

Dreamers experience righteousness and happiness simultaneously. Nondreamers indulge in wrongness and temporalities. Pure hearts over-power wickedness and falsification. Smiles try masking impurities and broken hearts. Be smart enough to avoid hell.

Holy Spirit. "Nevertheless, I tell you the truth; it is expedient for you that I go away: for if I go not away, The Comforter will not come unto you; but if I depart, I will send him unto you. And when he come, he will reprove the world of sin, and of righteousness, and of judgment. Howbeit when he, the Spirit of truth, is come, he will guide you into all truth: for he shall not speak of himself; but whatsoever he shall hear, *that* shall he speak: and he will shew you things to come." St. John 16:7, 8, 13.

The Holy Spirit teaches and guides believers. The Holy Spirit lives and acts, steering people to truth. The Word of God tells the truth. Itching ears only care to hear, recite, and recognize certain parts of God's Word, while ignoring others. The Spirit of Truth avoids adding to, or taking from, God's Word.

Itching ears are uncomfortable with the whole truth. Perpetually, itching ears feast on chaos and wickedness leading to illusions. Lifestyles are built on pretense, lies, uncertainty, and ill-gotten gain. Ill-gotten gain causes unrest and false security. Because of misdeeds, perpetuators are afraid. Unfortunately, their wickedness causes innocent, quiet, people suffering. "Thus saith the Lord...I will not turn away *the* punishment thereof; because they sold the righteous for silver, and the poor for a pair of shoes...and commanded the prophets, saying, Prophesy not. Behold, I am pressed under you, as a cart is pressed *that is* full of sheaves. Therefore the flight shall perish from the swift, and the strong shall not strengthen his force, neither shall the mighty deliver himself: Neither shall he stand that handleth the bow; and *he that* is swift of foot shall not deliver *himself:* neither shall he that rideth the horse deliver himself. And *he that* is courageous among the mighty shall flee away naked in that day, saith the Lord." Amos 2: 6, 12-16. "*There is* a genera-tion, whose teeth *are* as swords, and their jaw teeth as knives, to devour the poor from off the earth, and the needy from *among* men." *Proverbs 30:14.* "Woe to the rebellious children, saith the Lord, that take counsel, but not of me; and that cover with a covering, but not of my spirit, that they may add sin to sin…Now go, write it before them in a table, and note it in a book, that it may be for the time to come for ever and ever. That this is a rebel-lious people, lying children, children that will not hear the law of the Lord: Which say to the seers, See not; and to the prophets, Prophesy not unto us right things, speak unto us smooth things, prophesy deceits: Get you out of the way, turn aside out of the path, cause the Holy One of Israel to cease from before us. Wherefore thus saith the Holy One of Israel, Because ye despise this word, and trust in oppression and perverseness, and stay thereon: Therefore this iniquity shall be to you as a breach ready to fall, swelling out in a high wall, whose breaking cometh suddenly at an instant. And he shall break it as the breaking of the potters' vessel that is broken in pieces; he shall not spare: so that there shall not be found in the bursting of it a sherd to take fire from the hearth, or to take water withal out of the pit. For thus saith the Lord God, the Holy One of Israel; In returning and rest shall ye be saved; in quietness and in confidence shall be your strength: and ye would not. But ye said, No; for we will flee upon horses; therefore shall ye flee: and, We will ride upon the swift; therefore shall they that pursue you be swift. One thou-sand *shall* flee at the rebuke of one; at the rebuke of five shall ye flee: till ye be left as a beacon upon the top of a mountain, and as an ensign on an hill. And therefore will the Lord wait, that he may be gracious unto you, and therefore will he be exalted, that he may have mercy upon you: for the Lord is a God of judgment: blessed are all they that wait for him." Isaiah 30:1, 8-18. Surely, God recompenses deeds whether good or evil.

True believers desire to know and do what thus saith the Lord, seeking not to carve out segments or get around righteousness. God is truth. There is no getting around holiness. You cannot "get over on God." Appallingly, manipulators try manipulating God. This dangerous attitude needs correction now. Man needs God and to be right in God's sight. Mankind is justified through belief in Christ. Believing in, loving, and obeying God, is pathway to heaven. True believers live according to the Holy Bible. Therefore, lying, skirting, or evading truth, is intolerable. No form of sin is in heaven. The Holy Spirit works through God's people. Seek opportunities to share God's truth and His transforming power.

If not saved in time, nonbelievers have the same fate as the devil. The devil is the author of confusion, lies, jealousy, and hate.

Integrity. Dream fulfillments require discipline and stamina, because some – opposition tactics - obstacles are catastrophic. "Recompense to no man evil for evil. Provide things honest in the sight of all men." Romans 12:17. Godly stands give credence to perseverance.

J E S U S! Awesome! "Whosoever shall confess that Jesus is the Son of God, God dwelleth in him, and he in God." I John 4:15. For dreamers, leaving God is not an option! God never leaves you. His love is true and eternal.

Jesus-Reliant (Not Self-Made or Self-Reliant). Self-reliant people do not exist. God created the human race. He makes and owns all resources and wealth. "And the Lord God formed man *of* the dust of the ground, and breathed into his nostrils the breath of life; and man became a living soul." Genesis 2:7. "For ye are all the children of God by faith in Christ Jesus. For as many of you as have been baptized into Christ have put on Christ. There is neither Jew nor Greek, there is neither bond nor free, there is neither male nor female: for ye are all one in Christ Jesus. And if ye *be* Christ's, then are ye Abraham's seed, and heirs according to the promise." Galatians 3:26-29.

Admittedly, God is our Loan Officer. Upon death, nothing goes with us. While on earth, God's resources are used; but, everyone leaves them behind. Even when assets are buried with corpses, resources stay.

Jesus' Way. Everything you should know – earthly and heavenly – is found in the Holy Bible. "Jesus saith unto him, I am the way, the truth, and the life: no man cometh unto the Father, but by me." St. John 14:6. You cannot go wrong with Jesus. Be ecstatic about This Man! Jesus is Lord. Jesus' Team wins!

Jewels. Knowledge and opportunities provide power. "There is gold, and a multitude of rubies: but the lips of knowledge *are* a precious jewel." Proverbs 20:15.

Judgment. Dreamers hope achievements come easier. But, journeys have unexpected persecutors, persecutions, behaviors, and places; particularly in some church environments. Knowingly, judgment begins at the house of God gives a measure of comfort during afflictions. "For the time *is come* that judgment must begin at the house of God: and if *it* first *begin* at us, what shall the end *be* of them that obey not the gospel of God? And if the righteous scarcely be saved, where shall the ungodly and the sinner appear? Wherefore let them that suffer according to the will of God commit the keeping of their souls *to him* in well doing, as unto a faithful Creator." I Peter 4:17-19. "Now the Spirit speaketh expressly, that in the latter times some shall depart from the faith, giving heed to seducing spirits, and doctrines of devils; speaking lies in hypocrisy; having their conscience seared with a hot iron..." I Timothy 4:1-2.

Kin Violence. Dreamers are visionaries. As the premise of this book points out, Joseph's brothers' conspiracy against him, is abominable. Murderous, disloyalty, claws spill jealousy and disrespect.

Jealousy's discriminatory heart condition (mind abnormality) regarding the disabled, handicapped, race, gender, age, religion, family, acquaintances, and communities, intentionally hurts. God disapproves ungodly motives and intents. In other words, jealousy overrides common sense. Small-mindedness creates big problems. As in Joseph's case, when some dreamers share their hopes with nondreamers, evil opposition tactics and killings are proposed. Why? "For many are called, but few *are* chosen." St. Matthew 22:14.

Jealousy can be described as wedges driving anger and outrage. Nondreamers are offended and angry with themselves; so they deliberately strike out at dreamers. Dream robbery is worse than many other thefts. Dreams are mental first. Safeguard dreams. Safeguard assets.

Jealousy should not be misjudged or overlooked. When jealousy is underestimated, dreams and commodities are diminished – stolen. Underestimation, of jealous-filled hearts provide vindictiveness-flourishing environments. Slanderers balloon opposition against dreamers.

Sneaky, grinning, shysters, plot horrible acts. Grinning and pretending throws some people off-guard. Oftentimes, grinning intends to cover up evilness. Shysters despise openness. Repenting is righteousness. Overall, the goal is dream killing as well as other deadly ends.

Embrace opportunities leading to fulfillment. Regrets are disappointing. Ask nondreamers. They can vouch for this scenario. Layers of covetousness have different expressions. Brazen, volatile, foes seek oppression and other opposition tactics. Nondreamers despise dreamers' success. Beware of devilish invasions lest dreams, work, and success, are destroyed. Depression and nullification are prime opposition tactics. Nondreamers' tactics sank many dreams. Jealous oppressors are dream thieves, destroyers, and killers.

Wonderfully, for Christian dreamers, confidence in Jesus Christ, and dependence on Him, keeps life afloat. While witnessing dreamers' success, jealous foes become dauntingly dangerous. But, God's blessings and successes are invulnerable.

Unfortunately, thousands of dreams lie in cemeteries. Why? Shared with jealous nondreamers. Since nondreamers' wiring is jealousy, cruelty, hatefulness, depression, suppression, destruction, etc., they generally decelerate goodness and destroy dreams. Destruction devices operate on sinfulness which hampers positive fulfillment. Dreamers watch and pray.

God is the only One who can create clear minds and clean hearts. Mindfully, consider confidants. In Joseph's lifetime, his brothers plotted to hurt him. Today, family violence still plagues society. The Bible teaches requirements for all situations. "He hath shewed thee, O man, what *is* good; and what doth the Lord require of thee, but to do justly, and to love mercy, and to walk humbly with thy God?" Micah 6:8. Learn to do well;

seek judgment, relieve the oppressed, judge the fatherless, plead for the widow." Isaiah 1:17.

Sin lurks in deceitfulness; but exposure comes. Sadly, some family members are enemies - untrustworthy. "...they bend their tongues *like* their bow *for* lies: but they are not valiant for the truth upon the earth; for they proceed from evil to evil, and they know not me, saith the Lord. Take ye heed...trust ye not in any brother: for every brother will utterly supplant, and every neighbor will walk with slanders. And they will deceive every one his neighbor, and will not speak the truth: they have taught their tongue to speak lies, *and* weary themselves to commit iniquity. Thine habitation *is* in the midst of deceit; through deceit they refuse to know me, saith the Lord. Therefore thus saith the Lord of hosts, Behold, I will melt them, and try them...Their tongue *is as* an arrow shot out; it speaketh deceit: *one* speaketh peacefully to his neighbor with his mouth, but in heart he layeth his wait." Jeremiah 9:3-8.

Love, for family, does not necessarily imply trust. Arguably, love and trust, may have nil connection. "Why, seeing times are not hidden from the Almighty, do they that know him not see his days?...in the night is as a thief...The eye also of the adulterer waiteth for the twilight, saying, No eye shall see me: and disguiseth *his* face. In the dark they dig through houses, *which* they had marked for themselves in the daytime: they know not the light. For the morning *is* to them even as the shadow of death: *if* one know *them, they are i*n the terrors of the shadow of death. They are exalted for a little while, but are gone and brought low; they are taken out of the way as all *other*, and cut off as the tops of the ears of corn." Job 24:1, 14-17, 24. Safety is not found in untruths, whether it is thievery and/or deceit. Meltdowns show up. "For everyone that doeth evil hateth the light, neither cometh to the light, lest his deeds should be reproved. But he that doeth truth cometh to the light, that his deeds may become manifest, that they are wrought in God." St. John 3:20-21.

Victims of crimes should not allow perpetrators to oppress spirits. Perpetrators are villains. Scandals and reputation mutilation harasses and invades privacy. Firsthand, Joseph realized sinful acts committed against him did not make him a criminal. Perpetrators dare not own their evil deeds; but use dodging mechanisms inorder to mislead and cover misdeeds. Dodging responsibility may seem to work short-term. In final analysis, truth and responsibility shines through. Primarily, concealment is their definition of containment. God's eyes are uncontainable!

Knowing Who You Are in Christ. Rarely, if ever, do family enemies, or any, other enemies, boldly announce, "I am your enemy. I do not like you. I will destroy you if given the opportunity!" Discernment reveals some enemies. Verbalization and actions – opposition tactics – reveal others. Sadly, and seemingly, family enemies use the same type evil maneuvers as non-family members against their loved ones.

Dreamers, not only see nondreamer enemies' but feel them. Discernment knows. Ruthless, ungodly, tactics are not hidden from discerning spirits. "…I send you forth as sheep in the midst of wolves: be ye therefore wise as serpents, and harmless as doves." St. Matthew 10:16.

Actually, nondreamers are coward, back-working, pew villains. In order to hinder and destroy dreamers' dreams, back-workers solicit crews who help with maneuvering hostilities.

Continuously, nondreamers claim they are having so-called problems from dreamers. Of course, claims are without cause. Throwing dreamers, in pits, is their business. In Joseph's case, some of his brothers were willing to kill him. His brothers, were bothered – consumed – with jealousy, so they are willing to murder their brother in cold blood. Dreamer' alertness fosters prudence. Flagrantly, ignoring enemies displays imprudence. It is an *unwise approach* to disregard enemies' demonic, fallacious, deceptions.

God stops Satan from destroying dreamers' lives. Joseph's life shows how God turns Satan's plans in different directions. Dreamers lean on God for protection from opposition tactics. God helps us to keep moving and stay focused. ***Dreamers TRUST GOD!***

Dreamers are fighting a won battle because, "In the beginning was the Word, and the Word was with God, and the Word was God." St. John 1:1. "I am Alpha and Omeg'a, the beginning and the end, the first and the last." Revelation 22:13.

God holds time in His hands.

Satan's time is short and fated!

Leadership. Effectually, Eagle-tis-ti-cal dreamers manage priorities. Biblical insight incites godliness. Wrong, dishonest, leadership is not followed or patronized.

Nondreamers' pretense is used to gain followers. Disorderly priorities leap for mediocrity. "The wind shall eat up all thy pastors…surely then shalt thy be ashamed and confounded for all thy wickedness." Jeremiah 22:22.

God can give pastors; but, some choose their own. "And I will give you pastors according to mine heart, which shall feed you with knowledge and understanding." Jeremiah 3:15. The Bible teaches who to believe and disbelieve. Dreamers understand and support godly leadership. According to various situations, nondreaming leaders may or may not teach, or live, truth. Itching ears' truth-intolerance dictate men-pleasing lifestyles.

There are two places for each individual to spend eternity: heaven or hell. Wickedness is pervasive in tormentors' groups. Without appropriate consideration for actions, nonthinkers follow sinful leaderships. "For he that biddeth him God speed is partaker of his evil deeds." II John 11. (see Chapter 4, Nondreamer Opposition Tactics).

Titles or positions may, or may not, show hearts or wisdom. Undeservingly, authority is given without expertise. God is not fooled. He sees the heart. Outward appearances betray. Heart sanitation is possible. "Thus saith the Lord; Execute ye judgment and righteousness, and deliver the spoiled out of the hand of the oppressor: and do no wrong…For if ye do this thing…But if ye will not hear these words, I swear by myself, saith the Lord, that this house will become a desolation. And I will prepare destroyers against thee…many nations shall pass by this city, and they shall say every man to his neighbor, Wherefore hath the Lord done thus unto this great city? Then they shall answer, Because they have forsaken the covenant of the Lord their God, and worshipped other gods, and served them.

Woe unto him that buildeth his house by unrighteousness, and his chambers by wrong; *that* useth his neighbor's service without wages, and giveth him not for his work…Shalt thou reign…and do judgment and justice, *and* then *it was* well with him? He judged the cause of the poor and needy; then *it was* well *with him*: *was* not this to know me? saith the Lord. But thine eyes and thine heart *are* not but for thy covetousness…and for oppression, and for violence, to do *it*. The wind shall eat up all thy pastors, and thy lovers shall go into captivity: surely then shalt thou be ashamed and confounded for all thy wickedness." Jeremiah 22:3-5, 7-9, 13, 15-17, and 22. Economic opportunities and fairness matter.

Role models are expected in church and community settings. "For from the least of them even unto the greatest of them every one *is* given to covetousness; and from the prophet even unto the priest every one dealeth falsely." Jeremiah 6:13. "Thefts, covetousness, wickedness, deceit, lasciviousness, an evil eye, blasphemy, pride, foolishness: All these evil things come from within, and defile the man." St. Mark 7:22-23.

Sin is shameful; but, wicked promoters wrap it in pretty layers and packages. "…many antichrists…went out from us…But ye have an unction from the Holy One, and ye know all things. I have not written unto you because ye know not the truth, but because ye know it, and that no lie is of the truth." I John 2:18-21. When professed Christians willfully sin and continuously default on confessions and vows, questions and concerns arise. Sin adversely affects self and others. In many situations, upstanding, God-fearing, Christians are misrepresented as part of pew problems. "*If* a wise man contendeth with a foolish man, whether he rage or laugh, *there is* no rest." Proverbs 29:9. Wonderfully, God sees and knows every heart. The wheat and tares have separation times.

How does covetousness end? Many antichrists are here; but God's people need to stay focused. "O thou that dwellest upon many waters, abundant in treasures, thine end is come, *and* the measure of thy covetousness. The Lord of hosts hath sworn by himself, *saying*, Surely I will fill thee with men, as with caterpillars; and they shall lift up a shout against thee. He hath made the earth by his power, he hath established the world by his wisdom, and hath stretched out the heaven by his understanding. Every man is brutish by *his* knowledge; every founder is confounded by the graven image: for his molten image *is* falsehood, and *there is* no breath in them. They are vanity, the work of errors: in the time of their visitation they shall perish." Jeremiah 51:13-15, 17-18.

Leaving Some Resources for Poor People. With limited resources, poor people help others. Inhumane millionaires use helps as write-offs and promotion of personal agendas. Helping and acknowledging the poor is not on their list. If the top one percent millionaires cared and paid their fair share, there probably would not be any poor people. Inhumane millionaires' selfishness creates inequity and poor populations. Working in inhumane millionaires' workplaces can be a nightmare; because they do not care about, or support, their workers who keep their companies running. "And when ye reap the harvest of your land, thou shalt not make clean riddance of the corners of thy field when thou reapest, neither shalt thou gather any gleaning of thy harvest: thou shalt leave them unto the poor, and to the stranger: I am the Lord your God." Leviticus 23:22.

Joseph was a humane dreamer. Even though he was treated unfairly, he did good. Dreamers treat others as they want to be treated. Poor people deserve fair treatment. All people deserve fairness. Toleration plus mercy support justice for all.

Love. "If a man say, I love God, and hateth his brother, he is a liar: for he that loveth not his brother whom he hath seen, how can he love God whom he hath not seen? And this commandment have we from him, That he who loveth God, love his brother also." I John 4:20-21. God's Love is limitless and unconditional. No one is excluded from His loving arms; because, He loves each individual. Affirmatively and thankfully, His true, sure love, cannot be undermined or forfeited. Unquestionably, when Jesus says, "I love you," He speaks truth. He shows His love. Truthfully, and faithfully, God is Love and Truth.

Unmistakably, without love, you do not know God. He is love. Even if you do not love God, His unconditional love still abides. Miserably, human beings' love is sometimes conditional. If evil expectations are unmet, nondreamers throw dreamers in pits. God delivers dreamers from pits. Dethroning dreamers is nondreamers' enthrallment.

Undeniably, Joseph was a dreamer. His brothers hated him. He was different. His ambitions were different from theirs; so they made evil plans against him. "Come now therefore, and let us slay him, and cast him into some pit, and we will say, Some evil beast hath devoured him: and we will see what will become of his dreams." Genesis 37:20.

Joseph's brother, Reuben, spoke up for his brother. Acting on evil, foolish, instructions, is naive and shows lack of understanding. Reuben had a backbone. He ignored his brothers' wicked, murderous, enticements. Apparently, he is not gullible; thereby uninterested in participating in his brother's murder plot. Consequently, he persuaded his brothers not to shed Joseph's blood. "...Reuben heard *it*, and he delivered him out of their hands; and said, Let us not kill him. And Reuben said unto them, Shed no blood, *but* cast him into this pit...and lay no hand upon him; that he might rid him out of their hands...And it came to pass...Joseph was come unto his brethren...they stript Joseph out of...*his* coat of *many* colours that *was* on him; and they took him, and cast him into a pit..." Genesis 37:21-24.

Family members' enticements are not always godly or friendly. Reuben made a personal decision not to kill his brother. He did not side with his brothers. He did not want to be a murderer; but his brothers strive to get rid of their dreamer brother. If it had not been for God's protection and plans for Joseph's life...

Watching, who counsels us and who we follow, is vital. "My son, if sinners entice thee, consent thou not. If they say, Come with us, let us lay wait for blood, let us lurk privily for the innocent without cause: Let us swallow them up alive as the grave; and whole, as those that go down into the pit: We shall find all precious substance: We shall fill our houses with spoil: cast in thy lot among us; let us all have one purse: my son, walk not thou in the way with them; refrain thy foot from their path: for their feet run for evil, and make haste to shed blood. And they lay wait for their *own* blood; they lurk privily for their *own* lives. So *are* the ways of every one that is greedy of gain; *which* taketh away the life of the owners thereof. Wisdom crieth without; she uttereth her voice in the streets: How long, ye simple ones, will ye love simplicity? and the scorners delight in their scorning, and fools hate knowledge? Turn you at my reproof: behold, I will pour out my spirit unto you, I will make known my words unto you. Because I have called, and ye refused; I have stretched out my hand; and no man regarded; but ye have set at nought all my counsel, and would none of my reproof: I will laugh at your calamity; I will mock when your fear cometh…when your fear cometh as desolation, and your destruction cometh as a whirl-wind; when distress and anguish cometh upon you. Then shall they call upon me, but I will not answer; they shall seek me early; but they shall not find me: For they have hated knowledge, and did not choose the fear of the Lord: They would none of my counsel: they despised all my reproof. Therefore shall they eat of the fruit of their own way…prosperity of fools shall destroy them. But whosoever hearkeneth unto me shall dwell safely, and shall be quiet from fear of evil." Proverbs 1:10-16, 18-20, 22-33.

Disturbingly and sadly, some family members are foes. Some family members hate or dislike dreamer family members. Realistically, jealousy creates foes. Their jealousy seeks dreamers' ruin. Undeniably, when people are jealous of you, no matter what, you say or do, cruel feelings, postures, and evil ventures, toward you, persist. Joseph's brothers strip his clothing from his body. His brothers are negatively enthralled with Joseph's dreams. They rather see him dead or in a pit than to see his dream fulfillments. They are serious about hindering and hurting Joseph. "…Israel loved Joseph more than all of his children, because he *was* the son of his old age: and he made him a coat of *many* colours. And when his brethren saw that their father loved him more than all his brethren, they hated him, and could not speak peacefully unto him." Genesis 37:3-4.

Today, dreamers still face similar family members' opposition tactics. Some resort to opposition tactics; such as stealing, slandering, lying, destroying, and seeking to kill. Jealous individuals are in turmoil; because their minds are disquieted within themselves. They target dreamers. Dreamers love family members and dare not partake in evil deeds.

Joseph did not want his family to fear because of their misdeeds. God have plans for lives. Joseph's brothers thought retaliation for their opposition tactics was forthcoming; but, God's ambassadors' outlooks behold expected, mean-spirited, tactics. God made man in His image; therefore, he knows everything about mental and physical states. "And...they said, Joseph will peradventure hate us, and will certainly requite us all the evil which we did unto him. And they sent a messenger unto Joseph, saying, Thy father did command before he died, saying...Forgive, I pray thee now, the trespass of thy brethren, and their sin; for they did unto thee evil: and now, we pray thee, forgive the trespass of the servants of the God of thy father...Joseph wept when they spake unto him...his brethren also went and fell down before his face; and they said, Behold we *be* thy servants. And Joseph said unto them, Fear not: for *am* I in the place of God? But as for you, ye thought evil against me; *but* God meant it unto good, to bring to pass, as *it is* this day, to save much people alive. Now therefore fear ye not: I will nourish you, and your little ones. And he comforted them, and spake kindly unto them. And Joseph dwelt in Egypt, he, and his father's house: and Joseph lived an hundred and ten years." Genesis 50:17-22.

Personally, knowing God, and experiencing His Love, give dreamers unshakeable faith. Truly, dreamers love enemies and treat them right. God rewards righteousness. Joseph's experiences show God's power and deliverance. His brothers chose wrong paths. Although "unbrotherly" acts are unkind, his dreams are realized. God's purposes and plans are fulfilled.

Marriage. "For this cause shall a man leave his father and mother, and shall be joined unto his wife, and they two shall be one flesh." Ephesians 5:31. "Marriage *is* honourable in all, and the bed undefiled: but whoremongers and adulterers God will judge." Hebrews 13:4. Holy value traits honor God's Word. If marriage is not on your mind; don't waste time. Respect sacred unions. Unions are set up for monogamy.

Memory. God sees, knows, and has total remembrance throughout all ages. God is flawless. His records are accurate. Man's deeds are written in His Lamb's Book of Life. When standing before God, what will your record reflect? Are you preparing to go right or left? Now, is decision time! "Hear this, O ye that swallow up the needy, even to make the poor of the land to fail, saying, when will the new moon be gone, that we may sell corn? and the sabbath, that we may set forth wheat, making the e'phah small, and the she'kel great, and falsifying the balances by deceit? That we may buy the poor for silver, and the needy for a pair of shoes; *yea*, and sell the refuse of the wheat? The Lord has sworn by the excellency of Jacob, Surely I will never forget any of their works." Amos 8:4-7. "Though they dig into hell, thence shall mine hand take them; though they climb up to heaven, thence will I bring them down…*It is* he that buildeth his stories in the heaven, and hath founded his troop in the earth; he that calleth for the waters of the sea, and poureth them out upon the face of the earth: The Lord *is* his name." Amos 9:2, 6.

Pray to God. He is eager to help through persecutions. His guidance and strength is unmatched. Accountability is for everyone. No respect of persons! Jesus Christ is The True Lover of souls! God's Love is real! Trust His Pure Love. "But I trusted in thee, O Lord: I said, Thou *art* my God. My times *are* in thy hand, deliver me from the hand of mine enemies, and from them that persecute me. Make thy face to shine upon thy servant: save me for thy mercies' sake. Let me not be ashamed, O Lord: for I have called upon thee: let the wicked be ashamed, *and* let them be silent in the grave. Let the lying lips be put to silence; which speak grievous things proudly and contemptuously against the righteous. *Oh* how great *is* thy goodness, which thy hast laid up for them that fear thee; *which* thou has wrought for them that trust in thee before the sons of men! Thou shalt hide them in the secret of thy presence from the pride of man: thou shalt keep them secretly in a pavilion from the strife of tongues." Psalm 31:14-20. "Bless the Lord, O my soul. O Lord my God, thou art very great; thou art clothed with honour and majesty." Psalm 104:1.

Remember, God is not amnesia-prone. He loves each person and knows each person's deeds and needs.

Mentoring. Eagle-tis-ti-cal dreamers' contributions are invaluable. Eagle-tis-ti-cal dreamers are unordinary people, bold helpers, movers, and shakers, taking charge of dreams, insisting people see, and hear their godly visions.

Money. "Charge them that are rich in this world, that they be not highminded, nor trust in uncertain riches, but in the living God, who giveth us richly all things to enjoy; that they do good, that they be rich in good works, ready to distribute…Laying up in store for themselves a good foundation against the time to come, that they may lay hold on eternal life. I Timothy 6:17-19.

Dreamers use finance for spreading God's Word, Works, and Blessings. Dreamers handle God's money wisely. When money handles you, sorrow and debt prevails. "They shall cast their silver in the streets, and their gold shall be removed: their silver and their gold shall not be able to deliver them in the day of the wrath of the Lord: they shall not satisfy their souls, neither fill their bowels, because it is the stumblingblock of their iniquity." Ezekiel 7:19.

Mouth. Your mouth is a vessel for heaven upbuilding, not a cesspool. Humane environments help. Inhumane environments destroy. Help them go to heaven – not to hell. Your mouth is a member of the temple of the Holy Ghost.

Name Drop - "Jesus." Take every opportunity to spread **Jesus News**. Tell people about Jesus and shamelessly show love for Him. Proudly clap your hands to God. Talk, preach, and teach with the mouth God gives you. Praise God! He is Love! He is the Star of the World! He made the Universe! "Lift up your hands *in* the sanctuary, and bless the Lord." Psalm 134:2. "Hear the voice of my supplications, when I cry unto thee, when I lift up my hands toward the holy oracle." Psalm 28:2. "Thus will I bless thee while I live: I will lift up my hands in thy name." Psalm 63:4.

"Whosoever therefore shall be ashamed of me and of my words in this adulterous and sinful generation; of him also shall the Son of man be ashamed, when he cometh in the glory of his Father with the holy angels." St. Mark 8:38. Publicly, calling on Jesus' name is showing devotion and proudness to be His ambassador.

Name dropping is common practice for many activities. Ball players, kneel to pray - on television - on some sports' fields. Praise God for these motivational, precious acts. Spirits are lifted and give renewed sense of godly, bold responsibility, energy, and enthusiasm.

Inspiration abounds to soar in God's vineyard. Keep up great work for Jesus. Make righteous differences.

Noise. "Make a joyful noise unto God; all ye lands: Sing forth the honour of His name: make His praise glorious." Psalm 66:1-2. God's people love and adore Him. "For I am not ashamed of the gospel of Christ: for it is the power of God unto salvation to everyone that believeth..." Romans 1:16.

Make joyful, loud, sounds to the Lord. Draw attention. Let the world know God is the answer for life concerns.

Wholeheartedly and boldly, Eagle-tis-ti-cal dreamers' follow Christ. Reprehensibly, nondreamers give, and receive, worldly accolades for sinfulness. The world screams to show love for its own.

The One. "Who will have all men to be saved, and come unto the knowledge of the truth. For *there is* one God, and one mediator between God and men, the man Christ Jesus. Who gave himself a ransom for all, to be testified in due time." I Timothy 2:4-6.

Opposition Tactics. Pew villains ignore moral compasses. Clearly, detestable schemes are designed for goodness killings. Dreamers have positive influences on everything they put their hands to. Sadly, lies and rumors are concocted and spread in churches, communities, and homes. Whomever, wherever, and whatever, talebearers, are connected with, confusion, jealousy, and strife abounds.

Righteous living and soul-saving are pathways to heaven. Through God's light, His ambassadors' lights shine in the earth.

Dreamers' value traits defy wickedness. Though snares are plenty, God's Work moves forward. Souls are saved; therefore, Satan is angry with God's ambassadors. Prudently, many sinners are turning from wickedness to Jesus; because, now is the time to get right with God. Dreamers keep eyes on God and follow His Holy Bible teachings.

Sadly, and negatively, pew villains (talebearers) steadily deflect, thus counteracting some worshippers' mindsets. "As a *mad* man who casteth firebrands, arrows, and death, so *is* the man *that* deceiveth his neighbor, and saith, Am not I in sport? Where no wood is, *there* the fire goeth out: so where *there is* no talebearer, the strife ceaseth. As coals *are* to burning coals, and wood to fire; so *is* a contentious man to kindle strife.

The words of a talebearer *are* as wounds, and they go down into the innermost parts of the belly. Burning lips and a wicked heart *are like* a potsherd covered with silver dross. He that hateth dissembleth with his lips, and layeth up deceit within him; when he speaketh fair, believe him not: for there are seven abominations in his heart. *Whose* hate is covered by deceit, his wickedness shall be shewed before the *whole* congregation. Whoso diggeth a pit shall fall therein: and he that rolleth a stone, it will return upon him. A lying tongue hateth *those that are* afflicted by it; and a flattering mouth worketh ruin." Proverbs 26:18-28.

With their mouths, talebearing haters hurt. Their mouths and actions are intentional hurting machines without common sense, pause, or stop mediums. These "chaos vessels" – pew villains - would be better served if self's hurts and disappointments are addressed. Once personal problems are resolved, time could be used wisely accomplishing their dreams instead of implementing opposition tactics on dreamers.

Instead of disrupting sincere worshippers, talebearers should stop harassments and be a part of worship service as well. Unfortunately, talebearers enjoy implementing strife and hate among congregations. The term "villains" is used signifying wicked roles, not ill feelings toward anyone. Hopefully, talebearers and other troublemakers turn from wickedness before time is out.

Dreamers are watchful. Nondreamers' opposition tactics are deceitful, spiteful, careless, and wicked. "Answer not a fool according to his folly, lest thou also be like unto him. Answer a fool according to his folly, lest he be wise in his own conceit. The great *God* that formed all *things* both rewardeth the fool, and rewardeth transgressors. Where no wood is, *there* the fire goeth out: so where *there* is no talebearer, the strife ceaseth." Proverbs 26:4-5,10, 20.

Dreamers are attentive knowing talebearers have evil objectives; namely, speaking untruths and undermining dreams. Talebearers purposely inflict aggravation and sometimes death. Unfortunately, some peace-breaking habits start early in life. Early, righteous, training matters. Teaching others wickedness is evil. Ungodly, taught and learned, behaviors may or may not be erased because the devil loves corruptness. Keeping people away from God is the devil's quest. Disrespect, toward others, results from improper teaching, improper role-modeling, and inadequate accountability. Unaccountableness leads to false standings and false security. At some point, all persons are held accountable. Thank God for "no respecter of persons."

Joseph's brothers are an example of what some nondreamers have in mind for dreamers. Chapter Four describes some opposition tactics used to throw dreamers in pits. Specifically, opposition tactics' premeditation vehicles support disheartenment. Dreamers depend on God's help. Live for God. He is undefeated. God is The Dream Giver! Dreamers' safety lies only in His loving care.

Parents, are examples whether good or not. They plant and nurture dream instincts. Imprints are important and impressive. Scripture says, "Train up a child in the way he should go: and when he is old, he will not depart from it." Proverbs 22:6. "Hear counsel, and receive instruction, that thou mayest be wise in thy latter end." Proverbs 19:20. "Cease, my son, to hear the instruction *that causeth* to err from the words of knowledge." Proverbs 19:27.

Some parents' youngsters observe formulation and execution of pew disturbances. Scamming is hard to hide. Youths are exposed to disrespectfulness toward worshippers, elderly, and others. When discord needles are threaded, youngsters go down dangerous pew assault paths.

Hopefully wisdom rises up in hearts. Break the cyclone of thievery, embezzlements, slanders, and other evil plots and schemes.

As a whole, how do the aforementioned actions, and consequences, affect churches, families, homes, dreamers, nondreamers, communities, and planet?

The Bible teaches exhortation. On the other hand, nondreamers sit on pews teaching and practicing defamation. Nil accountability is shown for shattering morale, dreams, and lives. Jealousy and hate are combustible and ultimately explodes. Pew troublemakers cause extensive problems and dissatisfaction. *"Where there is* no vision, the people perish..." Proverbs

29:18. "And the Lord answered me, and said, Write the vision, and make *it* plain upon tables, that he may run that readeth it. For the vision *is* yet for an appointed time, but at the end it shall speak, and not lie: though it tarry, wait for it; because it will surely come, it will not tarry." Habakkuk 2:2.

The Holy Bible's teachings are constant reminders for living, teaching, and preaching godliness. Godly people see through culture lies, devilish stimulations, and dangerous friendships. People, in all age groups, are non-partakers of sin, challenging others to live righteously and master dream skills. Sin hinders dreams and fulfillment. Tampering with sin is risky, invasive, poisonous, and unhelpful.

Some peer pressuring bullies wrap sin in decorations. Early teachings - in the womb - of Who God is - is phenomenal. Early acquaintance is non-negotiable. Treatments, and reactions to people and situations, reveal inner feelings. Mouths say one thing; while hearts and actions say other things. As many men and women can attest, mouths flatter saying they love you or you look good; but, actions say the opposite. Believing talk, without discerning hearts, is negligence. Discerning spirits feel pew villains' opposition tactics. Some opposition tactics are seen <u>and</u> felt; whereas, others are seen <u>or</u> felt. Discernment is valuable.

Courage must be taught and shown. In dreamers' space, mediocrity conformity is amiss. In the midst of mediocrity, dreamers show smarts, bravery, and articulation.

At an early age, teaching, showing positivity and confidence provide some life cushions. Ungodly, unethical, parents are noticed. Righteous living, preaching, teaching, steers others in good paths. Necessarily, dreamers preach holiness through teaching and righteous living. Christian dreamers have charitable hearts. Christian, bold Eagle-tis-ti-cal, dreamers, encourage others to disentangle from mediocrity. Christian, bold Eagle-tis-ti-cal, dreamers are energetic believers, hearers, and doers.

Strive for goodness, which is godly and inspirational. In all situations, boldness and virtuousness overshadow mediocrity. Unexpected life circumstances; such as pit predicaments, job and friendship losses, etc., occur. During adversities, preferably, right choices, rather than wrong ones, are made. Otherwise, respect is lost; and, relationships with God are strained or possibly dissolved. Righteousness is key to eternal rest. While there is time, teach and live God's way of life. Advocate and leave godly legacies. Righteousness is godly; but, sin reproaches and confounds.

Persistence Pays. Perseverance is one of the main traits for dream accomplishments. "…There was in a city a judge, which feared not God, neither regarded man: And there was a widow in that city; and she came unto him, saying, Avenge me of mine adversary. And he would not for a while: but afterward he said unto himself, Though I fear not God, nor regard man; yet because this widow troubleth me; I will avenge her, lest by her continual coming she weary me. And the Lord said, Hear what the unjust judge saith. And shall not God avenge his own elect, which cry day and night unto him, though he bear long with them? I tell you that he will avenge them speedily. Nevertheless when the Son of man cometh, shall he find faith on the earth? And he spake this parable unto certain which trusted in themselves that they were righteous, and despised others…" St. Luke 18:2-9.

God avenges His elect. Dreamers applaud this widow because she "kept moving" eventually inspiring the <u>unjust judge's</u> movement on her behalf. Without determination, dreams are unachievable.

Planners. Beforehand, strategize godly action courses for dream accomplishment; such as, protocols, confirmations, and positive outcomes. If need be, make changes.

Hasty decisions are imprudent; because vital information and opportunities may be missed, overlooked, or lost. Haste creates wastefulness. Hastiness is recklessness. Without foresight, valuable assets, including time, money, opportunities, and other resources, are squandered. "Seest thou a man *that is* hasty in his words? *there is* more hope of a fool than of him." Proverbs 29:20.

Positive Peer Pressure expresses caring behavior leading people to Jesus. Jesus lovers are the light of the world having a duty to help others go to heaven. "Ye are the light of the world. A city that is set on an hill cannot be hid. Neither do men light a candle, and put it under a bushel, but on a candlestick; and it giveth light unto all that are in the house. Let your light so shine before men, that they may see your good works, and glorify your Father which is in heaven." St. Matthew 5:14-16. Plant seeds desirous of growth. Defiled roots grow into sin towers. Eventually, towers tumble; because underpinning is built on hypocrisy. God is Founder and Author of restarts – newness – clean hearts. The best decision you can make is making heaven eternal home. Where are you going? Heaven or hell?

Power. God's power supersedes every so-called power. Sustainability is uncompromised. "And Jesus came and spake unto them, saying, All power is given unto me in heaven and in earth. Go ye therefore, and teach all nations, baptizing them in the name of the Father, and of the Son, and of the Holy Ghost: Teaching them to observe all things whatsoever I have commanded you: and, lo, I am with you alway, *even* unto the end of the world..." St. Matthew 28:18-20.

God was, is, and always will be, in charge. According to His Will and Purpose, He institutes plans and missions. His servants are endowed with power. "But ye shall receive power, after that the Holy Ghost is come upon you: and ye shall be witnesses unto me...unto the uttermost part of the earth." The Acts 1:8. "...Christ sent me...to preach the gospel: not with wisdom of words, lest the cross of Christ should be made of none effect. For the preaching of the cross is to them that perish foolishness; but unto us which are saved it is the power of God...I will destroy the wisdom of the wise, and will bring to nothing the understanding of the prudent. Where is the wise?...where *is* the disputer of this world? hath not God made foolish the wisdom of this world? For after that in the wisdom of God the world by wisdom knew not God, it pleased God by the foolishness of preaching to save them that believe. Because the foolishness of God is wiser than men; and the weakness of God is stronger than men. For ye see your calling, brethren, how that not many wise men after the flesh, not many mighty, not many noble, *are called*: But God hath chosen the foolish things of the world to confound the wise; and God hath chosen the weak things of the world to confound the things which are mighty; and base things of the world, and things which are despised, hath God chosen, *yea*, and things which are not, to bring to nought things that are:

That no flesh should glory in his presence. But of him are ye in Christ Jesus, who of God is made unto us wisdom, and righteousness, and sanctification, and redemption...He that glorieth, let him glory in the Lord." I Corinthians 1:17-21, 25-27, 31.

God's Work cannot be undone, destroyed, or stopped. Throughout ages, His power display strength. God chooses trustworthy ambassadors whom He knows will carry out His will. "...Thy will be done in earth, as *it is* in heaven." St. Matthew 6:10.

At different times, and places, God appoints leaders, to fulfill His Will. His plans are thwart-proof and fulfillable. Self-absorption (egocentrism) is bent on carrying out plans through smarts, technology, and human strength. God's power defies all of these. He is Almighty God. "And Jesus came and spake unto them, saying, All power is given unto me in heaven and in earth. Go ye therefore, and teach all nations, baptizing them in the name of the Father, and of the Son, and of the Holy Ghost: Teaching them to observe all things whatsoever I have commanded you: and, lo, I am with you alway, *even* unto the end of the world..." St. Matthew 28:18-20.

Selfish individuals crave personal recognition, unconcerned with God's plans, missions, and is void of understanding. Millions of dollars plus hours are spent inducing, maintaining, and spreading wickedness. Regardless of monies spent and efforts applied, God's Will is done and His plans are carried out. Wicked attackers threaten God's called ambassadors; but He keeps their feet from slipping. The Lord lifts heads. "...the Lord raiseth them that are bowed down: the Lord loveth the righteous...but the way of the wicked he turneth upside down." Psalm 146:8-9. God makes choices and interventions. He put princes in power and removes others. "*It is* he that sitteth upon the circle of the earth...That bringeth the princes to nothing; he maketh the judges of the earth as vanity...the everlasting God, the Lord, the Creator of the ends of the earth, fainteth not, neither is weary...*there is* no searching of his understanding." Isaiah 40:22-23, 28. God has enemies and so does His ambassadors.

Automatically, power attaches responsibility. God is Creator. God has authority for calling who He chooses. God makes perfect choices. Man needs to understand God is in charge. "In whose hand *is* the soul of every living thing, and the breath of all mankind. He removeth away the speech of the trusty, and taketh away the understanding of the aged. He taketh away the heart of the chief of the people of the earth, and causeth them to wander in the wilderness *where there is* no *way*." Job 12:10, 20, 24.

Emphatically, the Lord leads and helps His chosen. His compassion expresses unconditional love. Explosive Holy Ghost Power of God! Awesome!

Pray. Communicate with Jesus. He wants to talk to you. "And he spake a parable unto them *to this end*, that men ought always to pray, and not to faint ..." St. Luke 18:1.

Preoccupation with Sin and Worldly Cares. Sin shows, bringing disgrace and eternal soul loss. Satan, and man, uses sin manipulations, sometimes through slander, bribery, exploitation, etc. Mind functions become perverse. Evil doings misplace trust. Senseless, displeasure with God causes dependency on man. Trust in God. He owns everything. Living for God brings bountiful blessings and eternal life. "The fear of man bringeth a snare: but whoso putteth his trust in the Lord shall be safe." Proverbs 29:25. "He that walketh uprightly walketh surely: but he that perverteth his ways shall be known." Proverbs 10:9.

Dreamers are wise-hearted. "The wise in heart will receive commandments: but a prating fool shall fall." Proverbs 10:8. Nondreamers' mouths stir hatred and strife. "He that winketh with the eye causeth sorrow: but a prating fool shall fall. The mouth of a righteous *man is* a well of life: but violence covereth the mouth of the wicked." Proverbs 10:10-11. Forsake the foolish, and live; and go in the way of understanding." Proverbs 9:6.

Self-respect generates respect for others. Pew villains lack self-respect, as well as, respect for others.

Dreamers are occupied with God thoughts. Righteousness lovers treat others fairly. When self has problems, problems with others are inevitable. Nondreamers' self-dejection denigrates relationships with others.

Prevention. Take care before something needs care. By the time circumstances need attention, it may be too late for finest options. Dreamers' keen insight precludes negative predicaments before breakages occur. Preventions cost less than nearsighted, naive, alternatives. Predictability-sensibility combinations reveal critical thinking.

Pursue. Chase – Jesus Christ - righteousness. "Depart from evil, and do good; seek peace and pursue it." Psalm 34:14.

Qualifications. God gives His called educations, wisdom, discernment, discretion, and opportunities. When God calls, His elect is unseatable and unbeatable. Opposition tactics, in any form, does not equate to, or with, God-given supernatural power. Dreamers live according to God's standards. Holiness is real; therefore, work.

Attention chasers use and trust unrighteous gadgets, such as slander, lies, immorality, etc., to gain access. What they view – as gain – is actually naught. "The Lord's voice crieth unto the city, and *the man of* wisdom shall see thy name: hear ye the rod, and who hath appointed it. Are there yet the treasures of wickedness in the house of the wicked, and the scant measure *that* is abominable? Shall I count *them* pure with the wicked balances, and with the bag of deceitful weights? For the rich men thereof are full of violence, and the inhabitants thereof have spoken lies, and their tongue is deceitful in their mouth. Therefore also will I make *thee* sick in smiting thee, in making *thee* desolate because of thy sins. Thou shalt eat, but not be satisfied; and thy casting down *shall be* in the midst of thee; and thou shalt take hold, but shalt not deliver; and *that* which thou deliverest will I give up to the sword." Micah 6:9-14.

Righteousness is gain. Unrighteousness is loss. God-given abilities cannot be seized or matched. Affirmatively, because of trust in God, dreamers soar above mediocrity.

Pursuit, of goodness, peace, and dreams, is personal responsibility. "Seest thou a man diligent in his business? he shall stand before kings; he shall not stand before mean *men*." Proverbs 22:29.

Realism. "For God so loved the world, that he gave his only begotten Son, that whosoever believeth in him should not perish, but have everlasting life." St. John 3:16.

One God. God's Son (Jesus Christ). One race (human). One heaven (eternal life). One hell (everlasting damnation). God loves you unconditionally. Take advantage of eternal, unearned, salvation gift, to the saving of souls.

Many people demean Jesus' crucifixion and His feelings toward mankind. "Ye therefore, beloved, seeing ye know *these things* before, beware lest ye also, being led away with the error of the wicked, fall from your own steadfastness." II Peter 3:17. God gave mankind The Salvation Gift - Jesus Christ. Guard your heart against wickedness and its perpetrators. Evil perpetrators coach wrongness and support pew villains' opposition tactics.

Recognition. God knows you forever. He wants total devotion, hot or cold – not lukewarm. "Then the word of the Lord came unto me, saying, before I formed thee in the belly I knew thee; and before thou camest forth out of the womb I sanctified thee, *and* I ordained thee a prophet unto the nations. Then said I, Ah, Lord God! behold, I cannot speak: for I *am* a child. But the Lord said unto me, Say not, I *am* a child: for thou shalt go to all that I shall send thee, and whatsoever I command thee thou shalt speak. Be not afraid of their faces: for I *am* with thee to deliver thee saith, the Lord. Then the Lord put forth his hand, and touched my mouth. And the Lord said unto me, Behold, I have put my words in thy mouth. See, I have this day set thee over the nations and over the kingdoms, to root out, and to pull down, and to destroy, and to throw down, to build, and to plant." Jeremiah 1:4-10.

God's power, and recognition, is irreplaceable. Rightfully, fear of God shows wisdom. Fear God, not man. Fear, of men's faces, is unnecessary.

Relationships, with some, hinder heed to God's call. Ill-advised associations are unwise, unhelpful, and dangerous. "These things have I spoken unto you, that in me ye, might have peace. In the world ye shall have tribulation: but be of good cheer; I have overcome the world." St. John 16:33.

Remember God and Obey His Commandments. Give Him glory, honor, and praise not merely in times of pleasant circumstances; but also in unpleasant situations.

Repentance. God forgives sin. Sins keep life in crisis-mode. Alignment with God affords harmony and comfort. "If we confess our sins, he is faithful and just to forgive us *our* sins, and to cleanse us from all unrighteousness." I John 1:9.

Requirements. God's Work is precious – not to be taken lightly. Christians depend on Jesus Christ. Faith, confession, profession, and sincerity, envelopes dreamers' portfolio. Distribution, of God's Word, should be done in season, out of season, decently, and orderly. Mockery, of God, is detrimental. Records – Book of Life – are kept. "And I saw the dead, small and great, stand before God; and the books were opened: and another book was opened, which is *the book* of life: and the dead were judged out of those things which were written in the books, according to their works. And whosoever was not found written in the book of life was cast into the lake of fire." Revelation 20:12, 15.

Riches. Give God glorification for achievements. Wealth should be used wisely. "Every man also to whom God hath given riches and wealth, and hath given him power to eat thereof, and to take his portion, and to rejoice in his labour; this *is* the gift of God." Ecclesiastes 5:19. Reliance on God gives purpose and life. Wealth dependency is failure. "He that trusteth in his riches shall fall: but the righteous shall flourish as a branch." Proverbs 11:28. Nondreamers worship man, places, objects, etc. – temporalities. "Thus saith the Lord, let not the wise *man* glory in his wisdom, neither let the mighty *man* glory in his might, let not the rich *man* glory in his riches..." Jeremiah 9:23.

Forgetting God's goodness is wrong and carries penalty. "And thou say in thine heart, My power and the might of *mine* hand hath gotten me this wealth. But thou shalt remember the Lord thy God: for *it is* he that giveth thee power to get wealth, that he may establish his covenant...And it shall be, if thou do at all forget the Lord thy God, and walk after other gods, and serve them, and worship them, I testify against you this day that ye shall surely perish...because ye would not be obedient unto the voice of the Lord your God." Deuteronomy 8:17-20.

Dreamers honor, praise, and worship God. "Thus saith the Lord, thy redeemer, and he that formed thee from the womb, I *am* the Lord that maketh all *things*; that stretched forth the heavens alone; that spreadeth abroad the earth by myself; that frustrateth the tokens of the liars, and maketh diviners mad; that turneth wise *men* backward, and maketh their knowledge foolish..." Isaiah 44:24-25. God's authenticity supercedes all gods. He speaketh things into existence. "But the Lord *is* the true God, he is the living God, and an everlasting king: at his wrath the earth shall tremble, and the nations shall not be able to abide his indignation." Jeremiah 10:10. "They that make a graven image *are* all of them vanity; and their delectable things shall not profit; and they *are* their own witnesses; they see not, nor know; that they may be ashamed. Who hath formed a god, or molten a graven image *that* is profitable for nothing? Behold, all his fellows shall be ashamed: and the workmen, they *are* of men: let them all be gathered together, let them stand up; *yet* they shall fear, *and* they shall be ashamed together. The smith with the tongs both worketh in the coals, and fashioneth it with hammers, and worketh it with the strength of his arms: yea, he is hungry, and his strength faileth: he drinketh no water, and is faint...shall I fall down to the stock of a tree?...a deceived heart hath turned him aside, that he cannot deliver his soul, nor say, *Is there* not a lie in my right hand?" Isaiah 44:9-12, 19, 20.

God is Perfect, irreplaceable, cannot make mistakes. God is the only True God. "I *am* the Lord, and *there is* none else, *there* is no God beside me...I form the light, and create darkness: I make peace, and create evil: I the Lord do all these *things*. Drop down, ye heavens, from above, and let the skies pour down righteousness: let the earth open, and let them bring forth salvation, and let righteousness spring up together, I the Lord have created it." Isaiah 45:5, 7-8. "I have sworn by myself, the word is gone out of my mouth *in* righteousness, and shall not return, That unto me every knee shall bow, every tongue shall swear. Surely, shall *one* say, in the Lord have I righteousness and strength: *even* to him shall *men* come; and all that are incensed against him shall be ashamed." Isaiah 45:23-24. "Fear ye not, neither be afraid: have not I told thee from that time, and have declared *it*? ye *are* even my witnesses. Is there a God beside me? yea, *there is* no God; I know not *any*." Isaiah 44:8. Other (small "g" gods) come and go and can do nothing, except fail.

How should wealth be attained? Honestly. Dishonesty dirties, clouding everyone and everything it touches. The devil and his angels are dishonest, encouraging stealing, killing, and destroying. Dishonest accumulations float away. "*There* is no peace, saith the Lord, unto the wicked." Isaiah 48:22.

God plus riches equal opportunities afforded for charity. Power results from knowledge and unleashes possibilities and benefits.

Righteousness brings peace and blessings. "And the work of righteousness shall be peace; and the effect of righteousness quietness and assurance for ever." Isaiah 32:17." For the kingdom of God is not meat and drink; but righteousness, and peace, and joy in the Holy Ghost." Romans 14:17.

Risks. With God, certainty abounds. God offers eternal life. His security is guaranteed offering options in every life area. With God, nothing is unmanageable.

On the other hand, the devil offers uncertainty and eternal damnation. He is a liar and bully. He uses ploys – lies, thievery, depression, oppression, murder, whoredom and other evils - to steal souls. If Satan creeps into your mind and body, he steals, kills, and, destroys. Some people have the wrong image of Satan. They think he is good; but, he is bad news - respecter of persons and thief. Take a lesson from one of the men who went to everlasting torment: "There was a certain rich man, which was clothed in purple, and fine linen and fared sumptuously every day...the rich man died, and was buried...And in hell he lift his eyes..." St. Luke 16:19, 22-23. He was tormented in flame. He asked the Father to send someone to warn his brothers so they would not come to this hot torment. His appeal is not granted. Obviously, his brethren already had Moses and the prophets. They should heed to them. Emphatically, pleasurable moments expire quickly; but hell is eternal - torment forever.

Beforehand, decision must be made not to make hell home. Afterwards, change is impossible. For worldly lusts, people take life-threatening risks. If your soul is gambled away, hell is waiting.

Salvation Plan. God's pathway leads to heaven. "If we confess our sins, he is faithful and just to forgive us *our* sins, and to cleanse us from all unrighteousness." I John 1:9. Unrighteousness is wickedness. God will not share his people with the world. He cleanses the **whole** man. "Behold, the whirlwind of the Lord goeth forth with fury...it shall fall with pain upon the head of the wicked. The fierce anger of the Lord shall not return, until he has done *it*, and until he have performed the intents of the heart: in the latter days ye shall consider it." Jeremiah 30:23-24.

Joseph, the dreamer, may have found resolution(s) in the pit. In crisis, peace, growth, and consolation, is possible. Whether before, during, or after pit escapement, realize God's call. He has plans. Analytically, and undeniably, friends and enemies see God's strong hands working. "Come unto me, all *ye* that labour and are heavy laden, and I will give you rest." St. Matthew 11:28.

Self-Commitment. Soar to, and in, excellence. Avoid regrets. Erase regrets. To avoid regrets, dreamers *consciously* practice prudent preventions and seize proper opportunities. "I can do all things through Christ which strengtheneth me." Philippians 4:13.

God's exaltation is purity and fairness. High self-esteem and motivation minimize peer pressure and nondreamers' opposition tactics. But, unmerited praise maximizes low self-esteem. Evil status quos diminish achievements. Soar high. Flee inappropriateness.

Exceptionally, dreamers understand "fitting in" is deception, contempt, and tokenism. Dreamers share outcast depictions. "Fitting out" is best.

Self-disparagement breeds poor portrayals. In turn, suicide and other problems arise. Self-fairness, and fairness toward others, is core. Despicably, exaltation and promotion are purposely withheld from deserving souls. Disdainfully, God's people are hated, mistreated, and ostracized. "These things I command you, that ye love one another. If ye were of the world, the world would love his own: but because ye are not of the world, but I have chosen you out of the world, therefore the world hateth you. If the world hate you, ye know that it hated me before it hated you. Remember the word that I said unto you, The servant is not greater than his lord. If they have persecuted me, they will also persecute you; if they have kept my saying, they will keep yours also. But all these things will they do unto you for my name's sake, because they know not him that sent me." St. John 15:17-21.

Dreamers encourage themselves in the Lord. "…David was greatly distressed…but David encouraged himself in the Lord his God." I Samuel 30:6.

Regrets create nondreamers. Nondreamers blame others for their disenchantments. Their low self-esteem is channeled to others. Self-worth determines whether you are a dreamer or not.

Simplification. Dreamers choose Life in Jesus Christ. Dreamers' holy calling is laser-focused entirely on Jesus. In pursuance of God's greatness, dreamers resist worldly distractions. Engrossment for worldliness is imprudence and lukewarmness leading to soul loss endangerments. Dreamers advocate wise choices.

Not accepting God's salvation leads to eternal damnation. God's ways are holy. You cannot live scandalously while claiming to be holy. "Enter ye in at the strait gate: for wide *is* the gate, and broad *is* the way, that leadeth to destruction, and many there be which go in thereat: Because strait *is* the gate, and narrow *is* the way, which leadeth unto life, and few there be that find it. Beware of false prophets, which come to you in sheep's clothing, but inwardly they are ravening wolves." St. Matthew 7:13-15. "Strive to enter in at the strait gate: for many, I say unto you, will seek to enter in, and shall not be able. When once the master of the house is risen up, and hath shut to the door, and ye begin to stand without, and to knock at the door, saying, Lord, Lord, open unto us; and he shall answer and say unto you, I know you not whence ye are: Then shall ye begin to say, We have eaten and drunk in thy presence, and thou hast taught in our streets. But he shall say, I tell you, I know you not whence ye are; depart from me, all *ye* workers of iniquity. There shall be weeping and gnashing of teeth, when ye shall see Abraham, and Isaac, and Jacob, and all the prophets, in the kingdom of God, and you *yourselves* thrust out. And they shall come from the east, and *from* the west, and from the north, and *from* the south, and shall sit down in the kingdom of God. And, behold, there are last which shall be first, and there are first which shall be last." St. Luke 13:24-30.

"For the time is *come* that judgment must begin at the house of God: and if *it* first *begin* at us, what shall the end *be* of them that obey not the gospel of God." I Peter 4:17.

If the "elect" is not watching and praying, the devil's enticements are likely working. Satan accepts any gullible souls.

Please do not go to eternal torment. Please do not go. Choose Jesus. He is knocking at your heart door. Please, do not wait too late. Ask the Lord to forgive all your sins. He forgives sins. He loves you. When you get right with God, joy and peace is immediate, knowing that He is waiting and watching over your soul.

Non-dreamers overcomplicate matters, facilitating wastefulness, discouragement, and soul loss. "Then shall he say also unto them on the left hand, Depart from me, ye cursed, into everlasting fire, prepared for the devil and his angels ...." St. Matthew 25:41.

Soul Fishers. Dreamers walk in deepness; however, nondreamers tread in shallowness. Nondreaming looters suck dreams, air, and strength, from unwise, weak souls. Nondreamers' lack necessary stamina for working through mazes or withstanding their own instigative opposition tactics. Mediocre endeavors flood naive spaces. Time and energy is sucked into mean-spiritedness.

"And Jesus said unto them, Come ye after me, and I will make you to become fishers of men." St. Mark 1:17. "And he taught them many things by parables...Hearken; Behold, there went out a sower to sow... as he sowed, some fell by the way side, and the fowls of the air came and devoured it up. And some fell on strong ground, where it had not much earth; and immediately it sprang up, because it had no depth of earth: But when the sun was up, it was scorched; and because it had no root, it withered away." St. Mark 4:2-6.

Spiritual Suicide. Dreamers observe associations and surroundings. Insight is profitable. In many cases, dissociations are necessary. "...if any man that is called a brother be a fornicator, or covetous, or an idolater... or a drunkard, or an extortioner; with such an one no not to eat." I Corinthians 5:11.

Association, with "itching ears," amounts to spiritual irresponsibility. Itching ears associate with sin. Worldly people are bewildered when they cannot see difference between godliness and ungodliness in the lives of those professing purity. Lukewarm lifestyles are careless, confusing, and upsetting. Expecting to see Christians live biblically, rather than just, teaching, is legitimate. Nonedification, for the Body of Christ, demonstrates unconcern for lost souls. Sin generates disrespect. Satan uses various stumblingblocks; including; confusion, deceits, etc. Saints cannot afford itching ears entanglements. Proudly, fakers and manipulators sponsor others' pitfalls, both physically and mentally. "Nor thieves, nor covetous, nor drunkards, nor revilers, nor extortioners, shall inherit the kingdom of God." I Corinthians 6:10. Company with pew villains spawn sinful spill-overs.

Stability is crucial. Simultaneously, "have" and "do" your dreams. Without adaptability and stability, minds become unfocused, contorted, and idle. Broken focus brutalizes spirits causing reckless behavior, sorrow, and destruction.

Stardom. True, everlasting stars, are people, preparing for eternity with God. God's superstars live among us. "And the light shineth in darkness; and the darkness comprehended it not." St. John 1:5. God does not reject anyone. Negatively, dreamers are oftentimes rejected. "...And whosoever will, let him take the water of life freely." Revelation 22:17. God's Stardom is **True** - **Eternal**.

Strong. Dreamers are strong, persistent warriors in the Lord's Army. God's Word teaches strength. "...be strong in the grace that is in Christ Jesus." II Timothy 2:1.

Time Management. Manage time wisely. Permitting others to burn your time and resources communicate imprudence. God's business is urgent. "Watch therefore: for ye know not what hour your Lord doth come." St. Matthew 24:42. "Therefore be ye also ready: for in such an hour as ye think not the Son of man cometh." St. Matthew 24:44. "But the day of the Lord will come as a thief in the night; in the which the heavens shall pass away with a great noise, and the elements shall melt with fervent heat, the earth also and the works that are therein shall be burned up." II Peter 3:10. Time is valuable. Time wasted equals time lost.

Tradition. Dreamers' protocol differs from worldly ways and temporalities. Affirmatively, holiness is righteousness. Worldliness is unrighteousness. Holiness and worldliness operate with opposite teachings and are like lightness and darkness. Fellowship with the world fosters evil communication and immoral behavior. "Beware lest any man spoil you through philosophy and vain deceit, after the tradition of men, after the rudiments of the world, and not after Christ." Colossians 2:8.

Trials and Tribulations. God is perfect. He was crucified for mankind's salvation.

Peacemaking dreamers personify optimism, welcoming kindness. It may seem unfair to fight inorder to do good; but Satan hates righteousness. He tries to make goodwill look like an evil trait. Satan loves persecutions and tribulations; because he is the author of lies. "If we suffer, we shall also reign with *him*: if we deny *him*, he also will deny ..." II Timothy 2:12.

Trophy Billboards. God puts dreamers on display so everyone sees His magnificent mercies, blessings and power. "But when thou doest alms, let not thy left hand know what thy right hand doeth: That thine alms may be in secret: and thy Father which seeth in secret himself shall reward them openly." St. Matthew 6:3-4.

When God puts His ambassadors on front rows, He is able to keep them there. But, when man put you on front rows, he might remove you at any time and for any reason. Dreamers seek God's exaltation; but nondreamers seek man's temporal, exaltation.

Trustworthiness is irreplaceable. God is holy - epitome of honesty. Maintenance of untainted reputations can show ability to make viable decisions. False accusations are not *genuine* taints. Perfect human beings are nonexistent. "A good name is rather to be chosen than great riches, and loving favour rather than silver and gold." Proverbs 22:1. "For all have sinned, and come short of the glory of God…" Romans 3:23. Willful sin is egregious.

Utopia is in heaven. Earth is Christian dreamers' workplace making sure God's Word is preached throughout the world. Ultimately, each person chooses their eternity place. Rest in everlasting peace or go to non-ending torment. "But as it is written, Eye hath not seen, nor ear heard, neither have entered into the heart of man, the things which God hath prepared for them that love him." I Corinthians 2:9.

Watchers are personal ambassadors for God – soul-winners. Be **courageous** – informed - stewards. Confession and profession are components of godly responsibilities.

God is complete. Dreamers realize problems stem from unfinished business. Staying focused on God keeps everything in proper focus. God's work provides earthly and heavenly benefits. God has whatever, and whoever, we need. The devil's work wreaks hellish catastrophes.

"So thou, O son of man, I have set thee a watchman…therefore thy shalt hear the word at my mouth, and warn them from me. When I say unto the wicked, O wicked man, thou shalt surely die; if thou dost not speak to warn the wicked from his way, that wicked *man* shall die in his iniquity; but his blood will I require at thine hand. Nevertheless, if thy warn the wicked of his way to turn from it; if he do not turn from his way, he shall die in his iniquity; but thy hast delivered thy soul." Ezekiel 33:7-9. Launch bold appeals for souls.

Who and What Was On the Ark? Eight souls were saved on the ark, but other souls perished. Lifestyles can show where preparations are being made to spend eternity. Righteous peoples' lives demonstrate they are on their way to heaven. Having, and maintaining, a personal relationship with God is wholesome and secures heavenly outcomes.

"And the Lord said, I will destroy man whom I have created from the face of the earth; both man, and beast, and the creeping thing, and the fowls of the air; for it repenteth me that I have made them. But Noah found grace in the eyes of the Lord. These *are* the generations of Noah:

Noah was a just man *and* perfect in his generations, *and* Noah walked with God." Genesis 6: 7-9. "And the Lord said unto Noah, Come thou and all thy house into the ark; for thee have I seen righteous before me in this generation." Genesis 7:1.

No one should risk going to eternal torment. Can you imagine how many times you might ask yourself "how did I get to this hot, never-ending, torment? The best thing to do is not go to eternal torment. Once you arrive, it is too late for questions? Now is the time for making everything right between you and God.

Men-pleasers seek man's attention and acceptance. While seeking worldly attention, pretenses and wicked acts are expected and required. Many souls are lost in pursuit of worldly fame, goods, and luxuries. Pretending you know Christ will not get you to heaven. Keeping God's commandments is the only pathway. Repetitively, this book points out how righteous words, without a righteous life, is insufficient. Confession and profession coincide. Quoting scriptures is good. Studying, and living, the scriptures is necessary.

"But as the days of No-é *were,* so shall also be the coming of the Son of man be. For as in the days that were before the flood they were eating and drinking, marrying and giving in marriage, until the day that No-é entered into the ark, and knew not until the flood came, and took them all away; so shall also the coming of the Son of man be." St. Matthew 24:37-39. "Behold, the eyes of the Lord *is* upon them that fear him, upon them that hope in his mercy; to deliver their soul from death, and to keep them alive in famine. Our soul waiteth for the Lord: he *is* our help and our shield. For our heart shall rejoice in him, because we have trusted in his holy name. Let thy mercy, O Lord, be upon us, according as we hope in thee." Psalm 33:18-22.

Relationship with Jesus leads to eternal peace. Living for Him commands serious commitment. Pitifully, some people spend all their time and endeavors on worldly pursuits. Worldly resources are left. Worldly pursuits cause sleeplessness, chaos, and in the end, much soul loss. Be wise! Go to heaven.

Winners. Eagle-tis-ti-cal Dreamers depend on God. "But they that wait upon the Lord shall renew *their* strength; they shall mount up with wings as eagles; they shall run, and not be weary; and they shall walk, and not faint." Isaiah 40:31. Dreamers give obeisance to God.

Non-dreamers worship graven images. "To whom then will ye liken God? or what likeness will ye compare unto him? The workman melteth a graven image, and the goldsmith spreadeth it over with gold, and casteth silver chains. He that *is* so impoverished that he hath no oblation chooseth a tree *that* will not rot; he seeketh unto him a cunning workman to prepare a graven image…" Isaiah 40:18-20.

Wise. Scripture likens the kingdom of heaven unto ten virgins. "They that were foolish took their lamps, and took no oil with them: But the wise took oil in their vessels with their lamps." St. Matthew 25:3-4. Dreamers frown on foolishness; whereas, nondreamers love, initiate, and follow folly.

Words. "He that hath knowledge spareth his words: and a man of understanding is of an excellent spirit." Proverbs 17:27. Words surmise power, whether positive or negative. Dreamers use words wisely and sparingly. Goals may be accomplished or foiled, depending on sayings' potency.

"But above all things, my brethren, swear not, neither by heaven, neither by the earth, neither by any other oath: but let your yea be yea, and *your* nay, nay; lest ye fall into condemnation." James 5:12.

Work Ethics. If anyone claims they have nothing to do, do not believe them and pray for them; because "…The harvest truly is plenteous, but the labourers *are* few; pray ye therefore the Lord of the harvest, that He will send forth labourers into his harvest." St. Matthew 9:37-38.

Worship. Bow down to God - Truth. "For though there be that are called gods, whether in heaven or in earth, (as there be gods many, and lords many) but to us there is but one God, the Father, of whom are all things, and we in him; and one Lord Jesus Christ, by whom *are* all things, and we by him." I Corinthians 8:5-6.

Daily Jesus doses cause Satan to flee.

Parents instill imprints in children's minds.
Dreaming requires motivation!

Remember, God loves you unconditionally.
Pit problems start early. Why?
Satan hates God's plans for your life.

4

Nondreamers' Opposition Tactics

"Where there is no vision, the people perish: but he that keepeth the law, happy is he."

PROVERBS 29:18

Nondreamers Stand Still and Obstruct Progress

DEALING WITH NONDREAMERS' mediocrity is uneasy and cumbersome. They stifle progress and progression seekers. Nondreamers deny deserved credit standing on wrong side(s) of times and issues which shows vision lack. They are perishing and cause others to perish. Watch your company.

Joseph's brothers were nondreamers. That is why they sought to kill him. Men-pleasers (nondreamers) despise Jesus association. They are ashamed of God Who created them in His own image. Straightforwardly, pew villains are nondreamers preferring to be dreamers but lack courage. Nondreamers lack positive initiatives. Also, nondreamers are respecters of persons, lacking courage, self-respect and discipline.

Pew villains use evil, sorted, inhumane tactics. Among pew myopias' plateaus, injustice escalations mount. Spiritual, humane, leaders disassociate from opposition tactics. Opposition tactics lead to respecter of persons. Justice thrives in humane administrations; but injustices thrive in non-God-fearing administrations. In God's eyes, man is equal. Man is God's creation. God made man in His image. Unfortunately, pew myopias downplay God's role in heaven and earth.

Nondreamers' non-enthusiastic, hope-draining, joy-stealing, and peace-breaking, attitudes provoke indecencies. Opposition tactics itemize negative-focused duplicities and complicities. Some pew villains concoct schemes alone; although, many connect with wicked networks. Dangerous pew villains wreak mayhem. Elevation and edification is downplayed. Nondreamers pretend to have dreamers' best interests in mind. But, at the same time, plot and hope for downfalls. Truth is faded from the scene; because, opposition tactics kill hope, peace and goodness. Nothing remains but lies, deceit, and slander. Constantly, nondreamers' wicked tradition full-blooms. Many souls fall victim to sinful plots.

Dreamlessness is like heartlessness. Figuratively, dreamers carry obstinate nondreamers on their backs. Realization, of important issues, is missing. Keep in mind, sometimes devils appear as angels of light. To the naked eye, they appear righteous, but are ravenous mockers.

Nondreamers, are followers structuring their lives for men-pleasers. How? They obey man rather than God and are mercy abusers and attackers. "…your faith should not stand in the wisdom of men, but in the power of God." I Corinthians 2:5. Their path is sown by mediocrity thinkers. By using unrighteous remedies, liars tend to think unsound judgments cover shortcomings and evil deeds. That is why many resources are plundered to pew villains' unseemly endeavors.

"…Love your enemies, bless them that curse you, do good to them that hate you, and pray for them which despitefully use you, and persecute you; that ye may be the children of your Father which is in heaven…For if ye love them which love you, what reward have ye?…And if ye salute your brethren only, what do ye more *than others*? …" St. Matthew 5:44-47.

Vast amounts of time consume malicious plots. As a whole, mediocrity mentalities are hindrances and slowdowns to churches and society. Shockingly, thousands of people participate in, and enjoy, thoughtless nondreaming undertakings. These actions make meaninglessness more pronounced and less preventable. Dealing with negativity, and stupidity, are two of the most agonizing jobs on earth. Empty minds make rackets but represents weakness. Excellence (dreamers) overpowers mediocrity (nondreamers). Dreamers discern nondreamers' evil deeds. Watching and praying is necessary.

Dreamers' primary interest, and mission, is soul-saving. In contrast, nondreamers subscribe to mediocrity and wickedness. Although differences between dreamers and nondreamers skyrocket, many nondreamers convert to dreamers. After prudent consideration of unrighteous opposition tactics, holy conversion follows. The Bible teaches, "Can two walk together, except they be agreed?" Amos 3:3. Wisdom says when you learn better, do things differently. Sadly, some evil mindsets are unchangeable. "Woe unto them that call evil good, and good evil; that put darkness for light, and light for darkness; that put bitter for sweet, and sweet for bitter! Which justify the wicked for reward, and take away the righteousness of the righteous from him!" Isaiah 5:20, 23.

Bold, righteous dreamers find naught encouragement from merciless deceivers. Nondreamers walk in darkness; because they fall in love with worldliness and seducing antichrists' lies – false sense of security. Their intent is to spread misery while implanting growth impediments. Outcomes are inevitable – hell eternal.

As this book emphasizes, Joseph is a dreamer; but his brothers are nondreamers. Mean-spirited tactics cause him and his family suffering. Oftentimes, nondreamers are pew, family, and community, enemies. *Opposition tactics – toward dreamers - include:*

Accusers. Basically, underpinnings, antics, and overlapping, are the same for accusers, credit denying foes, and pew villains. Credit denial comes in different forms: intellectual, philosophical, and monetary. Deceivingly, Satan leads pew villains into hateful cover-ups thinking these mentalities and actions deceive dreamers. They think safety lies in lying and conniving. Confess sins to God. God forgives. "If we confess our sins, he is faithful and just to forgive us *our* sins, and to cleanse us from all unrighteousness. I John 1:9.

Clearly, the Bible teaches confession. Cover-ups jumble matters. Confession and forgiveness institute redemption and growth – redeployments to higher places in the Lord. Otherwise, cover-ups prolong wilderness experiences.

Cover-ups' aim is to make wickedness seem right. The Bible teaches, "For from within, out of the heart of men, proceed evil thoughts…thefts, covetousness, wickedness, deceit, lasciviousness, an evil eye, blasphemy, pride, foolishness: All these evil things come from within, and defile the man." St. Mark 7:21-23.

God is our Creator and Truth. He loves us. He is interactive. He is not a liar, thief, cheater, or author of confusion. He pays whatever is right and fair, not condoning wrongness; but forgiving sin.

Angles. Admittedly, human beings "take sides." Without exception, truth counts on all sides. Let lumps fall in all deservable places. Verbally, sides are taken; however, deceitful sides attempt to hide behind silence. Damage is still done whether wrongness is committed verbally or silently.

Lies have several sides; because each untruth levy multiple layers. Lies can be hard to exterminate and overcome. Truth stands. For liars, reliability is implausibility.

Antichrists are deceiving, hostile, receptacles serving in various church roles. Avoidance is necessary. "For many deceivers are entered into the world who confess not that Jesus Christ is come in the flesh. This is a deceiver and an an'tichrist." II John 7. "For both prophet and priest are profane; yea, in my house have I found their wickedness, saith the Lord." Jeremiah 23:11. Antichrists reward evil and shun good. Antichrists insist on obstructing God's Work. These ruthless problem raisers - liars, deceivers, slanderers, thieves, witchcrafters, fornicators, adulterers, harassers – are members or attendees in many churches. Their pitches are evil – confusion and division.

The devil gives false scripts. He hopes you follow it; because the destination is "heat" eternal. "…it is the last time: and as ye have heard that an'-ti-christ shall come, even now are there many an'tichrists; whereby we know that it is the last time." I John 2:18. God is displeased with falsehood.

"That he might present it to himself a glorious church, not having spot, or wrinkle, or any such thing; but that it should be holy and without blemish." Ephesians 5:27.

Clearly, God's called shepherds and ambassadors have responsibilities. When His work is snubbed, flocks are prey. "Therefore, ye shepherds, hear the word of the Lord; *as* I live saith the Lord God, surely because my flock became a prey, and my flock became meat to every beast of the field, because *there was* no shepherd, neither did my shepherds search for my flock, but the shepherds fed themselves, and fed not my flock; therefore, O ye shepherds, hear the word of the Lord; Thus saith the Lord God; Behold, I *am* against the shepherds, and I will require my flock at their hand, and cause them to cease from feeding the flock; neither shall the shepherds feed themselves any more; for I will deliver my flock from their mouth, that they may not be meat for them. For thus saith the Lord God; Behold, I, *even* I, will both search my sheep, and seek them out." Ezekiel 34:7-11. God is the mindful and compassionate Shepherd of His flock. "As a shepherd seekest out his flock in the day that he is among his sheep *that are* scattered; so will I seek out my sheep, and will deliver them out of all places where they have been scattered in the cloudy and dark day." Ezekiel 34:12.

Figuratively, antichrists live in sewers, collecting mind trash, distributing to others, then taking advantage. Attitudes and actions are irresponsible causing immense tragedies. Ultimately, God delivers.

Attention Pursuers. Attention-pursuers take God's glory and give it to themselves. Disappointingly, nondreamers deny Jesus' glory while giving the devil praise. Jesus heals the sick and raises the dead; yet nondreamers give credit to men instead of Jesus. Why are we surprised when men deny rightful credits??? Liars and imposters are among us.

Dreamers do right whether given credit or not. Why? Because God gives deserved credit. Jesus teaches us not to grow weary. God pays what is right. Righteously, maintaining good works and not returning evil for evil, is important. ". . . why look ye so earnestly on us, as though by our own power or holiness we had made this man to walk? The God of

Abraham, and of Isaac, and of Jacob, the God of our fathers, hath glorified his Son Jesus; whom ye delivered up, and denied him in the presence of Pilate, when he was determined to let go. But ye denied the Holy One and the Just, and desired a murderer to be granted unto you; and killed the Prince of life, whom God hath raised him from the dead; whereof we are witnesses." The Acts 3:12-15.

When Jesus was on earth, he suffered. Now He is sitting on the right hand of God. The Bible teaches, we, His people, will have tribulations.

Dreamers shun attention; yet, receive it, leading to jealousy and opposition tactics. Contrastingly, nondreamers pursue and relish recognition; but are uncalled to leadership. Punishing, and ridiculing, "called leaders," is an age-old attention pursuers' evil practice.

Beware. Nondreamers outsides shows inconsistency with "insides." Clothing and salutations contribute to pretenses. Pew villains are literate in many forms of deception. "…Beware of the scribes, which love to go in long clothing, and *love* salutations in the marketplaces…" St. Mark 12:38. "Woe unto you…hypocrites! for ye devour widows' houses, and for a pretense make long prayer: therefore ye shall receive the greater damnation." St. Matthew 23:14. "Even so ye also outwardly appear righteous unto men, but within ye are full of hypocrisy and iniquity." St. Matthew 23:28.

Fast and pray to God. Stay close to Him. Dreamers discern hypocrites. Jesus' guidance shows life's paths. God-pleasers attention focuses on Him and His Work. On the other hand, men-pleasers appease men. If you have any questions, ask God. He loves helping you.

Boasting in Mischief. God is limitless. Evil doings are seen. To God, man's so-called hiding places are nonexistent. God sees everybody and all things. He sees through walls, partitions, earth, etc. Believeably, He sees and knows each act, whether good or not. He is Almighty God.

Behavior Documentation. Negative experiences, with pew villains, are akin to acid. Being there, seeing, and experiencing nondreamers' opposition networks conveys life-altering forwardness or backwardness. Josesph moved forward. Dreamers move forward. Going backward is senseless. Untameable tongues suscribe to enoromous triviality, nonsense, stupidity, insanity, and insincerity (nondreamers). Analyzing pew villians' opposition tactics reveal massive, negative, alignments and absurdness. Aggrievedness withhold much progress and compassion causing some dream loss or slowness. Strong dreamers survive opposition tactics. Pew villians' obstruction redefines bottomless pits. Joseph was thrown in a pit. Thankfully, God rescued him. Successfully, Joseph fullfiled his dreams. Wasted minds creep into peoples, times, and places. In times of trouble, dreamers seek God for help. God is True and Dependable.

"Why boastest thou thyself in mischief, O mighty man? The goodness of God *endureth* continually. The tongue deviseth mischiefs; like a sharp razor, working deceitfully. Thou lovest evil more than good; *and lying* rather than to speak righteousness..." Psalm 52:1-3. Lying, stealing, and using entrapment schemes, is wickedness. Schemes are devised against God's annointed believers. God's believers' prayers, and closeness to Him, prevent slips and downfalls. Enemies set traps seeking demises; but, God is The Deliverer. He holds His people up. He exalts His people. God is praised and exalted for His love, grace, and mightiness. Enemies are upset when their deceitfulness fails. "Thou lovest all devouring words, O *thou* deceitful tongue. God shall likewise destroy thee for ever, he shall take thee away, and pluck thee out of *thy* dwelling place, and root thee out of the land of the living...The righteous also shall see, and fear, and shall laugh at him: Lo, *this is* the man *that* made not God his strength; but trusted in the abundance of his riches, *and* strengthened himself in his wickedness." Psalm 52:4-7.

Trusting in God is life, wisdom, power, and days prolongment. "But I *am* like a green olive tree in the house of God: I trust in the mercy of God for ever and ever. I will praise thee for ever, because thou hast done *it*: and I will wait on thy name; for *it is* good before thy saints." Psalm 52:8-9.

Brain Commotion is mental head actions. Many look outside for solutions but never inside. Inside is where unsolved problems lie. As long as innards are victimized, outwards are also victimized. The two coexistent. Fix inside; then, outside flourishes.

Challenges and Payoffs. Living holy is eventful and fun. God's Holy Ghost warriors teach, preach, fight evil, laugh, cry, and stay ready for heaven. "Fight the good fight of faith, lay hold on eternal life, whereunto thou art also called, and hast professed a good profession before many witnesses." I Timothy 6:12. "I have fought a good fight, I have finished *my* course, I have kept the faith: Henceforth there is laid up for me a crown of righteousness, which the Lord, the righteous judge, shall give me at that day: and not to me only, but unto all them also that love his appearing." II Timothy 4:7-8.

Chaos Expectation. In the midst of God-fearing saints, snare factions set up heresies. They go from house to house, store to store, gathering to gathering, searching for timid, mindless, souls. Snare faction leaders organize busybodies, clone victims, seeking to slaughter God's peoples' reputations. Dreamers receive endless destruction messages. Unquestionably, dreamers, acknowledge and monitor nondreamers' long, dream-deprecation, list. By no means, should opposition threats deter dream fulfillment. Nondreamers' brokenness propels actions to look for answers in negative paths. Positively, working on self negates attaching "personal responsibility" on, or to, others. Self-responsibility, values, and equality, interlink. Fairness to self comes before fairness to others. Interlinks withstand impediments better than standalones.

These busybodies attend church and community functions. They read scriptures, preach, teach, sing, praise, testify, and hold church positions; but foster personal agendas – opposition tactics.

Recruitment, of others to chaotic disingenuous circles, is constant. Righteous non-compliance is taken casually and mockingly. Retaliation is furious. Criticism and disapproval solicitations are made against innocent, God-fearing saints. Some are swayed with lies and misinformation, but thank God, many are not. How many souls lose hope because of madness? Pew villains say a lot of honest things; but, lifestyles reflect dishonesty.

"Yea, and all that will live godly in Christ Jesus shall suffer persecution. But evil men and seducers shall wax worse and worse, deceiving, and being deceived." II Timothy 3:12-13.

Childish (Numeric Grown-Ups). How many grown-up children do you know? Physiological growth, without psychological growth, yields childish behaviors. These growths work together. One growth without the other causes societal dysfunctions. Unfortunately, some societies are not performing with full decks; namely, righteous, mature, grown-up, rational, individuals. In many cases, chronological grownups seem to be psychologically immature. Immature adults confuse "real children," making successful training difficult.

When "grown-ups" are immature, their behavior influences others to immaturity. Under these conditions, do you think society functions at full potential? "When I was a child, I spake as a child, I understood as a child, I thought as a child: but when I became a man, I put away childish things." I Corinthians 13:11. Apparently, many grown-ups refuse putting away childishness; therefore, everyone loses because improper protocols and orderliness are absent.

"-cisms", "-ists", and "-tries". God rewards righteousness. Apparently, in the church world, the devil creates the same types of mindsets as in non-church settings; namely, skepticism, racism, criticism, and contraries – evil opposition tactics. Sadly, he has numerous followers. Non-followers, of "cisms," "ists," and "tries," are often mistreated and renounced. Wrongness bows at righteousness' feet. "There hath no temptation taken you but such as is common to man: but God *is* faithful, who will not suffer you to be tempted above that ye are able; but will with the temptation also make a way to escape, that ye may be able to bear *it*." I Corinthians 10:13. Steadiness stands up to mediocrity; whereas, unsteadiness falls victim to vileness.

Complainers/Mummers market petty distractions, along with progress stoppers. While ignoring productivity, grumblers commit time to counter-productivity. Misery, unhappiness, and endless problems pacify unfulfillment. Because of whiners' self-inflicted problems, positive interactions are basically unexpected.

Core problems should be addressed and fixed. Complainers deal with symptoms only. As long as root causes remain unaddressed, negative exchanges continuously follow. "Do all things without murmurings and disputings." Philippians 2:14.

Conduct. Nondreamers say things, but oftentimes do the opposite. Trustworthiness is not their virtue. Purposely, this book describes vast differences between positive dreamers' traits and negative nondreamers' opposition tactics.

Do you encourage people to turn from wickedness or do you help them commit sin? Is your lifestyle helping or hurting? Do you cause erring from the faith? Itching ears cause chaos on pews and everywhere else. Dreamers' alertness is imperative; because enemies use opposition tactics hoping to destroy and defeat goodness.

"For both prophet and priest are profane; yea, in my house have I found their wickedness, saith the Lord. Wherefore their way shall be unto them as slippery *ways* in the darkness: they shall be driven on, and fall therein: for I will bring evil upon them …saith the Lord. And I have seen folly in the prophets…they prophesied…and caused my people…to err. I have seen also…an horrible thing: they commit adultery, and walk in lies: they strengthen also the hands of evildoers, that none doth return from his wickedness: they are all of them unto me as Sodom, and the inhabitants thereof as Gomorrah. Therefore thus saith the Lord of hosts concerning the prophets; Behold I will feed them with wormwood, and make them drink the water of gall…for from the prophets…is profaneness gone forth in all the land. Thus saith the Lord of hosts, Hearken not unto the words of the prophets that prophesy unto you: they make you vain: they speak a vision of their own heart, *and* not out of the mouth of the Lord. For who hath stood in the counsel of the Lord, and hath perceived and heard his word…a whirlwind of the Lord has gone forth in fury…it shall fall grievously upon the head of the wicked. The anger of the Lord shall not return, until he have executed, and till he have performed the thoughts of his heart: in the latter days ye shall consider it perfectly. I have not sent these prophets, yet they ran: I have not spoken to them, yet they prophesied. But if they had stood in my counsel and caused my people to hear my words, then they should have turned them from their evil way, and from the evil of their doings. *Am* I a God at hand, saith the Lord, and not a God afar off? Can any hide himself in secret places that I shall not see him? saith the Lord. Do not I fill heaven and earth? saith the Lord. I have heard what the prophets said, that prophesy lies in my name, saying, I have dreamed…How long shall *this* be in the heart of the prophets that prophesy lies? yea, *they are* prophets of the deceit of their own heart…he that hath my word, let him speak my word faithfully…saith the Lord. *Is* not my word like unto a fire, saith the Lord; and like a hammer *that* breaketh the rock in pieces?…I *am* against the prophets, saith the Lord, that steal my words every one from his neighbor…I *am* against them that prophesy false dreams, saith the Lord, and do tell them, and cause my people to err by their lies, and by their lightness; yet I sent them not, nor commanded them: therefore they shall not profit this people at all, saith the Lord…for every man's word shall be his burden; for ye have perverted the words of the living God, of the Lord of hosts our God." Jeremiah 23:11-16, 18-30, 32, 36.

Conspiracy. To kill dreams, enemies use subtlety and aggressiveness. Nondreamers consider lying and detractions more elusive than talebearing; but, both are deceitfulness and wickedness. While dreamers sleep, enemies plan demises. Scripture says, "He that hateth dissembleth with his lips, and layeth up deceit within him; when he speaketh fair, believe him not: for *there are* seven abominations in his heart. *Whose* hatred is covered by deceit, his wickedness shall be shewed before the *whole* congregation. Whoso diggeth a pit shall fall therein: and he that rolleth a stone, it will return upon him. A lying tongue hateth *those that are* afflicted by it; and a flattering mouth worketh ruin." Proverbs 26:24-28.

Contextual Environments. In addition to other scheming antics, pew villains use caricature for evil promotions. The Holy Bible's meanings and protocols are eternal. Speech mirrors the heart. In other words, speech says what your heart thinks. "O generation of vipers, how can ye, being evil, speak good things? for out of the abundance of the heart the mouth speaketh…an evil man out of the evil treasure bringeth forth evil things. But I say unto you, That every idle word that men shall speak, they shall give account thereof in the day of judgment. For by thy words thou shalt be justified, and by thy words thy shalt be condemned." St. Matthew 12:34-37. "Dearly beloved, avenge not yourselves, but *rather* give place unto wrath: for it is written, Vengeance *is* mine; I will repay, saith the Lord." Romans 12:19. Words and actions should not be taken out of proper venues.

Correlation Formula. Working on dreams requires business activities. Soaring signifies faith and works. Nondreamers miss the connection between faith and works. "Ye see then how that by works a man is justified, and not by faith only." James 2:24. "Even so faith, if it hath not works, is dead, being alone...a man may say, Thou hast faith, and I have works: shew me thy faith without thy works, and I will shew thee my faith by my works." James 2:17-18. Automatically, talk, without action, formalizes dream death.

Cynics' presentations constitute bullies' mediocrity. Sadly, shallowness constitutes nondreamers' normal behavior.

Eagle-tis-ti-cal dreamers are bold enough to ask "why"? Specifically, cynics congregate in churches and are staunch dream quenchers - betrayers. Nondreamers ignore confidentiality toward shepherds, congregation members, and all who have contact with them. Restless, unstable, dangerous, pew villains, start problems and hinder solutions. Enough "clean-up" crews are nonexistent for dismantling nondreamers' messes.

Amidst pew villains' opposition tactics, seemingly some soul-saving opportunities take rear seats. Mistakenly, some people assume church attendance and religious duties are equivalent to Christian living. Biblical teachings call for more. Much more is required; but cynics listen to satanic dogma and seemingly forget God's commandments. "...should not the shepherds feed the flocks? The diseased have ye not strengthened, neither have ye healed that which was sick, neither have ye bound up *that which was* broken, neither have ye brought again that which was driven away, neither have ye sought that which was lost; but with force and with cruelty have ye ruled them. And they were scattered, because t*here is* no shepherd: and they became meat to all the beasts of the field, when they were scattered." Ezekiel 34:2, 4-5.

Repercussions are forthcoming. Scattered flocks need godly attention and care. Pew villains tear congregations, communities, and homes asunder.

Defuse and Refuse. Take yourself from the devil. Give yourself – your life – to God. Reject lies, satanic advances, and bribes. Deceivingly, wickedness destroys minds, bodies, self-respect, and souls. Is the devil holding you hostage? Come to Jesus! Now!

Disguise is fake presentations. Treating people nicely at church, but treating people indignantly elsewhere, is deceitfulness. Abominable acts betray true values.

God is truth. His truth creates clean minds. He is displeased with untruth. He sees and knows heart intentions. Satan raids minds rewarding misrepresentation mediocrities. Ongoing fights rage between good and evil. God is Good! Satan is evil.

Lying, to self, is the root of problems. Truth flies the coup; while, lies grow bigger and bigger. Nondreamers forget God; because, their minds are turned upside down living in make-believe seas.

Reality loss creates theatric environments. Deceivingly, life is an act - portraying a Christian role, while living devilish. Two presentations are made: 1) Public persona – nice, calm and 2) home persona – mean, uncontrollable. When "goody" makeup is removed, the naked truth gets ugly.

Realists are heaven-bound. Fakers lie and beguile, headed to hell if changes are unmade. Hypocrites prefer undercover, cruel tactics; but, family, friends, church, and community, know their fruits. "Wherefore by their fruits ye shall know them." St. Matthew 7:20. "Even so ye also outwardly appear righteous unto men, but within ye are full of hypocrisy, and iniquity." St. Matthew 23:28.

Are you a - faker - Christian actor? Why pretend to be a Christian? "Create in me a clean heart, O God; and renew a right spirit within me." Psalm 51:10.

Defamation. God is strong upholding His people. Persecutors hope you fall. "For I heard the defaming of many, fear on every side...All my familiars watched for my halting, *saying*, Peradventure he will be enticed, and we shall prevail against him, and we shall take our revenge on him. But the Lord *is* with me as a mighty terrible one: therefore my persecutors shall stumble, and they shall not prevail: they shall be greatly ashamed for they shall not prosper: *their* everlasting confusion shall never be forgotten." Jeremiah 20:10-11.

Some ministries are blamed for defamation, offenses, and stumblingblocks. Mistrust, thievery, slander, persecutions, etc., cause pew down-sizing. Literally, evil, unexpected pew experiences, incites unfitting scenarios; especially to worldly audiences. "Even so hath the Lord ordained that they which preach the gospel should live of the gospel." I Corinthians 9:14.

Duplicity has two or more faces, and personalities, pretending to be one. Actually, nondreamers' "nice" faces hide behind venomous, opposition tactics. Nondreamers' objective is to set up footholds in various entities. They encourage wicked complicities and duplicities. These problem-makers steadily steal focus from kingdom work for sadistic pranks. Satanic forces invade congregations which may be overtaken or disintegrated. Posing as innocent bystanders, spiteful planners use fragmentation vices. These heads of self-serving divisions encourage gullible souls' falling into evil camps or fooled by shams. Selfish conspirators mercilessly hurt others. Watch those who always have a lot to say against others. "The righteous *is* more excellent than his neighbor: but the way of the wicked seduceth them. The slothful *man* roasteth not that which he took in hunting: but the substance of a diligent man is precious." Proverbs 12:26-27.

To cover mischievousness, nondreamers lie and talk against dreamers. Nondreamers' target fellow worshippers, as well as people in communities, homes, and workplaces. Truth disengagement spurs uncontrollable discordance urges.

Nondreamers lack courage; so they relinquish personal blame to others. They embrace "discouragement scenes" hoping to impart innocent impressions. That explains why bites are extremely toxic, disturbing, and abysmal. Because of pretenses, many victims do not see opposition tactics coming until it is too late. Stay watchful and prayful.

Everywhere pew villains go, some form of disintegration happens. No one is exempt from their onslaughts. They refuse to apologize for wrongs committed. Instead, whitewashes are forwarded. Their allies are groomed for torment. Undercurrents of unresolved wrongs flood the pews and suck life from gatherings. Disruption, and mindfulness, of lures are important.

Without proper Bible guidance and adherence, survival on some church pews can be challenging; because, nondreamers build tares among wheat. Sadly, they roll on as if God is not watching and as if nothing is happening. Unfortunately, tare-builders are fast and fierce destroyers.

Personal relationships with God, personal responsibility, and personal focus are dreamer requisites. Stay alert. Beware, because many gullible people are entrenched in opposition tactics' networks of falsehood and denigration. Horribly, many gullible souls never make progress or escape.

Opposition to righteousness is on the rise. God's people need vigilance. Fasting and praying keep alertness at the forefront.

Erosion. God wants the best for you. Lying, or any other sin, erodes spiritual relationship with God. One sin at a time is sometimes construed as small; but is huge because souls are at stake. The devil is patient. Sins mount. The devil wants only bad things for you. Watchfulness and prayfullness is always appropriate.

False Faces. Dreamers are forthcoming – not hiding behind – facades – smiles as big as horses. They are eagle-observant looking behind illusions; because frauds do not show heartfelt feelings. Smiling is an unspoken form of flattery. Analytically, what is behind smiles? The more smiles, the more you need to avoid their venom injections.

The Lord hates "A false witness *that* speaketh lies, and he that soweth discord among brethren." Proverbs 6:19. Acts of unkindness and fraud are abominable. "Deliver me not over unto the will of mine enemies: for false witnesses are risen up against me, and such as breathe out cruelty." Psalm 27:12.

Compassionate leadership makes targets; because, excellence outshines mediocrity. Fair, compassionate, Eagle-tis-ti-cal dreamers' courage make constructive differences. Just leaders pave prosperous ways for followers. Although, some leaders, may or, may not be comfortable in leadership roles, focus and movement in godly directions solidifies prudence.

Holy leaders desire followers; because teachings and lifestyles are based on God's Word. Holy followers need, and heed, sanctified leaders.

Claiming to know God differs from knowing Him. Dream haters grin while killing dreams. Dream haters cause tons of damage; all the while they never stop grinning. Grinning does not mean all is well. Oftentimes, grinning means "you had better run for cover; because you are looking in the face of your enemies." Concealment, of hate, is a treacherous weapon.

False Prophets are stumblingblocks; because they preach one thing, but live another. Their goal is attraction and wicked persuasion of unsuspecting victims – commonly labeled as weaklings or low-self esteemers. Ungodly behavior causes chaos in the Body of Christ and in society.

In many cases, members leave churches never returning. "Beware of false prophets, which come to you in sheep's clothing, but inwardly they are raving wolves. Ye shall know them by their fruits. Do men gather grapes of thorns, or figs of thistles? Even so every good tree bringeth forth good fruit; but a corrupt tree bringeth forth evil fruit." St. Matthew 7:15-17…for *the Lord seeth* not as man seeth; for man looketh on the outward appearance, but the Lord looketh on the heart…" I Samuel 16:7.

Carefully weigh tricksters; because for every false prophet you see there may be several unseen. By studying and obeying God's Word, antichrists and misrepresentations are discerned. Discerners feel the heart.

Foolishness and Wisdom - Mismatch. Wisdom is self-love. "He that getteth wisdom loveth his own soul: he that keepeth understanding shall find good." Proverbs 19:8.

"Be ye not as the horse, *or* as the mule. *which* have no understanding: whose mouth must be held in with bit and bridle, lest they come near unto thee." Psalm 32:9. Fools are void of understanding.

"He that begetteth a fool *doeth* it to his sorrow: and the father of a fool hath no joy." Proverbs 17:21. Wisdom does not rest in the bosom of fools. Wisdom and foolishness are enemies. "Go from the presence of a foolish man, when thou perceiveth not *in him* the lips of knowledge." Proverbs 14:7. "For the wisdom of this world is foolishness with God. For it is written, He taketh the wise in their own craftiness." I Corinthians 3:19.

Dreamers promote wisdom and foolishness abolition. If nondreamers work one-fourth as hard to encourage wisdom, as they do to encourage foolishness, the world would be a healthier place.

Mindsets can be changed. Some nondreamers become dreamers. "As a dog returneth to his vomit, *so* a fool returneth to his folly." Proverbs 26:11.

Fountains. Two-facers use aggressiveness and outsourcing for covering their tracks. Grappling, growling, and disturbing peace, are widening menaces. Actually, spreading false information and perceptions of their victims, among hand-picked people, is common. Hopefully, targeted groups discern, pray, and ask God to handle opposition tactics. Without prayer and research, many think lies are truth, furthering contamination. Alliances and friendships constantly diminish. Pew problems move around.

Drinking from right, and wrong, fountains simultaneously is impossible. At some point, choosing God's Way, or the other way, is a choice everyone is destined to make. "Doth a fountain send forth at the same place sweet *water* and bitter? Can the fig tree, my brethren, bear olive berries? either a vine, figs? so *can* no fountain both yield salt water and fresh. Who *is* a wise man and endued with knowledge among you? let him shew out of a good conversation his works with meekness of wisdom. But if ye have bitter envying and strife in your hearts, glory not, and lie not against the truth. This wisdom descendeth not from above, but *is* earthly, sensual, devilish. For where envying and strife is, there *is* confusion and every evil work. But the wisdom that is from above is first pure, then peaceable, gentle, and easy to be intreated, full of mercy and good fruits, without partiality, and without hypocrisy. And the fruit of righteousness is sown in peace of them that make peace." James 3:11-18.

Confess sins. Remember and reminisce, God forgives. God creates clean hearts.

Friendship. "Ye adulterers and adulteresses, know ye not that the friendship of the world is enmity with God? whosoever therefore will be a friend of the world is the enemy of God." James 4:4. Friendship with the world is opposition to God. As this book's subject matter illustrates, dreamers and nondreamers' relationship differences afford limited interactions.

Nondreamers obstructionist responses eliminate practical, positive, involvements. Even with rejections, dreamers remain focused and interested in all human beings' welfare.

God is your Creator and Friend. "Greater love hath no man than this, that a man lay down his life for his friends." St. John 15:13.

Sadly, "friend" is misrepresented, overused, scapegoated, and hijacked. Friends are sparse. Who are friends? Genuine, unbreakable, connections. Most, so-called, friends, who call others friends, are not friends. Without genuineness, clicks and hangouts are meaningless and hypocritical.

Frequently, companions disagree, but are committed, authentic, confidants. Compassion and bonds meet on many levels. Integrity is a mainstream component to steady, lasting, relationships. Consider not departure or hurt. Care triumphs. Understandably, agreements, and sometimes disagreements, are part of friendly relationships.

Pew villains' "so-called friendships" dispense hostility among themselves and others. Pew villains are deceiving crooks. Information is sought only for customized, oppressive, plots. So-called friends are dreamers' oppositionists. Using time for holy projects display faith, stability, and sociability. Thankfully, integrity-based, wholesomeness, outpaces mediocrity. Mediocre systems are incompatible and counterproductive for soaring aspirations and friendships; because, "high" self-esteem is missing. When hypocrites show who they are, wise people take heed. Showing blind eyes to mediocrity magnifies stupidity. Society needs more sensibility and much less folly.

Self-love is the basis for loving others and forming sincere commitments and relationships. On all levels, true friends value one another's concerns and privacy.

Biblical principles are irrefutable. Relationships built on worldly principles fall; because; foundations are unsound and unfair. "...be ye therefore wise as serpents, and harmless as doves." St. Matthew 10:16. Biases, and its participants are faulty, therefore, mechanisms misfire.

Universally, friendships are abused. The noun, friend, is thrown around, abused, misused, taken suspiciously, and lightly. "*Friends*" are, and can be, sources of pain, sorrow and death. "Trust ye not in a friend, put ye not confidence in a guide: keep the doors of thy mouth from her that lieth in thy bosom." Micah 7:5.

Gangster Tactics. Church members are expected to be godly role models; but, worldly tactics infiltrate, confuse and stunt growth. While hypocrites, sit in some pulpits, others sit on some church pews. Instead of worshipping, pew villains' actions induce troublesome behaviors.

"For the pastors are become brutish, and have not sought the Lord: therefore they shall not prosper, and all their flocks shall be scattered." Jeremiah 10:21. "His watchmen *are* blind: they are all ignorant, they are *all* dumb dogs, they cannot bark; sleeping, lying down, loving to slumber. Yea, *they are* greedy dogs *which* can never have enough, and they *are* shepherds *that* cannot understand: they all look to their own way, every one for his gain, from his quarter." Isaiah 56:10-11. "Beware of dogs, beware of evil workers..." Philippians 3:2. Worship assemblies ought not blend with sinful, infectious, plots.

"...Every plant, which my heavenly Father hath not planted, shall be rooted up. Let them alone: they be blind leaders of the blind. And if the blind lead the blind, both shall fall into the ditch. But those things which proceed out of the mouth come forth from the heart; and they defile the man. For out of the heart proceed evil thoughts, murders, adulteries, fornications, thefts, false witness, blasphemies: These are *the things* which defile a man..." St. Matthew 15:13-14, 18-19, 20.

Widespread problems permeate some congregations. Hard-hearted troublemaking nondreamers proclaim they know God. Liars, slanderers, confidence breakers, and bullies, are commonplace.

In case you are unaware, these are Bible-carrying, church-going members. Because of pew villains' violence, assumption might be made they are worldly persons who do not profess knowing God. "Deliver me, O Lord, from the evil man: preserve me from the violent man; which imagine mischiefs in *their* heart; continually are they gathered together *for* war. They have sharpened their tongues like a serpent; adders' poison is under their lips...Keep me, O Lord, from the hands of the wicked; preserve me from the violent man; who have purposed to overthrow my goings." Psalm 140:1-4.

For righteousness' sake, abolition of worldly corruptions, on church pews, is desirable, but not probable. Inevitably, the great falling away is being fulfilled. Prayer and vigilance is prudent.

According to Biblical teachings, problematic situations should be handled. On many levels, stumbling occurs inside and outside of church walls. Why? Sinful (careless) lifestyles scorch hearts of many souls. Distrust and hurt fume, boil over, and cripple.

Seriously, pew gangsters' manipulation, fakeness, lying, slander, thievery, cover-ups etc., sow discord. Subsequently, sinister actions, and behaviors, harden hearts and minds toward church attendance. Furthermore, some soul loss may occur. Ramifications are serious; but perpetrators act and treat their wickedness as folly. "*It is* as sport to a fool to do mischief: but a man of understanding has wisdom." Proverbs 10:23.

Interconnecting Biblical teachings, and personal responsibility, toward your fellow man, provides honorable traction. Satan tells fakers creating false pictures succeed. Consequently, these dishonest pictures generate deceitful securities. Satan and his workers pretend. Counterfeiters, pose as selfless, caring, goodwillers. In essence, when Satan gives you something, it is not for good, but for evil doings and outcomes.

When God gives gifts and wealth, there is no sorrow with it; but when Satan gives wealth, the price is high and the heat is smothering. "The blessing of the Lord, it maketh rich, and he addeth no sorrow with it." Proverbs 10:22. Jesus Christ is the epitome of love, change, hope, and promise.

Getting Along with People. Is it possible to get along with everyone? "If it be possible, as much as lieth in you, live peaceably with all men." Romans 12:18.

Although Joseph is a dreamer, his brothers are nondreamers. They hate him and cannot speak peaceably to him. Is it Joseph's fault that he is a dreamer with nondreaming siblings? No. In spite of Joseph's siblings' persecutions, he maintains and pursues his dreams. Dreamers are about Jesus' business. In order to fulfill dreams, withdrawal from foolishness is essential. Fools' perverse lips fill despair pits. "… discretion…deferreth… anger; and *it is* his glory to pass over a transgression." Proverbs 19:11.

God Deprivation. Without God, life is incomplete and distorted. In all areas of life, incompletion and distortion cause slowdowns, meltdowns, and shutdowns leading many to eternal fire and brimstone.

God Treatment. Do you respect God as your Creator? Do you know God loves you? Do you love Him? Do you know God is not crazy, senile, or stupid? Do you know He has no respect of persons? Do you know He knocks on your heart door? Aforementioned questions are thought-provoking. Many people discount, disrespect, and deny God's Word, status, and glory. Thoughts, behavior, and eternity count. Preparations start now! Taking chance(s) on missing heaven frighten prudent souls straight into heaven.

"To have respect of persons *is* not good: for for a piece of bread *that* man will transgress." Proverbs 28:21. "Behold, the Lord's hand is not shortened, that it cannot save; neither his ear heavy, that it cannot hear. But your iniquities have separated between you and your God, and your sins have hid *his* face from you, that he will not hear: For your hands are defiled with blood, and your fingers with iniquity; your lips have spoken lies, your tongue hath muttered perverseness. None calleth for justice, nor *any* pleadeth for truth: they trust in vanity, and speak lies; they conceive mischief, and bring forth iniquity." Isaiah 59:1-4.

Reality mirrors keenness. Justice, righteousness, cries out for all. Rightly, justice is a birthright for all. Wrongly and oftentimes, justice is promoted as privileges. Dream crushers seek to devour brilliant-minded goals and acquisitions. Dousing dreams wreak peril. Watch out for dream crushers!

Harlot. This book focuses on Joseph's dreams and some problems encountered toward his pursuits. He is falsely accused and imprisoned; because, he refuses to lie with King Pharaoh's wife. Her unethical behavior triggers Joseph's imprisonment. Joseph was not guilty of King Pharaoh wife's accusation; yet, he was imprisoned.

Routinely, innocent souls suffer false charges, criticism, and skepticisms. Believing, and acting on, unreliable information, rather than proof, places blame and jeopardies on wrong people, places, and things. Falsity hurts, and deprives, freedom. When making claims, make sure proof is available. Truth protects innocents. "Blessed *are* the poor in heart: for they shall see God." St. Matthew 5:8. Some people have no respect for themselves or anyone else. Unfortunately, dreamers face "nondreamer opposition tactics" from some family members, church members, coworkers, and community members. Sadly, pew villains form evil webs. Dreamers detach from nondreamers' mazes.

Hate. Living requires choices whether good or bad. Loving God and hating people simultaneousness is incompatible and impossible. Why? Because God is love. "Whosoever hateth his brother is a murderer: and ye know that no murderer hath eternal life abiding in him." I John 3:15.

Prejudice manifests hearts, which may stem from various sources. Appropriate guidance aligns with The Holy Bible teachings. Holiness teaches against hatred and biasness. Loving God means loving everyone. God is unconditional love's author.

Favoritism structures unfairness support. Equality frightens unfairness. Fairness' goal is unfairness elimination. One is equal; but one is unequal.

Inequality participants use imbalanced scales. Their criteria are worldly, evil, and tainted. Scale imbalance inhabits ungodliness and contentiousness. Unfairness creates prisons, both physical and mental. Infestation occurs in wicked affiliations. Hate-infectivity mongers require Biblical teachings, repentance, purification, adherence, and soul-searching. Repentance and cleansing annul ungodly views. "For godly sorrow worketh repentance to salvation not to be repented of: but the sorrow of the world worketh death." II Corinthians 7:10.

Honesty exudes majesty, and excellence, on peaceful hilltops. Soon, or maybe later, every person has their time. Workers, in God's vineyard, are treated and paid fairly; because, He is not respecter of persons. Eventually, favoritism fades. Why? Dishonesty is sinful.

Hell. God gives time for everyone to make things right with Him. Earthly, summer, heat is cool compared to hell eternal. "But the fearful, and unbelieving, and the abominable, and murders, and whoremongers, and sorcerers, and idolaters, and all liars, shall have their part in the lake which burneth with fire and brimstone: which is the second death." Revelation 21:8.

Hypocrites are bullies, crybabies, and pity partiers, teaching one thing; but, living another. They intend on hiding irresponsibility and misdeeds by attention-shifting from themselves, to others. Shame and deceit are used to impede dreams. Appetite, for peace breaking, is extraordinary. "A hypocrite with *his* mouth destroyeth his neighbor: but through knowledge shall the just be delivered." Proverbs 11:9. "He that goeth about *as* a talebearer revealeth secrets: therefore meddle not with him that flattereth with his lips." Proverbs 20:19.

Hypocrites' short spans and memories pander to mediocrity. Imprudently, impending life choices and ideas are discounted. Dreaming requires foresight. Sin and foolishness choke major decisions and benefits. Hypocritical mindsets are prime real estate for Satan's purposes. Holy living generates long-term gain - eternal life. Nondreamers lose themselves among unfulfillment, dishonest, tangles. However, truth last forever; whereas, dishonesty self-destructs.

Eagles fly to lustrous dreams while chickens languish in messy coops. Temporary power, goods, and services contribute to short-term pleasure. "Knowest thou *not* this of old, since man was placed upon earth, that the triumphing of the wicked *is* short, and the joy of the hypocrite *but* for a moment? Because he hath oppressed *and* hath forsaken the poor; *because* he hath violently taken away an house which he builded not; surely he shall not feel quietness in his belly, he shall not save of that which he desired. In the fullness of his sufficiency he shall be in straits: every hand of the wicked shall come upon him...a fire not blown shall consume him; it shall go ill with him...The heaven shall reveal his iniquity; and the earth shall rise up against him. The increase of his house shall depart, *and his goods* shall flow away in the day of his wrath. This *is* the portion of a wicked man from God, and the heritage appointed unto him by God." Job 20:4-5, 19, 20, 22, 26-29.

Dreamers have confidence in God. Oppositely, nondreamers trust earthly man-made underpinnings, undertakings, cultures, goods, and services. Emphatically, God owns, and made, all things. His blessings are pure and sure. His promises and appointments are divine, thus unbreakable. Count on Jesus; because He is the only One Who can help mankind. He knows everything. He cares about each individual. His love is unconditional. Trust in the True God. The one Who made man. Who is He? Almighty God!

Idols. Worship not! Graven images are counterfeits. Prayfully, and carefully, charter life courses. Be Bible-living ambassadors. "Ye shall make ye no idols nor graven image, neither rear you up a standing image, neither shall ye set up *any* image of stone in your land, to bow down unto it: for I *am* the Lord your God." Leviticus 26:1. "...we know that an idol *is* nothing in the world, and that *there is* none other God but one." I Corinthians 8:4.

Ludicrously, many accept images/idols when "...the Spirit and the bride say, Come. And let him that heareth say, Come. And let him that is athrist come. And whosoever will, let him take the water of life freely." Revelation 22:17.

Ignorance and doubt lurk quietly but destroy dreams. Orally, most people do not intend to announce their stupidity; but, it still shows through mannerisms and verbalization antics. If anyone thinks God is unreal, and is not returning, is misled. "And that, knowing the time, that now *it is* high time to awake out of sleep: for now is *our* salvation nearer than when we believed. The night is far spent, the day is at hand: let us therefore cast off the works of darkness, and let us put on the armour of light." Romans 13:11-12. The devil lies and seeks to blind righteous souls.

"Study to show thyself approved unto God, a workman that needeth not to be ashamed, rightly dividing the word of truth." II Timothy 2:15. Potentiality depends on motivated minds.

Instability depletes growth and is akin to quicksand – destruction. "A double-minded man *is* unstable in all his ways." James 1:8.

Interconnections. "Even so faith, if it hath not works, is dead, being alone." James 2:17. Belief, without behavior, is futility; because, fruits do not support mouth sayings. Truthful living is based on Jesus Christ. He is eternal truth. Jesus Christ is The Truth. Living for God and walking with Him is spiritual lifestyle. Deviation, from God's Word, is sin. God desires you to be cold or hot, not lukewarm. "I know thy works, that thou art neither cold nor hot: I would thou wert cold or hot. So then because thou art lukewarm, and neither cold nor hot, I will spue thee out of my mouth." Revelation 3:15-16.

Believers, holding fast to God, enduring to the end, goes to heaven. Belief and behavior are inseparable, kinfolks. These partners are not foreign to each other but have mutual interests and outcomes. Faith and works' relationship intertwine.

Loving Jesus, keeping His commandments, and loving mankind, protect believers from pew villains (deceivers and corrupters). Be alert! Pew villains seek integrity destabilization of believers.

Judgment. What will God say to you? Words make noise. Fruits act. "Not every man that saith unto me, Lord, Lord shall enter into the kingdom of heaven; but he that doeth the will of my Father which is in heaven." St. Matthew 7:21.

Taking people, and circumstances, at face value disseminates mistakes. Fakers and grinners use facials for evil plots' concealment. Faking's goal is to misguide victims' thus diverting attention from evil doings. "Beloved, believe not every spirit, but try the spirits whether they are of God: because many false prophets are gone out into the world." I John 4:1. "For the gifts and calling of God *are* without repentance." Romans 11:29. Heaven preparation time is now.

Lies. Untruths stink like filthy pens. One of the biggest lies Satan tells is: When you hurt someone, they never know. Wrong! God is there. He sees, hears, and knows. God warns His people - through discernment – who hurt them. "A faithful witness will not lie: but a false witness will utter lies." Proverbs 14:5. "Blessed *are* they that do his commandments, that they may have right to the tree of life, and may enter in through the gates into the city. For without *are* dogs, and sorcerers, and whoremongers, and murderers, and idolaters, and whosoever loveth and maketh a lie. I Jesus have sent mine angel to testify unto you these things in the churches. I am the root and the offspring of David, *and* the bright and morning star. And the Spirit and the bride say, Come. And let him that heareth say, Come. And let him that is athirst come. And whosoever will, let him take the water of life freely." Revelation 22:14-17.

Lights Shining. "Let your light so shine before men, that they may see your good works, and glorify your Father which is in heaven." St. Matthew 5:16. God's ambassadors' lights shine forth edification.

When pew villains deceive and instigate confusions, souls inside and outside, congregations see ungodliness. Even sinners expect you to live what you preach and teach to them. Otherwise, they may not want to hear you; although you quote truth. Hypocrites are stumblingblocks.

Christ's ambassadors role model for the world. God is watching. People are watching. Matches, among confessions, conversations, and lifestyles, are expected. Confessing is one thing, but lifestyle is another. Confession, profession, and lifestyle compatibility is to line up with the Holy Bible.

Wicked insinuations are noticed, unappreciated, and ill-advised. Souls are at stake. Stop chasing worshippers out! Time is moving. Pew villains' foolishness need to stop! Souls need saving now!

God's Word teaches holiness. Stop lying and keeping up confusion. Tell the truth. God already knows whether you are saved, or not. Truthfully, no one fools God! Preaching and teaching, alone, is not enough. Righteous living displays His teachings. Get serious! "Wherefore laying aside every malice, and all guile, and hypocrisies, and envies, and all evil speakings, as newborn babes, desire the sincere milk of the word, that ye may grow thereby: If so be ye have tasted that the Lord is gracious. But ye *are* a chosen generation…that ye should show forth the praises of him who hath called you out of darkness into his marvelous light…Having your conversation honest among the Gentiles: that, whereas they speak against you as evildoers, they may by *your* good works, which they shall behold, glorify God in the day of visitation." I Peter 2:1-3, 9, 12.

Little is Lots. Ill-gotten gain disperses venom-like magnets and guilt carriers. Ill-gotten gain leaves undesirable legacies, trails of dishonesty, despair, and fear. Multiplication, complication, and troubles travel throughout ill-gotten gains. Stolen goods and services are disadvantageous. They never add up. Vaporization takes place. Authentic pleasure is denied from stolen properties. Affirmatively, stolen goods may seem like "easy" accumulations and accomplishments, but are sinful and troublesome. Taking and holding on to items that are not yours is time- and energy-consuming. Dangerously, worldly emotions, psychology, and finances, are connected to ill-gotten items. Outwardly, some people appear happy but inwards show thorough unhappiness. Who is the root of unhappiness? Satan.

God gives happiness, hope, and help. Ask Him for needed goods and services. When He gives you someone or something, He takes care of it. He protects you and your belongings. Righteous accumulation of wealth avoids needless suffering for yourself and others.

"Thou shalt not steal." Exodus 20:15. "Ye shall not steal, neither deal falsely, neither lie one to another." Leviticus 19:11. "And be renewed in the spirit of your mind; and that ye put on the new man, which after God is created in righteousness and true holiness. Wherefore putting away lying, speak every man truth with his neighbor: for we are members one of another. Neither give place to the devil. Let him that stole steal no more: but rather let him labour, working with his hands the thing which is good, that he may have to give to him that needeth." Ephesians 4:23-25, 28. "Better is a little with righteousness than great revenues without right." Proverbs 16:8. "Better is little with the fear of the Lord than great treasure and trouble therewith." Proverbs 15:16. "A little that a righteous man hath *is* better than the riches of many wicked." Psalm 37:16. "But godliness with contentment is great gain." I Timothy 6:6. "And God is able to make all grace abound toward you; that ye, always having all sufficiency in all *things*, may abound to every good work..." II Corinthians 9:8. "Let your conversation be without covetousness; *and* be content with such things as ye have: for he hath said, I will never leave thee, nor forsake thee. So that we may boldly say, The Lord is my helper, and I will not fear what man shall do unto me." Hebrews 13:5-6. Inevitably, Christian walks incur persecutions.

Longsuffering coincide with dreaming and is not weakness. Jesus is forgiving, patient, and compassionate, toward mankind. If He was intolerant, mankind could not survive. "The Lord is longsuffering, and of great mercy, forgiving iniquity and transgression, and by no means clearing *the guilty*, visiting the iniquity of the fathers upon the children unto the third and fourth *generation*." Numbers 14:18. "The Lord is not slack concerning his promise, as some men count slackness; but is longsuffering...not willing that any should perish, but that all should come to repentance." II Peter 3:9.

While pretending adherence to purity, church bullies conduct vicious quandaries. Misguidedly, bullies equate abusing God's people's compassion with gullibility. Equating mismatches ill-advises providing invalid senses of security. Supposedly, evilness means the same as shrewdness. Evilness wreaks ungodly radicalism. Villains' menus include evil and limited entrees. Main courses dish out thievery and lying. Desserts enclose talebearing, confusion, and slander. Nondreamers brag saying, "you can never stop them from talking about you." Prudently, consider sources and courses.

Dreamers analyze corruption; however, nondreamers do not Whatever pew troublemakers say, or do, pacifies and satisfies itching ears. Compassion exploitation, of saints, or anybody, demonstrate degradation. Satanic imaginations prompt arrogance leading to unrealistic reasoning; including, self-inflicted physical, mental, and financial encumbrances.

God-fearing saints sense bullies' game plans. Dreamers pray for hostile parties (oppositionists). Nondreamers do evil for evil. God's prescriptions are advantageous; because, vengeance belongs to Him. "Be not overcome of evil, but overcome evil with good." Romans 12:21. "And we know that all things work together for good to them that love God, to them who are the called according to *his* purpose." Romans 8:28. Trust God, for everything, always.

Mazes Haze. Sin is like a twisted muddle. Fun, at first, seeming easy to find your ways. Excitement is stirring! Suddenly! Paths are lost. Running into walls, curbs, and dead ends. Panic and screaming ensue. Help needed! Finally, you cry out to God saying, "Lord, please help me. You alone are my Rescuer from wicked, sinfulness. Steadily, things change. So-called enjoyment equals momentary pleasures. Satan claims worldly mazes yield fun. Worldliness endangers souls for eternal torment." God comes to the rescue! "...Lord, remember me when thou comest into thy kingdom. And Jesus said unto him, Verily I say unto thee, To day shalt thou be with me in paradise." St. Luke 23:42-43.

Meddling. "It is an honour for a man to cease from strife: but every fool will be meddling." Proverbs 20:3. Fools treat excellence and greatness disdainfully. In mediocre circles, understanding is despised.

Mediocrity. God's Work deserves prioritization. Tribulations come. God's faithfulness allows dreamers' steadfastness maintenance. "These things I have spoken unto you, that in me ye might have peace. In the world ye shall have tribulation: but be of good cheer; I have overcome the world." St. John 16:33. Dreamers encourage excellency while discouraging mediocrity. Nondreamers' mediocre behavior shows shortsightedness and shallowness. Frivolity causes nondreamers to commit much time on opposition tactics rather than valuable life-changing experiences and heavenly homegoing preparations. Working, in God's vineyard, helps lost souls come to Christ while facilitating spiritual and psychological growth. Soar in God! Can't win with sin!

Men-pleasers, have divided hearts succumbing to wicked peer pressure. Fearfulness, of man, creates men-pleasers, and is liableness. Indebtedness controls behavior. Read the Word of God aloud. Self, talk positivity. Remind self of His love and blessings. "There is no fear in love; but perfect love casteth out fear: because fear hath torment. He that feareth is not made perfect in love." I John 4:18. Men-pleasers attempt to serve two masters - God and Satan - which is impossible and intolerable. God is Jealous. Fearing God is appropriate. "The fear of the Lord *is* the beginning of knowledge: *but* fools despise wisdom and instruction." Proverbs 1:7. **"Go from the presence of a foolish man, when thou perceiveth not in him the lips of knowledge." Proverbs 14:7.**

Mercy Abusers. Intentional sinning, then asking forgiveness, compares to game-playing. Game-playing puts souls at risk for hell fire and brimstone. Those who do not fear God and think manipulation works follow misguided manuals. These actors look and pretend to be religious. Satan uses misguided hypocrites to commit atrocities against God's people.

Middle. Stuck? The Bible teaches right and left, not luke warmness. "When the Son of man shall come in his glory, and all the holy angels with him, then shall he sit upon the throne of his glory...and he shall separate them one from another, as a shepherd divideth *his* sheep from the goats: And he shall set the sheep on his right hand, but the goats on the left." St. Matthew 25:31-33.

Where is middle? Nondreamers' (pew villains) murky character present legitimate concerns and questions. Indecisiveness present itself. Fence straddlers' (friends with the world) lifestyles go neither left nor right. Is this is called "middle ground." "... whosoever therefore will be friend of the world is the enemy of God." James 4:4. "Love not the world, neither the things *that are* in the world. If any man love the world, the love of God is not in him. For all that *is* in the world, the lust of the flesh, and the lust of the eyes, and the pride of life, is not of the Father, but is of the world. And the world passeth away, and the lust thereof: but he that doeth the will of God abideth forever...it is the last time: and ye have heard that an'-ti-christ shall come, even now there are many an'-ti-christs; whereby we know it is the last time." I John 2:15-18.

Mind-Killer. Satan's job description entails stealing, killing, and destroying. When he obliterates minds, eventually bodies follow; then, possibly soul loss.

Misjudgment. Nondreamers underestimate urgency and importance of righteousness, knowledge, and eternal life. For many souls, miscalculation is deadly; because, recalculations are unmade in time for eternal life.

Money. Money lovers rely on worldly goods and services rather than God. They loathe fair distribution of rights and opportunities while selfishly indulging in temporalities (ill-gotten resources, immoral activities, etc.). "For the love of money is the root of all evil: which while some coveted after, they have erred from the faith, and pierced themselves through with many sorrows." I Timothy 6:10.

Much money is made from sin commercialization. Satan set up vicious, temporal, schemes. Satan exploits and purchases as many one-way destruction tickets as he can. "...Take heed, and beware of covetousness: for a man's life consisteth not in the abundance of the things which he possesseth." St. Luke 12:15.

Deservingly, praise and worship Jesus Christ. Good is in the beginning, middle, and end. Mixed-up priorities explode and implode. Order flows through proper prioritization pipelines. Society spends millions of dollars on clothing, tickets, transportation, parties, vehicles, etc., honoring personalities and temporalities. God loves celebrities as well as noncelebrities. Most celebrities are probably known from distances, but love and public connection link parties.

God is displeased when others receive more praise than He. He is Jealous. God deserves glory and praise! God is not distant. "God *is* our refuge and strength, a very present help in trouble." Romans 46:1.

Jesus loves, knows, and takes care of you. Mankind is made in His image. Jesus suffered for us. He died for us. He saves souls. We should live for Him. Everything we do for Him last. Temporal, earthly doings, fade. Jesus' presence is powerful. Jesus calls, woos, and shows His love.

Time, money, and resource investments count for, or against, you, depending on where they are made. Investing, in your Creator's kingdom, is safe. Jesus investments have heavenly returns – eternal life. "Be not thou therefore ashamed of the testimony of our Lord...but be thou partaker of the afflictions of the gospel according to the power of God; who hath saved us, and called *us* with an holy calling, not according to our works, but according to his own purpose and grace, which was given us in Christ Jesus before the world began, but is now made manifest by the appearing of our Saviour Jesus Christ, who hath brought life and immortality to light through the gospel: whereunto I am appointed a preacher, and an apostle, and a teacher...For the which cause I also suffer these things: nevertheless I am not ashamed: for I know whom I have believed, and am persuaded that he is able to keep that which I have committed unto him against that day." II Timothy 1:8-12.

Jesus' everlasting love surpasses any other love. He came so mankind can have eternal life and peace. He deserves glory, honor, praise, and sacrifices. Living life, in Christ's honor, rewards handsomely. Giving our lives to Jesus, and glorifying Him, determines destinies. God's people love Him and make sacrifices for His sake. Living for Jesus is not in vain. Sacrifices are not in vain. He is our Saviour and avenger. "And let us not be weary in well doing: for in due season we shall reap, if we faint not." Galatians 6:9. "THEREFORE seeing we have this ministry, as we have received mercy, we faint not; but have renounced the hidden things of dishonesty, not walking in craftiness, nor handling the word of God deceitfully; but by manifestation of the truth commending ourselves to every man's conscience in the sight of God." II Corinthians 4:1-2.

Naivety. Before acting, search into matters. Consider outcomes. "The simple believeth every word: but the prudent *man* looketh well to his going." Proverbs 14:15.

Negative Peer Pressure premier bullying formats. Wickedness-lovers prefer corrupt company. "Enter not into the path of the wicked, and go not in the way of evil *men*. Avoid it, pass not by it, turn from it, and pass away. Avoid it, pass not by it, turn from it, and pass away." Proverbs 4:14-15.

Bullies have membership in club darkness eating and drinking mediocrity, chaos, and foolishness. "But the wicked *are* like the troubled sea, when it cannot rest, whose waters cast up mire and dirt. *There* is no peace, saith my God, to the wicked." Isaiah 57:20-21.

Nondreamers (dream saboteurs) epitomize life-sucking leaders and partakers of unrighteousness using opposition tactics. Their intention is robbing dreamers of their visions. Self-deceiving enemies lack positive motivation.

Deceivers (pew villains) are unrighteousness enemies to the church; because pretenses are impediments and offensives. "For he that biddeth him God speed is partaker of his evil deeds." II John 11. Believing and acting on God's Word infuses conquering mentalities and strength.

Dreamers believe God's Word. Partnerships, with deceitful pew villains, violate Gospel teachings and value traits. Belief in God and holy lifestyles match.

Nondreamers are deceived. Their actions say, "I can treat people any way I please. All I have to do is lie, steal, cause confusions, and hide." Shamefully, nondreamers display ungodly behaviors, inviting, enticing, and encouraging others' wickedness and floundering.

Dreamers are not deceived by pew villains. Praying and watching afford steadfastness in God and His principles. Unfeelingly, nondreamers disregard spiritual and psychological welfares of others. "If there come any unto you, and bring not this doctrine, receive him not into *your* house, neither bid him God speed: For he that biddeth him God speed is partaker of his evil deeds." II John 10-11. The apostle warns faithful believers to walk in obedience and avoid association with false teachers. In today's society, pew villains may also be described as false teachers and antichrists – enemies of the church. Faithful believers ought not use time, finances, or resources, unwisely. Energies should be used for godliness.

Keeping company with, antichrists, and deceivers, is sharing in false teachings as well as other ungodly acts. John's warnings concerning deceivers are relevant today. He lets us know not to let deceivers in our houses and not bid "God speed." He also lets us know that you are partaking in false teachers' evilness if they are allowed in your homes or if giving "to be well" salutations. Partaking in deceitfulness is dangerous. Anyone who truly knows God lives His Word in hearts, minds, and bodies. Live God's Word full-time; so, when God comes, your soul is ready to meet Him. Part-time is lukewarmness. Righteousness seeds flow with positive harvests, placements, and actions.

Partakers with Those in Others' Blood. "…Woe unto you…hypocrites! Because ye build the tombs of the prophets, and garnish the sepulchers of the righteous, and say, If we had been in the days of our fathers, we would not have been partakers with them in the blood of the prophets. Wherefore ye be witnesses unto yourselves, that ye are the children of them which killed the prophets. Fill ye up then the measure of your fathers. *Ye* serpents, *ye* generation of vipers, how can ye escape the damnation of hell? Wherefore, behold, I send unto you prophets, and wise men, and scribes: and *some* of them ye shall kill and crucify; and *some* of them shall ye scourge in your synagogues, and persecute *them* from city to city: That upon you may come all the righteous blood shed upon the earth, from the blood of righteous Abel unto the blood of Zacharias son of Barachias, whom ye slew between the temple and the alter. Verily I say unto you, All these things shall come upon this generation…*thou* that killest the prophets, and stonest them which are sent unto thee, how often would I have gathered thy children together, even as a hen gathereth her chickens under *her* wings, and ye would not! Behold, your house is left unto you desolate. For I say unto you, Ye shall not see me henceforth, till ye shall say, Blessed *is* he that cometh in the name of the Lord." St. Matthew 23:29-39.

Committing persecutions are perpetrated in different ways; both physical and mental abuse. Some people physically kill others. Others assist with silence, money, lies, slander, get-away mechanisms, etc. But, all are complicities and duplicities. All are guilty and reap what is sown.

"THEN spake Jesus to the multitude, and to his disciples, Saying, The scribes and the Pharisees sit in Moses' seat: All therefore whatsoever they bid you observe, *that* observe and do; but do not ye after their works: for they say, and do not. For they bind heavy burdens and grievous to be borne, and lay *them* on men's shoulders; but they *themselves* will not move them with one of their fingers. But all their works they do for to be seen of men: they make broad their phylacteries, and enlarge the borders of their garments, and love the uppermost rooms at feasts, and the chief seats in the synagogues, and greetings in the markets…he that is greatest among you shall be your servant…whosoever shall exalt himself shall be abased; and he that shall humble himself shall be exalted…woe unto you…hypocrites! for ye shut up the kingdom of heaven against men: for ye neither go in yourselves, neither suffer ye them that are entering to go in. Woe unto you, scribes and Pharisees, hypocrites! for ye devour widows" houses, and for a pretence make long prayer: therefore ye shall receive the greater damnation. Woe unto you… hypocrites! for ye pay tithe of mint and anise and cumin, and have omitted the weightier *matters* of the law, judgment, mercy and faith: these ought ye to have done, and not to leave the other undone. *Ye* blind guides, which strain at a gnat, and swallow a camel. Woe unto you…hypocrites! for ye make clean the outside of the cup and of the platter, but within they are full of extortion and excess. *Thou* blind Pharisee, cleanse first that *which is* within the cup and platter, that the outside of them may be clean also. Woe unto you…hypocrites! for ye are like unto whited sepulchres, which indeed appear beautiful outward, but are within full of dead *men's* bones, and of all uncleanness. Even so ye also outwardly appear righteous unto men, but within ye are full of hypocrisy and iniquity." St. Matthew 23:1-7, 12-14, 23-29.

Evil's followers responsibility lies in participation in wicked strategies, acts, and implementations. Righteous dreamers decline sinful enticements and involvements. Stay vigilant. Know who you follow. Spiritually and soberly, stop and think about your actions. God sees and knows each intention and action. When the Lamb's Book of Life is opened, what will your record show? Where will you spend eternity?

Partridge Egg Riches. Riches claimed but not owned is called thievery. Stolen riches reap pandemonium. Thievery attaches trouble. Thieves constantly, lie, cover, and maneuver, attempting to keep stolen goods. Agony and restlessness are hatched from partridge eggs. Winking, gesturing, evading, and searching avenues inorder to conceal sinful secrets, is outrageous. Taking others' properties, controls and, destroys lives and legacies. Hearts and minds' imprisonment dislocate all fairness semblances. Stolen properties belong to others, not claimants. Stolen properties sit in bank accounts, houses, and vehicles. Minds are covetous. Burdens are heavy.

Peace and enjoyment rest in rightful accumulations, not in stolen properties - unrighteousness. *"As* a partridge sitteth *on eggs,* and hatchest *them* not; *so* he that getteth riches, and not by right, shall leave them in the midst of his days, and at his end shall be a fool." Jeremiah 17:11.

Path. Know intended life missions. Shun evil. Dreamers realize gains in this life do not compare with glorious eternity with God. Dreamers love God, live for Him, and make daily preparations for eternity in heaven! Praise Jesus!

Even though pew villains create divisions in congregations, families, homes, workplaces, etc., trusting Jesus, praying, and fasting, negate opposition tactics. For pew villains, attempting ostracism and defeatism of God's elect is hard and dangerous propositions. God's people pray for deliverance and God answers! That is why dreamers steadfastly keep moving.

Dreamers travel on different roads from nondreamers. Goals differ. "The way of the wicked *is* as darkness: they know not at what they stumble." Proverbs 4:19. Dreamers are prudent. Contrastingly, nondreamers exhibit random, irresponsible behaviors - instability elements.

Money, fame, or luxury, does not compare with Jesus' heaven. Dreamers' heavenly home cannot be compromised or taken away. Minds are made up. Living for Jesus is wise, unsurpassed.

Payback. Be careful what you do. Recompense comes. "Be not deceived; God is not mocked: for whatsoever a man soweth, that shall he also reap." Galatians 6:7.

Personal Agendas. Unfortunately, Eagle-tis-ti-cal (courageous), truth warriors, are strongly resisted. Bullies forego compassion for ungodly, self-gratifications. These mobs deploy several disorientations, dismantlement, antennas. Through nonparticipation, or leaving, anguished congregators express frustrations. True worshippers would rather not witness lying, confusion, slandering, and pretending, on pews. Church bullies do not seem to care about discord perpetration. Life enrichment flows through unclogged pipes, not clogged ones. Personal agendas are like impassable tunnels. Nothing comes in. Nothing goes out. Nothing gets done. Millions live on planet Earth. Without any rules or regulations how can the planet survive? Wild Wild Earth cannot survive. Sensible rules, regulations, and fairness, permit survival for all. Unfair, lawless, societies, disintegrate. Wise leaders understand sensible measures; whereas, unwise leaders do not.

Have you forgotten God's agenda? Sadly, many individuals are intent on "saving face." Disproportionate self-interests contaminate, causing friction, hurt, and fall aways. Intentionally, ungodly, unfair (crooked), foundational scopes abound proliferating structural instability. Sneakily, nondreamers - troublemakers - propagate confusion behind dreamers' backs. Such behavior disturbs local congregations as well as the whole Body of Christ.

Unfortunately, reporting of lies, thefts, broken confidences, broken promises, mistreatments, as well as other problems, permeate congregation fabric. This shameful setup mirrors secular dogma.

Sadistic plots execute sadistic maneuvers. During assembly with fellow worshippers, souls suffer. Unsuspecting members experience exploitation. Pitiful precedents trample commonsense procedures. Satan uses opposition formats for intimidation, discouragement, and soul loss. Unfortunately, negativity works. Because of hindrance experiences, souls leave congregations. Intrusiveness takes minds off worship and discourages returns.

Perpetrators grin and pretend while their actions negatively impact fellow church members and non-church people. In some assemblies, disinformation and dysfunction seem to take center stage. But, soul-saving should not be lost for any reasons.

Beware of church bullies. They hijack the truth and hope everyone turns blind eyes and pretend all is well. Nondreamers crave Christian distinction (good name labels), but act no different from worldly bullies. Some might argue that pew bullies act worse than worldly bullies. Damages caused and imposed on true Christians' church reputations intensify pew troubles.

Since church bullies disregard sentiments for others, wise judgments are made to avoid snares and entrapments. Realistically, troublemakers prowl everywhere, including churches. "...The effectual fervent prayer of a righteous man availeth much." James 5:16. "Then came the disciples to Jesus apart, and said, Why could not we cast him out? And Jesus said unto them, Because of your unbelief: for verily I say unto you, If ye have faith as a grain of mustard seed, ye shall say unto this mountain, Remove hence to yonder place; and it shall remove; and nothing shall be impossible unto you. Howbeit this kind goeth not out but by prayer and fasting." St. Matthew 17:19-21.

Condoning sinister behavior is sin. Sinful, misleading, conduct conveys confusion and falling away. Drama does not just arrive on pews. Intentional components, such as, planning, participation, invitation, and association, engender devious actions. Take responsibility for your drama and leave other people out of your messes. Positive, proactive, spirits are absent. Chaotic, divided, divisive ships, sink. Unfortunately, many innocents sink, along with guilty perpetuators.

Sincere worshippers enjoy holy assembly but dissociates from any malicious deception. Are you sentencing souls to eternal heat because of unholy talk, walk, and fake smiles? Hatred and jealousy retreat behind smiles. Firmly, smiles are often deadly, cannonballs of make-ups and masks. Dreams drown while pew villains play church.

Indispensable, lifestyle, reflection measures ethical conduct. If holiness is not reflected, questions arise.

Pew Villains and surrogates' itching ears displease true worshippers. Regular recruitments are made. Wicked insurgence obliterates many dreams. For positive focus, dreamers' dissociate from troublemakers. Positivity uplifts.

"Be not deceived: evil communications corrupt good manners." I Corinthians 15:33. Prudent associations stimulate positivity; however, evil associations taint dreamers' value traits. Nondreamers start and keep acrimonies alive. Ultimately, operations established on rot flounder and fail. Evil cores corrupt and transport evil flows. Objectable subscriptions flood markets. Sludge partakers buy into, and administer, hopelessness. Dreamers respect truth. Nondreamers muzzle truth (authenticity). Lies and disquietness are generated in homes, families, and congregations. Obstructionists' dangerous, ruthless, tactics endanger opportunities and lives. Without discernment, storytelling, concerning others, pictures truths. It is foolish to believe everything said. Jealousy speaks lies.

Tongues are uncontrollable and loaded with fear and violence. Obstructionists' unclear thinking hunts for, and entertains, deceitfulness. "...this *is* a rebellious people, lying children, children *that* will not fear the law of the Lord: Which say to the seers, See not; and to the prophets,

Prophesy not unto us right things, speak unto us smooth things, prophesy deceits: Wherefore thus saith the Holy One of Israel, Because ye despise this word, and trust in oppression and perverseness, and stay thereon: Therefore this iniquity shall be to you as a breach ready to fall, swelling out in a high wall, whose breaking cometh suddenly at an instant." Isaiah 30:9-10, 12-13.

Villains' efforts bear scrutiny – not to be underrated or overlooked. Predators embrace, and encourage, selfishness and misery. Thinking non-dreamers observe friendship loyalties predicate wrong impressions. **"For the time will come when they will not endure sound doctrine; but after their own lusts shall they heap to themselves teachers, having itching ears; and they shall turn away *their* ears from the truth, and shall be turned into fables." II Timothy 4:3-4.**

Pew villains use gangster, premeditation, tactics. In other words, they seek preplanned reactions from their prey. If responses, to evil setups, are not in accordance with pew villains' plans, anger creeps in seeking revenge. **"Having a form of godliness, but denying the power thereof: from such turn away." II Timothy 3:5. "They profess that they know God; but in works they deny *him*, being abominable, and disobedi-ent, and unto every good work reprobate." Titus 1:16.**

Valuation of God's purpose and soul-saving do not appear on oppo-sition tactics' priority list. "For men shall be lovers of their own selves, blasphemers...unthankful, unholy...false accusers, incontinent, fierce, despisers of those that are good, traitors, heady, high-minded, lovers of pleasures more than lovers of God." II Timothy 3:2-4.

Many cave in because prayer lives are not strong enough to withstand adversity. Presumably, witchcraft may be a part of inducements for pew violence; because attacks are satanic, constant, and rigid. Dreamers expe-rience unpleasant cover-ups and polarizations. Negatively, Satan influ-ences minds and emotions. Unhappiness and dream unfulfillment trigger instabilities. Evil amusement comes from ridicule investments. God can clean filthy minds and hearts from sin and shame. Nondreamers charge others with their self-inflicted unhappiness.

Under these circumstances, concentration on worship services is difficult. Pew villains savagely hamstring many worshippers' pew enjoyment. Of course, dreamers neither sell or buy adversity; but nondreamers support evilness. Vehemently, personal motivations cannot override God's purposes. "Woe unto them that call evil good, and good evil …" Isaiah 5:20.

Prayer keeps instability at bay. Confidence in Christ Jesus gives hope, comfort, and happiness. Keeping His commandments assures eternal life.

Pit Diggers experience self-inflicted punishment because of wickedness imposed on others. Unfairly, blaming others for self-inflicted consequences presents psychotic formulations. "Whoso diggeth a pit shall fall therein: and he that rolleth a stone, it will return upon him. Proverbs 26:27. Predestinations are set for godly people as well as worldly bullies.

Planet Earth is treated as a port for individuals to do anything they want, how they want, when they want, and where they want. Spirituality, logic, and common sense defy this wicked, man-made, philosophy (tradition).

Illogical thinkers criticize necessary rules, and/or regulations; yet at the same time say, "I do not understand why there is turmoil in the world." Often, individuals desiring order, and structure, oppose godly remedies necessary for civil order for all. Concocting ungodly, obstruction recipes, disrupt smooth flows. For civility's sake, radioactive relationships must be approached cautiously and eliminated. Dreamers' prudence ward off nondreamer affronts. Irrationality follow nondreamers.

Poor Treatment. Oppression, of the poor, is unacceptable. Treat everyone with respectability and fairness. "He that oppresseth the poor reproacheth his Maker: but he that honoureth him hath mercy on the poor." Proverbs 14:31. "He that oppresseth the poor to increase his riches, *and* he that giveth to the rich, *shall* surely *come* to want." Proverbs 22:16.

"So God created man in his *own* image, in the image of God created he him; male and female created he them. And God saw every thing that he had made, and behold, it *was* very good…" Genesis 1:27, 31. Joseph's brothers ridiculed him for dreaming. Mistreating others is mean and corrupt. Regardless of ethnicity, economic status, demographics, etc., God created, and loves, all people. *Every human being is created equal.* Whoever is responsible for inequality reaps recompense. God made humanity in many shades, heights, weights. Anyone who has problems with His Work needs to consult with Him. Frankly, is anyone idiotic enough to question God why He made people differently? God has all the answers. Mankind answers to God. "Rob not the poor, because he is poor: neither oppress the afflicted...For the Lord will plead their cause, and spoil the soul of those that spoiled them." Proverbs 22:22-23.

Condescending treatment, to the poor, shows outwardly who you are inwardly. Insensitive authorities and powers are culprits responsible for traditions and excuses for mistreating and vexing the poor. Flocks of cowards follow these con artists to their deaths. "The instruments also of the churl *are* evil: he deviseth wicked devices to destroy the poor with lying words, even when the needy speaketh right. But the liberal deviseth liberal things; and by liberal things shall he stand." Isaiah 32:7-8.

"He that hath pity upon the poor lendeth unto the Lord..." Proverbs 19:17. "Whoso mocketh the poor reproacheth his Maker: *and* he that is glad at calamities shall not be unpunished." Proverbs 17:5.

Previously, some rich people were poor. However, now their paychecks are six or seven figures; so, they seek food and other humanitarian programs' eradication. Evil audacities, of this nature, are uncaring. When they were poor, records show they used and accepted help from the same programs they are now attempting to destroy. Most likely, they would not be rich if humanitarian assistance was unavailable. Selfishness is sinful and cantankerous.

Clearly, the Lord has heaven prepared for the righteous. *Final destination for the right side:* "Then shall the King say unto them on his right hand, Come, ye blessed of my Father, inherit the kingdom prepared for you from the foundation of the world: For I was a hungred, and ye gave me meat: I was thirsty, and ye gave me drink: I was a stranger, and ye took me in." St. Matthew 25:34-35.

Certainly, hell is torment. *Final destination for the left side:* "Then shall he say also unto them on the left hand, Depart from me, ye cursed, into everlasting fire, prepared for the devil and his angels: For I was an hungred, and ye gave me no meat: I was a thirsty, and ye gave no drink… "Inasmuch as ye did *it* not to one of the least of these, ye did *it* not to me. And these shall go away into everlasting punishment: but the righteous into life eternal." St. Matthew 25:41-42, 45-46.

Which is your choice? Right or left – heaven or hell? Can you live in fire and brimstone forever?

Poverty. Robbing God causes unpleasant situations (problems), including poverty. Robbing God cheats self. Robbing God consummates the worst financial blunder of all times. Affects sift through life. Crevices swallow stolen property.

Thieves encounter unexpected losses and complications. Stop hemorrhages! Give God His due. He disapproves cheating. He is Truth! He is Almighty God!

"Will a man rob God? Yet ye have robbed me, But ye say, Wherein have we robbed thee? In tithes and offerings. Ye *are* cursed with a curse: for ye have robbed me, *even* this whole nation. Bring ye all the tithes into the storehouse, that there may be meat in mine house, and prove me now herewith, saith the Lord of hosts, if I will not open you the windows of heaven, and pour you out a blessing, that *there shall* not *be room* enough *to receive it.* And I will rebuke the devourer for your sakes, and he shall not destroy the fruits of your ground; neither shall your vine cast her fruit before the time in the field, saith the Lord of hosts. And all nations shall call you blessed: for ye shall be a delightsome land, saith the Lord of hosts." Malachi 3:8-12. Kingdom work requires commitment, faithfulness, finances, and upkeeps – FINANCIAL STEWARDSHIP.

PRAISE JESUS! God performs miracles. Miraculously, God saves lives. Oftentimes, tributes are given to people, institutions, and animals. Unfairly, in many situations, God is not mentioned. God gives life, skills, firefighters, hospitals, health care, professions, professionals, etc. Without God, mankind cannot learn or do anything. Without God, mankind's incomprehensibility would render inabilities to learn applicable professional content or do jobs.

Thanking God, and giving Him praise, is one of the main focuses of Christian dreamers' lives. Thank God for blessings with professions, jobs, etc. "Whosoever therefore shall be ashamed of me and of my words in this adulterous and sinful generation; of him also shall the Son of man be ashamed, when he cometh in the glory of his Father with the holy angels." St. Mark 8:38. "...We give thee thanks, O Lord God Almighty, which art, and wast, and art to come; because thou hast taken to thee thy great power, and hast reigned. And the nations were angry, and thy wrath is come, and the time of the dead, that they should be judged, and that thou shoudest give reward unto thy servants the prophets, and to the saints, and them that fear thy name, small and great; and shouldest destroy them which destroy the earth." Revelation 11:17-18.

Priority Mix-Ups. Do you pay tithes and give offerings? Are most funds spent on personal items like homes, apartments, clothings, vehicle, entertainment, etc. God deserves firstfruits, not leftovers. Are you getting on hands and knees cleaning/scrubbing floors? Are you spending hours and days in rain-soaked conditions (for leisure activities); but offering criticism for dreamers spending, one or two hours, in godly worship services.

Unashamedly, kneel and pray. Many forget Who creates life, mouths, hands, knees, and floors. God gives; but, He also takes away. God is Jealous. He does not share His glory. "Lest ye corrupt *yourselves*, and make you a graven image, the similitude of any figure, the likeness of male or female...Take heed unto yourselves, lest ye forget the covenant of the Lord your God, which he made with you, and make you a graven image, *or* the likeness of any *thing*, which the Lord thy God hath forbidden thee. For the Lord thy God is a consuming fire, *even* a jealous God...if thou shalt seek the Lord thy God, thou shalt find *him*, if thou seek him with all thy heart and with all thy soul. When thou art in tribulation, and...things come upon thee, *even* in the latter days, if thou turn to the Lord thy God, and shalt be obedient unto his voice; (For the Lord thy God *is* a merciful God;) he will not forsake thee, neither destroy thee, nor forget the covenant of thy fathers which he sware unto them." Deuteronomy 4:16, 23-24, 29-31.

Embarrassed to kneel and pray – but unembarrassed to kneel and clean? Is God pleased? When time comes for your final appointment, do you think man-composed explanations are sufficient for Him? God's Word instructs us how to live holy. Ignoring God causes pain, humiliation, and soul loss. Live for Him today! Stay with Him forever!

Question. Are you self-helping? Working out soul salvation is personal. Obey God's Word so you are prepared for heaven homegoing. Jesus wants us to live with Him forever. "Behold, I stand at the door, and knock: if any man hear my voice, and open the door, I will come in to him, and will sup with him, and he with me. To him that overcometh will I grant to sit with me in my throne, even as I also overcame, and am set down with my Father in his throne." Revelation 3:20-21.

Rendering Just Punishments. "Who will render to every man according to his deeds: To them by patient continuance in well doing seek for glory and honour and immortality, eternal life: But unto them that are contentious, and do not obey the truth, but obey unrighteousness, indignation and wrath, tribulation and anguish, upon every soul of man that doeth evil...for there is no respect of persons with God." Romans 2:6-9, 11.

Destruction masterpieces contain various pieces, tiers, and networks. For reputation-tarnishing purposes, the devil and cohorts devise ferocious plans. Intentional, reputation smudging, leads to false depictions of dreamers. Liars, jealous foes, have layouts for dreamers' demises. Repeatedly, reputation destruction prioritizes opposition tactics' list. Why? Good names publish positive, upstanding, and outstanding accomplishments. "A GOOD name *is* better than precious ointment..." Ecclesiastes 7:1.

Nondreamers conduct business like their master – Satan. Nondreamers' misplaced, anger, results in self-inflicted poor choices plus illogical determinations minus happiness and mercy. Opposition tactics strike at dreamers attempting dream sabotages. Beware of dream sabotagers – pew villains. "An ungodly man diggeth up evil: and in his lips *there is* as a burning fire. A froward man soweth strife: and a whisperer separateth chief friends. A violent man eticeth his neighbor, and leadeth him into the way *that is* not good." Proverbs 16:27-29.

Reiteration. Deafness, blindness, and disobedience plague some church pewers. Talebearers are negative role players swarming church pews and society. They are deceived, misguided, demolitionists. Stings, of Satan's concoctions, freeze sensibility. Gossip and mistreatment detonations alienate and chase people from churches.

God's perfect eyesight is not hidden from so-called cover-ups or evil stashes under rugs. God's records reflect why, how, when, and where, tales are told. He knows all guilty parties. God's judgments are unmistaken.

Oftentimes, man's judgments are unfairly given and administered. Intentionally, from the start, frameworks are set up for biased outcomes and deliveries. Many earthly systems are designed for unfairness. Many innocents are confined; while guilty parties walk free.

Contrastingly, heavenly systems were, are, and always will be fair. Worldly systems deliberately trafficking unfairness have a judgment day. In heavenly systems, there is no respect of persons. Every knee bows. Every tongue confesses. God's heavenly Lamb's Book of Life reflects truth. Deed are accounted for. "...for the Lord God Almighty and the Lamb are the temple . . . And there shall in no wise enter into it any thing that defileth, neither *whatsoever* worketh abomination, or *maketh* a lie: but they which are written in the Lamb's Book of Life." Revelation 21:22, 27.

Talebearers have short-term memories and shortsightedness. Consumed in pew violence, they seem to forget why God died and his redemption plan for mankind. Biblical – true - principles – are unobserved. Personalities fight. So-called facts are manufactured and passed along to targeted circles. Lies and deceit flood their airways. God knows all culprits and victims. God knows the truth. Satan convinces culprits that their lies and ill-gotten gain are hidden. But, culprits are accountable and not escapees. God is merciful and longsuffering. But, reaping season does come. For repentance and amends, time is now. Sin does not evaporate. Sin confession has to be done; then room is there for forgiveness.

What God says matter. Talebearers claim quietness, and slowness to anger, is naivety. "*He that is* slow to anger *is* better than the mighty; and he that ruleth his spirit than he that taketh a city." Proverbs 16:32.

Quietness' virtue leads to peace and comfort. Talebearers' mouths steadily move. Mouths and ears never rest. Therefore, busybodies communicate confusion, anger, jealousy, and unreliability – tangled webs. Their advice and assessment should be carefully diagnosed. The company you keep counts. Sinful webs uphold torment. Talebearers become entrapped in their own confinements – worlds. They are sneaky plus unreliable.

Sincere worshippers assemble in God's Houses for praise and worship. Talebearers' make their overbearing negative presence known; therefore, many sincere worshippers seek other assemblies. Talebearers are extremely disruptive. Sincere worshippers cannot afford wasting valuable time with meddlers. Talebearers' hearts need transformation and regeneration. When false lips rule, lies and abominable acts compound.

Runaway Dreamers are beholden. Independence and integrity is long, long, diminished or was never there. Miserably, despair-filled individuals abandon dreams. Lives are negatively changed because hopes are unfulfilled. Unfairly, blaming and causing problems for others are common opposition tactics.

Positively and realistically, dream accomplishment contributes to quality of life. Hopes dictate and activate dreams; whereas, despair deactivates dreams. Certain aspects of speech and action are scripted and followed. Dreamers do not accept interference, with personal aspirations; but nondreaming busybodies do. Mediocre-euphoria traps tosses dreams in garbage disposals. Nondreamers suffer regrets because courage is lacking for pursuit convictions. Allowance of others, to ruin your life, is cowardice and pathetic.

Some would-be preachers, teachers, evangelists, scientists, doctors, lawyers, morticians, carpenters, etc., feel like prisoners. These would-be dreamers fear labels. Why? Shamefulness of Jesus Christ and fear of unacceptability. Realistically, ***smart or nerd,*** *are compliments*. What is your preference name? Jesus-lover, smart, nerd, or prisoner? Other than Jesus, it seems as though, almost any other name, is acceptable.

<u>*Life lesson*</u>: Be not afraid of men-pleasing labels. Step out! Soar to hopes or have regrets! The choice is – personal – yours! Through tiredness, keep soaring!

"And let us not be weary in well doing: for in due season we shall reap, if we faint not." Galatians 6:9. "THEREFORE seeing we have this ministry, as we have received mercy, we faint not; but have renounced the hidden things of dishonesty, not walking in craftiness, nor handling the word of God deceitfully; but by manifestation of the truth commending ourselves to every man's conscience in the sight of God." II Corinthians 4:1-2.

Sadness. Devastatingly, talebearers lie and prowl, causing sadness and chaos pathways. "Because with lies ye have made the heart of the righteous sad, whom I have not made sad; and strengthened the hands of the wicked, that he should not return from his wicked way, by promising him life: Therefore ye shall see no more vanity...for I will deliver my people out of your hand: and ye shall know that I am the Lord." Ezekiel 13:22-23. "...Touch not mine anointed, and do my prophets no harm." Psalm 105:15.

Alertness interrupts both physical and mental attacks. Particularly, nondreamers' gangs, pits, and snares, are devised against dreamers. Ultimately, opposition tactics kill, or halt, many dream fruitions. Opposition tactics are restraints. In the Name of Jesus, talebearers are subdued.

Satan is a Serpent, Predator, Bully, Hope Killer, Liar, and Thief. Firstly, Satan caused his destiny predicament. Secondly, he is angry and unhappy. Why? He is headed to everlasting torment. His fate is hopeless and unchangeable. "And the great dragon was cast out, that old serpent, called the Devil, and Satan, which deceiveth the whole world: he was cast out into the earth, and his angels were cast out with him." Revelation 12:9. "...Woe to the inhabiters of the earth and under the sea! for the devil is come down unto you, having great wrath, because he knoweth that he hath but a short time." Revelation 12:12.

Why listen to the devil? Why follow him? He has an unsolvable problem. His ticket to eternal turmoil is irreversible. He has an active, recruitment, sign-up and a full-time work staff (specifically, liars, thieves, manipulators). Mankind is his prey. "Be sober, be vigilant; because your adversary the devil, as a roaring lion, walketh about, seeking whom he may devour…" I Peter 5:8. "Ye are of your father the devil, and the lusts of your father ye will do: He was a murderer from the beginning, and abode not in the truth; because there is no truth in him. When he speaketh a lie, he speaketh of his own: for he is a liar, and the father of it." St. John 8:44.

Where it is due, give Satan credit: He gives bribe gifts, with intent, to steal souls from heaven's gate. Why accept gifts from, or brag on, the serpent? You are aware; he bites. "If ye then, being evil, know how to give good gifts unto your children, how much more shall your Father which is in heaven give good things to them that ask him?" St. Matthew 7:11.

Recognition, of Satan's evil agenda, toward you is essential. Logically speaking, the devil has "zero tolerance" for God's people. His outcomes yield catastrophes. Do you want to go where he is going? "But the fearful, and unbelieving, and the abominable, and murderers, and whoremongers, and sorcerers, and idolaters, and all liars, shall have their part in the lake which burneth with fire and brimstone: which is the second death." Revelation 21:8.

Satan's Marketing Tool. Sin is abominable. Being the deceiver he is, Satan shows sin as good, not evil. Sin is evil and causes – permanent - soul loss. Eternal damnation awaits Satan and his followers.

Scapegoats. Exposure, to sin, is inexcusable for committing wickedness. Sin is damaging and chargeable. Divestments should be made. "So then every one of us shall give account of himself to God." Romans 14:12. "And that servant, which knew his lord's will, and prepared not *himself*, neither did according to his will, shall be beaten with many stripes. But he that knew not, and did commit things worthy of stripes, shall be beaten with a few *stripes*. For unto whomsoever much is given, of him shall be much required: and to whom men have committed much, of him they will ask the more." St. Luke 12:47-48. "…the righteous shall be recompensed in the earth: much more the wicked and the sinner." Proverbs 11:31.

Even in the presence of sinfulness and worldliness, the Lord teaches Christians to remain holy.

Don't Be Scared! Be Ready! Preparation for, heavenly, homegoing, consists of holiness, prayer, study, and helps. Heaven - or hell – is chosen eternal destinations. No one goes, to either place, accidentally or haphazardly. Mankind can make freewill choices. Living right, or wrong, determines eternal home. Focus on Jesus!

God is in His own class; but, the devil would have mankind believe he is equal to God. Simply, two life plans are available: 1) **God's plan** and 2) the devil's plan. The aforementioned plans are dissimilar. **God's plan is Life.**

The devil's plan is death. Do you want to go where he is going? Everyone preaches their own eulogy. Truthfully, the fruits you live speak for themselves. "If any man worship the beast and his image, and receive *his* mark in his forehead, or in *his* hand, the same shall drink of the wine of the wrath of God, which is poured out without mixture into the cup of his indignation; and he shall be tormented with fire and brimstone in the presence of the holy angels, and in the presence of the Lamb: And the smoke of their torment ascendeth up forever and ever: and they have no rest day nor night, who worship the beast and his image, and whosoever receiveth the mark of his name." Revelation 14:9-11.

Scorners accuse God-fearing saints. Disdain, and distaste for sin, seems to be lost among these opponents. They are disrespectful to dreamers and wisdom; because, they are slaves to mediocrity. Nondreamers are aggressive, tough to teach, and void of understanding. Inclination for creation of bizarre stunts – on pews – takes precedent.

Minds are cluttered with foolishness and ill will. "Forsake the foolish, and live; and go in the way of understanding. Reprove not a scorner, lest he hate thee: rebuke a wise man, and he will love thee." Proverbs 9:6, 8.

Obviously, scorners are unappreciative of instruction. "He that reproveth a scorner getteth to himself shame: and he that rebuketh a wicked *man getteth* himself a blot." Proverbs 9:7.

Self is you. Even through deception (pretense), someone else cannot become you. Stop trying. Decide whether you dream or not. God's instructions are nourishment for body, soul, and mind. According to your decisions, lead your life. Refrain from lying about, and meddling in, others affairs. "A righteous *man* hateth lying: but a wicked *man* is loathsome, and cometh to shame." Proverbs 13:5.

Self-Haters. Disturbingly, wholesale distributions of pettiness and ignorance spread undue chaos. Hastily taking unrelenting shots toward dreamers continuously unfold. Their mission comprises management and facilitation of evil plans for dreamers' suffering, while discounting pain. They strategize downfalls hoping dreams die.

Without seeing the premise of long-term glory, haters pander to short-term schemes – opposition tactics. Because of nondreamers' self-inflicted problems, struggle ensues making evil the main component of their wicked landscape. "Whoso rewardeth evil for good, evil shall not depart from his house." Proverbs 17:13.

Self-Validation. High esteem standards indicate life experiences and preparedness. Heaven or hell is not inheritable. Life lived, decisions made and opportunities taken, determine eternity destinations. "Know ye not that the unrighteous shall not inherit the kingdom of God? Be not deceived: neither fornicators, nor idolaters, nor adulterers, nor effeminate, nor abusers of themselves with mankind, nor thieves, nor covetous, nor drunkards, nor revilers, or extortioners, shall inherit the kingdom of God." I Corinthians 6:9-10. Choices validate finality.

Set-Asides. God is our help. Christian Eagle-tis-ti-cal dreamers trust God; whereas, nondreamers trust "people that could not profit them, nor be an help nor profit, but a shame, and also a reproach." Isaiah 30:5. Itching ears disregard portions of scripture; because, they only want to hear smooth things. Overlooking and pretending do not dissolve, or prevent, God's Word from fulfillment. "The Lord is not slack concerning his promise, as some men count slackness; but is longsuffering to us-ward, not willing that any should perish, but that all should come to repentance." II Peter 3:9.

Overlooking, and pretending, shows imprudence and lack of wisdom. Heaven is real. Hell is real too. "Now go, write it before them in a table, and note it in a book, that it may be for the time to come for ever and ever…this *is* a rebellious people, lying children, children *that* will not hear the law of the Lord: Which say to the seers, See not; and to the prophets, Prophesy not unto us right things, speak unto us smooth things, prophesy deceits: Get you out of the way, turn aside out of the path, cause the Holy One of Israel to cease from before us. Wherefore thus saith the Holy One of Israel, Because ye despise this word, and trust in oppression and perverseness and stay thereon: Therefore this inequity shall be to you as a breach ready to fall, swelling in a high wall, whose breaking cometh suddenly at an instant." Isaiah 30:8-13. "As in the days of No'e, so shall it be also in the days of the Son of man. They did eat, they drank, they married wives, they were given in marriage, until the day that No'e entered into the ark, and the flood came, and destroyed them all. Likewise also as it was in the days of Lot; they did eat, they drank, they bought, they sold, they planted, they builded; But the same day that Lot went out of Sodom it rained fire and brimstone from heaven, and destroyed *them* all. Even thus shall it be in the day when the Son of man is revealed." St. Luke 17:26-30.

Reality is filled with some pleasures, delicacies, persecution, and tribulation. Righteousness leads to eternal life. "Blessed be the God and Father of our Lord Jesus Christ, which according to his abundant mercy hath begotten us again unto a lively hope by the resurrection of Jesus Christ from the dead, to an inheritance incorruptible, and undefiled, and that fadeth not away, reserved in heaven for you, who are kept by the power of God through faith unto salvation ready to be revealed in the last time." I Peter 1:3-5. Wickedness leads to everlasting fire and brimstone.

Sin Insanity is a mind-altering, deadly, state. Momentary pleasures infiltrate all life chapters. The more you do right, the better you feel; but temporal immoralities lead to eternal damnation. As more wrongdoings are committed, more are desired. Satan lies pretending sin makes you feel better. In essence, this is another satanic trick for blocking souls from God's eternal glory. To nondreamers, temporality looks, sounds, and feels, satisfactory but fades and bites with eternal punishment. Righteousness and wrongness differ. Meshing right and wrong is impossible. Whether you live <u>holy</u> or <u>unholy</u> is your choice. Holiness saves souls. Unholiness destroys

Dreamers are committed to righting wrong; but nondreamers perpetuate wrongness. Righteousness breaks sin transmission chains. Surrendering, to God's Call, ensures eternal survival. "On," and "off," relationships with God is re-crucifixion. "For *it is* impossible for those who were once enlightened…if they fall away, to renew them again unto repentance; seeing they crucify to themselves the Son of God afresh, and put *him* to an open shame." Hebrews 6:4, 6. *Time is here for holy living*.

Sin enslaves. Settlement, for devil-inspired fixes, amounts to short-term so-called enjoyment. A few moments of worldly pleasure can cost a lifetime of pain – as well as - eternal destruction. "For the wages of sin *is* death; but the gift of God *is* eternal life through Jesus Christ our Lord." Romans 6:23.

Soon or later, snake heads are cut off; then tails automatically die. Befriending people snakes permit bites. After all, biting is their calling card - lifestyle. Is the serpent at fault, when you fall for his subtlety bites, especially if you were previously bitten? How many snake friends do you have?

Sin simmers, implodes, and then explodes. People serpents are enemies, cynics, liars, thieves, slanderers, and talebearers. Conclusively, sin does not win. Sin detoxification is necessary!

Situation Control. Understand **why** things happen. People and things cause situations to happen. Figure out why and how; then apply solutions.

Sowing/Reaping. Sowing time is here. Reaping time is coming. "Be not deceived; God is not mocked: for whatsoever a man soweth, that shall he also reap." Galatians 6:7. Foolishly, nondreamers live as if present actions have no bearing on future conditions.

Stagnation is unproductivity and inexcusability. Souls await rescue from hell's pit. "…behold, now, *is* the accepted time; behold, now *is* the day of salvation…" II Corinthians 6:2. Time is a valuable asset. Wasting time is senseless liability.

Stupidity blocks excellence. God's Word teaches wisdom and excellency. "Wise *men* lay up knowledge: but the mouth of the foolish *is* near destruction." Proverbs 10:14. "…he that followeth vain *persons is* void of understanding." Proverbs 12:11.

"The labour of the righteous tendeth to life: the fruit of the wicked to sin. He *is in* the way of life that keepeth instruction: but he that refuseth reproof erreth. He that hideth hatred with lying lips, and he that uttereth a slander, is a fool. In the multitude of words there wanteth not sin: but he that refraineth his lips *is* wise. The tongue of the just *is as* choice silver: the heart of the wicked *is* little worth. The lips of the righteous feed many: but fools die for want of wisdom. The blessing of the Lord, it maketh rich, and he addeth no sorrow with it." Proverbs 10:16-22. Unfortunately, mediocrity appeals to nondreamers; consequently, divisiveness is ever present.

Swamp Creators. Swamp creators make needless problems. Wickedness is abominable. Incredibly, psychology between swamp creators and pit throwers, denote similar linkages. To impede progress both use opposition tactics. Both are prideful. Pride imposes on everyone and everything touched. Family, teachers, communities, and the general public are negatively affected. Pride has a way of squeezing and upsetting normalcy. Supervisors, personnel directors, worldwide, have come in contact, or supervised, swamp creators. Usually, swamp creators hire a lot of people. Hirees' responsibility is to help cesspools handle unscrupulous-type business which creates various hazards. No one really benefits from swamp ill-gotten gains.

Swamp creators/bullies' pathetic doings must be handled through necessary blockages inorder to secure fairness and intimidation elimination. Although Joseph suffered without cause, he pursued dreams. Dreamers' stamina accelerates, exhilarates excellency.

Taking Undeserved Credit. Deceitfully and irresponsibly, nondreamers give undue (false) credit. Intentionally, they give credit among nondreamers; therefore, excluding deserving souls - dreamers. Falsity networks ignore truth. Undue credit is false – undeserving. Dreamers deserve earned credit. "Withhold not good from them to whom it is due, when it is in the power of thine hand to do *it*." Proverbs 3:27.

Talebearers –Gloominess and Falsehood Artists. Negatively, nondreamers are skillful brainwashers and sinister schemers who promote prejudice. Appallingly, talebearing is their profession and is treated seriously and discriminately. Intentionally, dreamers are oftentimes sought out, and campaigned against, for victimization mockeries.

Abomination brushes paint canvases filled with naivety and weakness. Talebearers showcase opposition tactics as truth, and lies as truth.

Repetitively and knowingly, dreamers are sought-out targets. Inter-circles (nondreamers) are given some immunity from talebearing attacks; but outer-circles (dreamers) are not, at all, immunized. Wonderfully, dreamers build courage. "Yea, though I walk through the valley of the shadow of death, I will fear no evil: for thou *art* with me; thy rod and thy staff they comfort me. Thou preparest a table before me in the presence of mine enemies: thou anointest my head with oil; my cup runneth over. Surely goodness and mercy shall follow me all the days of my life: and I will dwell in the house of the Lord forever." Psalm 23:4-6.

Nondreaming, talebearers' main goals include denigration, impo-tence, and imposition, toward dreamers' value traits. As a matter of fact, intimidation and humiliation slaughter good names and dreams. Nondreamers ruin their reputations. Instead of repairing bad names, they attack dreamers' good names. Be ardently careful how interactions are made with cold-hearted culprits (corruption defenders) on pews. In many cases, persons' and properties' jeopardy dispels common sense. Evil influ-ence retards expansion. Nondreamers punch hard and low; because hits are - about them – not you. Low self-esteem issues should be addressed. Possibly, opposition tactics' projection against dreamers, is because of cov-etousness, jealousy, and mediocrity.

Painstaking efforts like confusion (mixed messages) impose dream kills. Intertwined offenses, into pew fabrics, seem to be one of nondream-ers' favorite tricks. In the Body of Christ, conspirator bands cause and create drama. Responsibility, to themselves and others, escapes them. Somehow, conspirators convene on large scales. With side shows, they undermine good people. While goodness rewards are withheld, wicked-ness rewards flow freely. Simultaneously, lips flatter and faces smile; but, demise nets maximize surroundings. "A talebearer revealeth secrets: but he that is of a faithful spirit concealeth the matter." Proverbs 11:13. "He that goeth about *as* a talebearer revealeth secrets: therefore meddle not with him that flattereth with his lips." Proverbs 20:19.

Jesus ambassadors must remain attentive and observe scrutiny. "BELOVED, believe not every spirit, but try the spirits, whether they are of God: because many false prophets are gone out into the world. Hereby know ye the Spirit of God: Every spirit that confesseth that Jesus Christ is come in the flesh is of God: And every spirit that confesseth not that Jesus Christ is come in the flesh is not of God: and this is that *spirit* of an'-tichrist, whereof ye have heard that it should come; and even now already is it in the world. Ye are of God...and have overcome them: because greater is he that is in you, than he that is in the world. They are of the world: therefore speak they of the world, and the world heareth them. We are of God: he that knowest God heareth us; he that is not of God heareth not us. Hereby know we the spirit of truth, and the spirit of error...let us love one another: for love is of God; and everyone that loveth is born of God, and knowest God. He that lovest not knowest not God; for God is love." I John 4:1-8.

Thanks. Although God deserves praise and gratitude for His might works, praises go to other gods. In many cases, everybody is praised but God. Planes fall from the sky. Cars are torn apart. God spares lives; but, few proudly announce Jesus saves lives. "I *am* the Lord: that *is* my name: and my glory will I not give to another, neither my praise to graven images." Isaiah 42:8.

"Whosoever therefore shall confess me before men, him will I confess also before my Father which is in heaven. But whosoever shall deny me before men, him will I also deny before my Father which is in heaven." St. Matthew 10:32-33.

Acknowledgement of God's marvelousness stirs worship anew. "If *it had* not *been* the Lord who was on our side, when men rose up against us: Then they had swallowed us up quick..." Psalm 124:2-3. Whether in valleys, pits, or on mountaintops, God walks with His people. Foolhardily, engagement in sin invites and permits sorrows.

Thievery. "AND God spake all these words, saying...Thou shalt not steal." Exodus 20:1, 15. Thieves are liars and imposters pumping and fueling confusion. Convincingly, they lie to themselves saying others' property belong to them. When confronted, reputation bombardment results. Cycles persist. Because cycles continue, pits become deeper and parameters broader. Disheartening, company consist of chaotic, evil, duplicitous dens, complicities' associations, and irrelevant issues. Peace is absent; only strife and divisions abound.

Somehow, prideful, brazen, thieves paint false pictures portraying themselves as victims. In other words, they say they have a right to steal and claim to pay you back later. Stolen monies, or belongings, never return nor reparations made. Instead, lies mount - on victims. Itching ears listen to thieves' untruths, as well as, develop strange attitudes toward victims. In the meantime, thieves float through while their victims suffer persecutions resulting from their ungodly behavior.

After thefts and misbehaviors, they go back to pulpits and pews acting as though nothing is stolen. Systematically, false implications and lies are concentrated, long-term, and widespread. Evidently, plans, time, and thoughts go into nondreamers' evil plots. Sadly, these type situations may occur regularly or irregularly. Whether regularly or irregularly, evil plots' intentions are to dampen spirits.

Crime victims question "how does this happen?" Even on pews, the devil works with whoever lets him. His job consists of hiring liars, slanderers, and thieves. Satan enjoys wrongness anywhere, any time, it occurs; especially, on pews.

Complicity, with thieves, has dire consequences. Influences should be monitored. Evil influences exude harmfulness. Using wise precautions evoke wisdom and structure. "When thou sawest a thief, then thou consentedst with him, and hast been partaker with adulterers. Thou givest thy mouth to evil, and thy tongue frameth deceit. Thou sittest *and* speaketh against thy brother...These *things* hast thou done, and I kept silence; thou thoughtest that I was altogether *such an one* as thyself: *but* I will reprove thee, and set *them* in order before thine eyes. Now consider this, ye that forget God, lest I tear *you* in pieces, and *there be* none to deliver. Whoso offereth praise glorifieth me: and to him that ordereth *his* conversation *aright* will I shew the salvation of God." Psalm 50:18-23.

Partnerships can be fruitful; but some spree destruction and unfeasibility. Actually, certain relationships cause soul loss. Sin infringements change focus from heavenly affections to worldliness. "Whoso is partner with a thief hateth his own soul: he heareth cursing, and bewaryeth *it* not. The fear of man bringeth a snare: but whoso putteth his trust in the Lord shall be safe. An unjust man *is* an abomination to the just: and *he that is* upright in the way *is* abomination to the wicked." Proverbs 29:24-25, 27.

Seemingly, some thieves create safe havens. These oppressors plant and cultivate cruelty strongholds. Armed with untruths, cover-ups, and reputation mutilation, audacities including saying to those stolen from, "you have to forgive." This is true. Forgiveness is done; but this does not give thieves rights to steal your belongings and act as though they did not.

Embellishment is a past-time. Yet, another thieves' priority is concealment of evil deeds. After stealing others' belongings, they lie to select audiences that victims did acts demoralizing to them. Culprits use reverse psychology hoping to block suspicions of their thieveries. They suppose twisting truth works. Specifically, selected audiences are crutches, chosen as sympathizers, for their personal schemes. Be wise; so you are not drawn into these ungodly maneuvers.

Clearly, nondreamers' victimization pool is twofold: 1) persons stolen from, and 2) selected audiences (sympathizers). Consideration, of soul-saving efforts and reprisals, seems to escape recompense equations.

Restitution payments remain unpaid. Overtime, in attempts to cover robberies, perpetrators pit others against innocent theft victims. Continuous lying, spreading rumors, and keeping up confusion, may deflect attention from the thefts and real perpetrators; but, those thefts happened. God sees and knows guilty thieves. Affirmatively, both perpetrators and victims know what truly happened.

Gleefully, real perpetrators watch and salivate as their evil conspiracies unfold. Particularly, victims' reactions are closely monitored; because perpetrators enjoy hurting others. Jealous, of their victims, contributes to scoffs, winks, deceitful smiles, while inflicting hurtful, harmful schemes. Efforts to steal dreamers' calmness permeate several spaces. Nondreamers glow if anxiety and tears are seen; but seem upset and saddened to see God's bountiful blessings which never stop pouring into dreamers' lives. "Thou preparest a table before me in the presence of my enemies: thou anointest my head with oil; my cup runneth over. Surely goodness and mercy shall follow me all the days of my life: and I will dwell in the house of the Lord forever." Psalm 23:5-6.

Straightforwardly, "reaping time is coming and deeds resurface whether good or bad." Rightfully and cheerfully, prosperity is gained through giving, not by taking. "Every man as he purposeth in his heart, *so let him give*; not grudgingly, or of necessity: For God loveth a cheerful giver." II Corinthians 9:7.

Ill-gotten resources diminish success capacity. "Wealth *gotten* by vanity shall be diminished: but he that gathereth by labour shall increase." Proverbs 13:11.

Stolen resources are like drain clogs. Also, ill-gotten gains cause losses, shortages, stagnation, imbalances, sorrows, and dryness. Instead of blackness, balance sheets show redness. Problem-solving mechanisms are insufficient; because so-called assets belong to someone else - stolen. When profits are sought from ill-gotten gains, losses occur. At first, the devil masks so-called gains as profitability. But, in the end, losses ensue. In some cases, losses pursue and consume. The devil provides truth dislodgements. After all, he is a liar. "A FALSE balance is abomination to the Lord: but a just weight *is* his delight." Proverbs 11:1.

Oftentimes, men-pleasers overlook theft side effects. "Treasures of wickedness profit nothing: but righteousness delivereth from death. The Lord will not suffer the soul of the righteous to famish: but he casteth away the substance of the wicked." Proverbs 10:2-3. Dream suckers kill time and attempt hiding behind falsehood layers. "He that justifieth the wicked, and he that condemeth the just, even they both *are* abomination to the Lord." Proverbs 17:15.

Common sense discloses remorsefulness. Deniability is unreasonable.

Disharmonious environments should be distanced from hearts and pocketbooks, is prudent and necessary. Enemies take advantage of kindness. Unwisely, enemies misdiagnose dreamers compassion as gullibility and stupidity. Dreamers are neither gullible or stupid. Dreamers are cheerful givers and helpers. Dreamers' bedrock trademark is enthusiasm.

Jealousy leads to stealing and hurting in many, and any, ways. Jealousy convolutes hearts. Hardheartedness (dehumanization philosophies) distorts views, leading to criminal acts. When jealousy is suspected, take heed. Take steps denying adversaries' access.

Dreamers are nonparticipants in duplicities and complicities. Dreamers soar in the midst of obstacles. Win with God. Some challenges and unforeseen problems are repercussions of sin; but, adversity is a part of life. God is our Deliverer.

Thresholds. "Wisdom is too high for a fool...The thought of foolishness is sin: and the scorner is an abomination to men." Proverbs 24:7, 9. Dreamers display excellence, having low foolishness tolerance.

Dreamers set high standards, having no time or effort for evil, opposition tactics' duplicities, and complicities. Mischievous, sinful, plots destroy helpful avenues, including temperance. Foolishness and its perpetrators drag others into malicious circles. Knowingly, some talebearers are willing (volunteering) perpetrators; whereas others are unsuspecting, unwilling, victims. Sinful, horror, halls align with worldly temporalities. Worldly pleasures require misdeeds. Hurters cling to cruelty. Worldly, short-term, gratifications are unworthy of souls. "What? know ye not that your body is the temple of the Holy Ghost *which is* in you, which ye have of God, and ye are not your own? For ye are bought with a price: therefore glorify God in your body, and in your spirit, which are God's." I Corinthians 6:19-20.

Time Allotment. Valuable time assets should be managed appropriately. Bible study keeps you out of other peoples' business. Particularly, time <u>management</u> utilizes prudence. Rewards contain exceptionality and positive opportunities.

"The beginning of strife *is as* one letteth out water: therefore leave off contention, before it is meddled with." Proverbs 17:14. "And that ye study to be quiet, and to do your own business, and to work with your own hands…I Thessalonians 4:11. "Seest thou a man diligent in his business? he shall stand before kings; he shall not stand before mean *men*." Proverbs 22:29.

Attendance to personal business formula follows:

6 months – *Take care* of self-business.
<u>6 months – *Do not take* care of others' business</u>.
12 months = one year. The year is gone.

By taking care of your business and leaving others to them, years are more fruitful. When taking care of self's business properly, time does not permit meddling in other peoples' affairs.

Timidity. Nondreamers follow; therefore weakness is main trait. Fearful, covetous, followers promote cruelty. Also, they are too afraid for self-truth; thus, dreams are unpursued. (Blind + blind = blindness). Nondreamers' protocols are taken from unreliable sources; such as liars, slanderers, thieves, and antichrists. Pew villians tear others apart. Prudently, dreamers' associations upbuild.

God loves and helps everyone – dreamers and nondreamers. "…Of a truth I perceive that God is no respecter of persons…" The Acts 10:34.

Toleration. God fosters justice and esteems uprightness. In some circles, righteousness is not tolerated; but, mistreatment is encouraged and compensated. "They…hate him that speaketh uprightly." Amos 5:10.

Satan enables injustice. "Forasmuch therefore as your treading *is* upon the poor, and ye take from him…ye have built houses…but ye shall not dwell in them…ye have planted pleasant vineyards, but ye shall not drink wine of them. For I know your manifold transgressions and your mighty sins: they afflict the just, they take a bribe, and they turn aside the poor in the gate *from their right*." Amos 5:11-13.

When excluded from ungodly, ominous, circles, be not discouraged. Surely, participation in unholy, inhumane, forums debase integrity. By disrespecting your Creator, respect for His creation automatically crumbles. Reckoning day comes. God's side is The Right Side - leading to heaven.

Tree-Bearers. Where does fruit come from? Life fruits produce mind-expressing motivations and feelings. Fruits tell, and show, where one stand. Words, alone, are an incomplete process. Actions show wordings' feelings. Apple trees are not orange producers. When lifestyles conflict with holiness professions, stumbling blocks and confusions persist. Sinners watch Christians' lives. Many skeptical sinners claim "no one lives holy." But, that is a lie from Satan. There is a difference between living righteous and unrighteous. Clearly, Satan attempts to blur righteous and unrighteous differences (value traits vs. opposition tactics). God's Word teaches sin is wrong. Stay watchful and pray. Satan tries to make sin look right.

God's Word says live holy. God, Himself, is holy. He does not tell us to do what we cannot. He knows holy living is achievable, if we choose. He gives mankind freewill (choices). Living for God is righteousness. Living for the devil is unrighteousness. "Dearly beloved, I beseech *you* as strangers and pilgrims, abstain from fleshly lusts, which war against the soul; having your conversation honest...that whereas they speak against you as evildoers, they may by *your* good works, which they shall behold, glorify God in the day of visitation." I Peter 2:11-12.

Correctly, sinners expect God's people to live different from them. After all, right and wrong is totally different. Sinners have a right to see Christians live what the Holy Bible teaches. Intolerabilities, for lying, thievery, evil complicities, duplicities, and other wicked tactics, are expected. Stumblingblocks decay progress. "For it had been better for them not to have known the way of righteousness, than, after they have known i*t*, to turn from the holy commandment delivered unto them. But it is happened unto them according to the true proverb, The dog *is* turned to his own vomit again; and the sow that was washed to her wallowing in the mire." II Peter 2:21-22. Mixing righteousness and sinfulness funnel lukewarmness. Hot or cold is required. "For even hereunto were ye called: because Christ also suffered for us, leaving us an example, that ye should follow his steps: Who did no sin, neither was guile found in his mouth... Who his own self bare our sins in his own body...that we, being dead to sins, should live unto righteousness: by whose stripes ye are healed. For ye were as sheep going astray; but are now returned unto the Shepherd and Bishop of your souls." I Peter 2:21-22, 24-25.

Satan's limited powers deceive. He uses opportunities, lavishness, etc., for enticing saved men and women to commit sin. Satan works through nondreamers. Nondreamers refuse God's Word; but, dreamers' focus is continuously solvent. "*Even him*, whose coming is after the working of Satan with all power and signs and lying wonders, and with all deceivableness of unrighteousness in them that perish; because they received not the love of the truth, that they might be saved. And for this cause God shall send them strong delusion, that they should believe a lie: that they all might be damned who believed not the truth, but had pleasure in unrighteousness." II Thessalonians 2:9-12. Pew villains fuel anxieties and skirmishes. Through Christ, dreamers maintain composure, along with analytical balance.

Nondreamers' opposition tactics permit perishing ruins. "Ye are of *your* father the devil, and the lusts of your father ye will do. He was a murderer from the beginning, and abode not in the truth, because there is no truth in him. When he speaketh a lie, he speaketh of his own: for he is a liar, and the father of it. And because I tell you the truth, ye believe me not. Which of you convinceth me of sin? And if I say the truth, why do ye not believe me? He that is of God heareth God's words: ye therefore hear *them* not, because ye are not of God." St. John 8:44-47.

Basically, most nondreamers assault verbally rather than physically. Slandering, and other opposition tactics, exemplifies cowardice. Dreamers' relationships with God supersede lies, slander, and all other smear tactics.

God saved Joseph's life and his family's lives. God did not permit Joseph's brothers to kill him. But, God permitted Joseph to help his whole family, love them, and take care of them. When you love God, you love your enemies. "…Love your enemies, bless them that curse you, do good to them that hate you, and pray for them which despitefully use you, and persecute you; that ye may be the children of your Father which is in heaven… For if ye love them which love you, what reward have ye? …And if ye salute your brethren only, what do ye more *than others*?…Be ye therefore perfect, even as your Father which is in heaven is perfect." St. Matthew 5:44-48. God turns situations in directions human capacities do not understand.

Triviality quenches aspirations. The so-called "new norm" should not consist of sinful, careless, reckless, behaviors. Pools of false prophets, haters, bullies, liars, deceivers, witchcrafters, fornicators, adulterers, thieves, etc., dampen church and societal spirits. Unscrupulously, the aforementioned ploys lure unsuspecting individuals.

Eve second-guessed God. She listened to the snake, which caused her and Adam's relationship collapse from God. "But I fear, lest by any means, as the serpent beguiled Eve through his subtilty, so your minds should be corrupted from the simplicity that is in Christ...For Satan himself is transformed into an angel of light. Therefore *it is* no great thing if his ministers also be transformed as the ministers of righteousness; whose end shall be according to their works." II Corinthians 11:3, 14-15.

Viewing God's mandates secondarily, and unrepentantly, garners possible soul loss unless corrected. The devil caters to people who take God insincerely. "Therefore if any man *be* in Christ, *he is* a new creature: old things are passed away; behold, all things are become new." II Corinthians 5:17. "And be renewed in the spirit of your mind; and that ye put on the new man, which after God is created in righteousness and true holiness." Ephesians 4:23-24.

God's Word is unchangeable. Mankind must change for God.

Troublemakers intentionally practice unfairness – inhumaneness. Calculating, disgusting, conspiracies, kill dreams. Innocent-looking pew villains, and their approaches, snare people. Treacherous villains (nondreamers) realize cruel actions create problems. By the time many naive people realize entrapments, they are already consumed by them. Some escape, while others perish.

Pray and focus; so troublemakers' tricks are disabled. For protection and joy, stay in the Lord's presence. Where is eternity for unrepentants? "...He that soweth the good seed is the Son of man; the field is the world; the good seed are the children of the kingdom; but the tares are the children of the wicked *one*; the enemy that sowed them is the devil; the harvest is the end of the world…As therefore the tares are gathered and burned in the fire; so shall it be in the end of this world. The Son of man shall send forth his angels…they shall gather out of his kingdom all things that offend, and them which do iniquity; and shall cast them into a furnace of fire: there shall be wailing and gnashing of teeth." St. Matthew 13:37-42.

To avoid the furnace, repentance of sins, as well as receiving salvation, is essential. "So shall it be at the end of the world: the angels shall come forth, and sever the wicked from among the just, and shall cast them into the furnace of fire…" St. Matthew 13:49-50.

For starting chaos, peacebreakers receive compensations. When repayment packages arrive, some are surprised because opposition tactics were supposedly hid. Not so! God sees you and every plot, scheme, and theft, committed. Without respect of persons, God vindicates. "See *it is* a righteous thing with God to recompense tribulation to them that trouble you; and to you who are troubled rest with us, when the Lord Jesus shall be revealed from heaven with his mighty angels, in flaming fire taking vengeance on them that know not God, and that obey not the gospel of our Lord Jesus Christ: Who shall be punished with everlasting destruction from the presence of the Lord, and from the glory of his power; when he shall come to be glorified in his saints, and to be admired in all them that believe…in that day." II Thessalonians 1:6-10.

Understand. You must know God to comprehend His ways and keep His tamper-proof commandments. "…if any man shall take away from the words of the book of this prophecy, God shall take away his part out of the book of life, and out of the holy city, and *from* the things which are written in this book." Revelation 22:19.

Natural eyes cannot see spiritual doings. Christians walk in the spirit – light - discerning both spiritual and natural. God's light shines eternally bright. "But the natural man receiveth not the things of the Spirit of God: for they are foolishness unto him: neither can he know *them*, because they are spiritually discerned." I Corinthians 2:14.

Unmovable Kingdom. God's Word prevails forever leading to eternal life in His Kingdom. Nursing temporalities and injustices eat up time and other valuable resources. Lies, slander, and other opposition tactics, misappropriate God-given talents and resources. Hereafters do come. "…Yet once more, signifieth the removing of those things that are shaken, as of things that are made, that those things which cannot be shaken may remain. Wherefore we receiving a kingdom which cannot be moved, let us have grace, whereby we may serve God acceptably with reverence and godly fear: For our God *is* a consuming fire." Hebrews 12:27-29. "Ye shall do no unrighteousness in judgment, in meteyard, in weight, or in measure. Just balances, just weights…ye shall have: I *am* the Lord your God…Therefore shall ye observe all my statutes, and all my judgments, and do them: I *am* the Lord." Leviticus 19:35-37. "…ye have been called unto liberty; only *use* not liberty for an occasion to the flesh, but by love serve one another. For all the law is fulfilled in one word, *even* in this: Thou shalt love thy neighbor as thyself." Galatians 5:13-14.

Emphasis on God's Word helps mankind. Mismanaging authority, worldly goods and so-called love, exposes souls to err. Worldliness emphasizes earthly matters. In other words, what man calls love is not love. Man fakes love. Once one gets whatever they seek, the victims find out there is no love. God is truth. He is love. We count on God. God answers truthfully. When someone say they love you, ask God is that person telling the truth. God gives true answers. When someone says they love you, make sure red flags are flying at full staff. "…be…wise as serpents, and harmless as doves." St. Matthew 10:16.

Biblical responses require fasting and praying; otherwise, avenging ourselves is attractive. God is our Avenger. When God avenges, all matters are in order.

Usability. Truth and charity paths lead to eternal life. Engagement in futility is misery leading to eternal damnation.

God is The Giver. Dreamers cheerfully give time, finances, talents, skills, education, and resources, for His glorification and edification; so there is meat in His storehouse. "Will a man rob God? Yet ye have robbed me, But ye say, Wherein have we robbed thee? In tithes and offerings. Ye *are* cursed with a curse: for ye have robbed me, *even* this whole nation. Bring ye all the tithes into the storehouse, that there may be meat in mine house, and prove me now herewith, saith the Lord of hosts, if I will not open you the windows of heaven, and pour you out a blessing, that *there shall* not *be room* enough *to receive it.* And I will rebuke the devourer for your sakes, and he shall not destroy the fruits of your ground; neither shall your vine cast her fruit before the time in the field, saith the Lord of hosts. And all nations shall call you blessed: for ye shall be a delightsome land, saith the Lord of hosts." Malachi 3:8-12. "Neither yield ye your members *as* instruments of unrighteousness unto sin: but yield yourselves unto God, as those that are alive from the dead, and your members *as* instruments of righteousness unto God. Romans 6:13.

God is the Creator and Owner of every ounce of our bodies. Body members should be used for His glory. Unless God allows us to think and perform, intellect would be nonexistent. Without God, bodies and minds are incapable of functionality.

Talent misuse sparks various problems. Unrighteousness leads down error-prone avenues. Money love causes erring from the faith. Pure money flow exfoliates taint. "For the love of money is a root of all *kinds of* evil, for which some have strayed from the faith in their greediness, and pierced themselves through with many sorrows." I Timothy 6:10. "Therefore, as we have opportunity, let us do good to all, especially to those who are of the household of faith." Galatians 6:10.

God gives skills, talents, and money. How is appreciation shown? Sadly, forgetfulness of God is common. Unless God is in heads and minds, misusing talents abound. Anxiety kindles frustrations. "Who changed the truth of God into a lie, and worshipped and served the creature more than the Creator...For this cause God gave them up unto vile affections ...And even as they did not like to retain God in *their* knowledge, God gave them over to a reprobate mind, to do those things which are not convenient; being filled with all unrighteousness, fornication, wickedness, covetous-ness, maliciousness; full of envy, murder, debate, deceit, malignity; whis-perers, backbiters, haters of God, despiteful, proud, boasters, inventors of evil things, disobedient to parents, without understanding…unmerciful: Who knowing the judgment of God, that they which commit such things are worthy of death, not only do the same, but have pleasure in them that do them. (Romans 1:25-26, 28-32). God is pleased with performances to Him and for Him – glorification and edification.

Many dreams and talents sit, on shelves, packed in storage bins. Why? God is rejected; while flips are turned to please man. Nondreamers' flippant behavior runs amuck. Talents can vanish. Where are they? Why are they gone? Ungodly misuse, and abuse of talents, create and further ungodliness, as well other sorrows occur.

Vainness. Do you use God's name appropriately? Do you jokingly minimize His standing? "Thou shalt not take the name of the Lord thy God in vain; for the Lord will not hold him guiltless that taketh his name in vain." Exodus 20:7.

Victim Mentalities. Careful! Dreamers cope poorly with prey mentalities. These mentalities hate self, thus using hate for spite and fighting high self-esteemers/self lovers. Mindlessness and thanklessness allow dream destructions Sitting, on life sidelines, deepens weaknesses. Get on, and stay on, **God's** timing.

The devil accepts employment applications. His company's name and address is the same - hell. Employment rates are high. Sadly, less people prefer right than wrong. "Enter ye in at the strait gate: for wide *is* the gate, and broad *is* the way, that leadeth to destruction, and many there be which go in thereat. Because strait *is* the gate, and narrow *is* the way, which leadeth unto life, and few there be that find it." St. Matthew 7:13-14.

Nondreamers covet dreamers' accomplishments, but lack willingness for performing necessary requirements for dream attainment. They are "would-be dreamers", lacking motivation, inspiration, edification, and boldness. Unfortunately, gulfs exist between dreamers and nondreamers. Naturally, right and wrong disagree.

Essentially, sustenance (time, effort, resources, finances) must be given to dreams not just talk and tradition. Work lips less. Give hands time to work and catch up. The formula, for dream accomplishment, is very simple: God first. Dreams, plus work, equal dream fulfillments. Continuously, work on dreams. Reality: Lip service plus tradition, minus work, equal dream death.

God – First - is the prioritization key to successfulness. With Jesus, life is great and promising!

Vows. Keep promises made to the Lord. Presumably, intentions are to keep them. "Better *is it that* shouldest not vow, than that thou shouldest vow and not pay." Ecclesiastes 5:5. "I will go into thy house with burnt offerings: I will pay thee my vows, which my lips uttered, and my mouth hath spoken, when I was in trouble." Psalm 66:13-14. "When thou vowest a vow unto God, defer not to pay it; for *he hath* no pleasure in fools: pay that which thou hast vowed." Ecclesiastes 5:4.

Vulnerability. God heals and strengthens. In every area of life, He knows motives and understands emotions.

Holy Bible scriptures show how Joseph's brothers plotted to hurt him. He dreamed and talked about his dreams. Low self-esteem liabilities open evil doors. Dreamers enjoy high self-esteem; regrettably, nondreamers have low self-esteem. It is like one party operates on mountaintops; whereas the other operates in valleys. Dreamers (optimists) believe in helping nondreamers realize holy life way. God lifts souls from depths of despair. He places souls in heavenly environments here on earth. By staying in God's presence, dreamers live some heaven while still living on earth. Godly dreamers' mission is upbuilding which includes rescuing nondreamers from opposition tactics' pits.

Warnings. Holiness does not cater to itching ears. Daily self-examinations, such as confessing and repenting, of sins, master evils. Forsake sin. "When I say unto the wicked, Thou shalt surely die; and thou givest him not warning, nor speakest to warn the wicked from his wicked way, to save his life; the same wicked *man* shall die in his iniquity; but his blood will I require at thine hand. Yet if thou warn the wicked and he turn not from his wickedness, nor from his wicked way, he shall die in his iniquity; but thou hast delivered thou soul." Ezekiel 3:18-19.

Warnings extend opportunities. Ignoring desensitizes. In part, consequences' dissipation lies in repenting, praising, worshipping, sayings, and doings.

Weapons. Scare tactics (emotional, and physical barriers) are used against dreamers. Specifically, church talebearers (slanderers) are notorious displacers - dream terminators. Their mouths denounce "stop cues" and "reset" devices starting unquenchable suffering and despair fires.

To kill dreams, nondreamers' tongues devise deceitful and catastrophic plots and are mockers and torchbearers for vindictiveness. Nondreamers' plant wickedness seeds they dread reaping; but they plant them anyway. Informational twisters ("people users") lacking integrity.

Itching ears plus tongues have proclivities for swaying and impeaching good environments. Watching and praying is always prudent. "But the tongue can no man tame; *it is* an unruly evil, full of deadly poison." James 3:8. Sadly, positive dreaming can be a dangerous undertaking. Many nondreamers are enemies. Tongues are small, but powerful. Power should be used for goodness, not evil. Wicked nondreamers recruit other wicked nondreamers. God protects and helps dreamers fulfill His calling and realize their dreams. Keep going forward. Even though negative talk hurts feelings, make sure pew villains are not hindering your dreams. Beware! Dreamers upplay exceptionalness; but, nondreamers downplay brilliance. Dreamers' value traits exemplify prudence. Regrettably, nondreamers' opposition tactics impede goodness; namely, fairness and progression. Entitlement, to fairness, is expected and should be protected without dissimilation.

Window dressers use one hundred percent of their time maintaining insignificances. These dressers keep outsides tidy; while insides remain filthy. Sides contradict. In order to effectively get along, insides and outsides should agree with one another. Divided houses fail. Oftentimes, and falsely, deadly foes parade as gentle souls.

Woe! Do you allow God to make you happy? Are you depending on ungodly measures? "Who has woe?...They that tarry long at the wine; they that go to seek mixed wine. Look not thou upon the wine when it is red, when it giveth his colour in the cup, *when* it moveth itself aright.

At the last it biteth like a serpent, and stingeth like an adder. Thine eyes shall behold strange women, and thine heart shall utter strange things." Proverbs 23:29-33.

God is first, and right, everlasting. Obedience, to God, is personal responsibility, vital for happiness, and heavenly homegoing.

Wrath of God. God deals with sin malignancy. Noah was a perfect man who walked with God. Notice who God appointed to build the ark. He was given an assignment of a lifetime. "The earth also was corrupt before God, and the earth was filled with violence. And God looked upon the earth, and, behold, it was corrupt; for all flesh had corrupted his way upon the earth. And God said unto Noah, The end of all flesh is come before me; for the earth is filled with violence through them; and…I will destroy them with the earth." Genesis 6:11-13.

God sees man's wickedness, angering Him daily. "God judgeth the righteous, and God is angry *with the wicked* every day." Psalm 7:11. "…every imagination of the thoughts of his heart *was* only evil continually." Genesis 6:5. The Lord was grieved. Man's wickedness was so vast that "…the Lord said, I will destroy man whom I have created from the face of the earth; both man, and beast…for it repenteth me that I have made them." Genesis 6:7.

Noah fulfilled God's commandments. God has purposes for lives and gives His people divine appointments. "And the Lord said, My spirit shall not always strive with man…" Genesis 6:3. Noah heard Him, listened, and is saved, along with family which was with him in the ark. "…every living substance was destroyed which was upon the face of the ground, both man, and cattle, and the creeping things, and the fowl of the heaven; and they were destroyed from the earth: and Noah only remained *alive* and they that *were* with him in the ark. And the waters prevailed upon the earth an hundred and fifty days." Genesis 7:23-24.

As dreamers reflect on Noah's time period, it looks and sounds current. Hearts are heavy. Because of fear, souls shiver. "The earth also was corrupt before God, and the earth was filled with violence." Genesis 6:11. But, God's people are shouting for joy because His peace is planted in hearts and minds. His word is being fulfilled. Surely, judgment day comes, not a debate but confirmation. Evidently, people who perished, in the flood, did not seriously consider prior warnings. Inobservance causes death. Obeying God illustrates preventive care. Preventive care keeps souls from eternal fire.

As in Noah's time, corresponding, wicked actions happen in the earth. Attention to earthly idols occupy vital time. Irresponsibility displeases God. "The great day of the Lord *is* near, it *is* near, and hasteth greatly, *even* the voice of the day of the Lord: the mighty man shall cry there bitterly. That day *is* a day of wrath, a day of trouble and distress…wasteness…darkness and gloominess…And I will bring distress upon men, that they shall walk like blind men, because they have sinned against the Lord: and their blood shall be poured out as dust, and their flesh as the dung. Neither their silver nor their gold shall be able to deliver them in the day of the Lord's wrath: but the whole land shall be devoured by the fire of his jealousy: for he shall make a speedy riddance of all them that dwell in the land." Zephaniah 1:14-15, 17-18.

Today is action time. Neither negotiations, nor money, purchase heavenly tickets. Sell-out, to worldly fame and luxuries only offer temporal gratification. In exchange for precious souls, Satan can only offer meager, earthly, temporal items. Satan's capabilities amount to short-term hype. Hell enlarges because the devil signs up many recruits. So-called luxuries; including, cars, houses, jewelry, positions, bribes, etc., pacify short-term. Ready souls spend eternity in heaven. The choice is yours. We all make numerous choices; however, eternity choices outmatch all. Personal chosen, destinations, earmark eternal home whether heaven or hell. Your eternal future is at stake. Once this choice is made and you arrive, there is no switching places. Make sure the heavenly choice is made; otherwise…"For what shall it profit a man, if he shall gain the whole world, and lose his own soul? Or what shall a man give in exchange for his soul? Whosoever therefore shall be ashamed of me and of my words in this adulterous and sinful generation; of him also shall the Son of man be ashamed, when he cometh in the glory of his Father with the holy angels." St. Mark 8:36-38.

Is eternal burning insaneness? The answer is yes; but, the choice belongs to you. You have a choice to live with God peaceably forever. God's salvation plan is the only way to make heaven home.

Hell is a hot, forever tormenting, place set aside for disobedient, unrepentant, sinners. When earthly days are ended, where is your home? Heaven or hell? "He that hath an ear, let him hear what the Spirit saith unto the churches; To him that overcometh will I give to eat of the tree of life, which is in the midst of the paradise of God." Revelation 2:7. "And I saw the dead, small and great, stand before God; and the books were opened: and another book was opened, which is *the book* of life: and the dead were judged out of those things which were written in the books, according to their works." Revelation 20:12. "And whosoever was not found written in the book of life was cast into the lake of fire." Revelation 20:15. Salvation, through Christ Jesus, stands forever as path to glorious homegoing. No exceptions! God is The Magnificent Eternal Bright and Morning Star. Heaven is Paradise. If you miss heaven, you have missed Jesus Christ forever.

In every sense, hell is unattractive. Hell consists of total, forever, unpleasantness, including fire and brimstone.

Wrongness. Right and wrong is likened to unmixable oil and water. "An unjust man *is* an abomination to the just: and *he that is* upright in the way is abomination to the wicked." Proverbs 29:27.

5

Resisting Mediocrity

Unfortunately, *WORLDLY* PROVISIONS and luxuries are freely doused, and set aside, for those who deny God. Despite subjection to devil-inspired riches and power, dreamers are not sin conformists endangering walking with God. Through faith and trust in Him, God-given riches and power come. God owns riches, power, luxuries...everything. Furthermore, dreamers' authority bolsters. God promotes. God created the universe. Christian dreamers sojourn on earth, not belonging to this world.

Nondreamers use opposition tactics against dreamers, hoping to turn hearts and minds from God. Wrongly, harmful tactics shape, and steer, many life courses. While sojourning in this sinful world, determining whether you dream righteously, or wrongly, is personal. Wrongly, nondreamers presume "original sin(s)" have no bearing on their lives' consequences, outcomes. For eternal life, confession, repentance, and doing right is important and essential.

As this book points out, Joseph's righteousness impacted his family's, and others', lives. Even though Joseph's brothers contemplated killing him, God allowed him to save their lives. Joseph did not hold their sins against them. He did not do evil for evil.

Absurdly, attempting to cover wrongness, instead of repenting, projects imprudence. God forgives. Living holy, in the midst of trials and tribulations, consummates right choice. During sufferings, trials, and tribulations, choose righteousness. Affirmatively, God's Way is always perfect. Christ's ambassadors' sufferings end. "For our light affliction, which is but for a moment, worketh for us a far more exceeding *and* eternal weight of glory; while we look not at the things which are seen, but at the things which are not seen: for the things which are seen *are* temporal; but the things which are not seen *are* eternal." II Corinthians 4:17-18.

Introspection

Who, and what, creates chaos on pews? Differences between dreamers' value traits, and nondreamers' opposition tactics, solidify moral programming differences. Dreamers follow Holy Bible teachings; however, nondreamers follow Satan's opposition tactics.

Dreamers are God-appointed ambassadors in the earth. Eagle-tis-ti-cal dreamers dedicate themselves to His assignments. Time and resource appropriations are for goodness' sake. Dreamers are not too busy to help; because their mission is God-driven. "And be not conformed to this world: but be ye transformed by the renewing of your mind, that ye may prove what *is* that good, and acceptable, and perfect, will of God." Romans 12:2.

Dream leaders take self-inventories. Why? Because godly, inward, mentalities sway outward decisions and behaviors. Oppositely, nondreamers overlook inward examinations, blaming others for negative, personal, choices and outcomes. Nondreamers neglect accountability. Whether personal or corporate, blame is not taken for anything. Unfairly, negative implications toward dreamers are customary.

God strengthens dreamers – leaders – spiritually, mentally, and physically. He gives wisdom and discernment needed to excel in the world and go to heaven. God also provides needed leadership skills. Firmly, dreamers believe God's instructions give expertise no matter the time, location, or circumstances. He is faithful. "...God gave them knowledge and skill in all learning and wisdom: and Daniel had understanding in all visions and dreams." Daniel 1:17. God educates.

Christian dreamers are not spared wickedness, foolishness, or unfairness – oppositions. Dreamers expect nondreamers' bouts against excellence. Dialogue exchanges tell predispositions. One entity practices goodness. Others support naughtiness. Dreamers' hope in Jesus Christ. Irresponsibly, nondreamers put confidence in man. Dreamers' trials are temporal. Without fainting, the end result is eternal salvation.

Befriend Jesus Christ. Ascend on wisdom wings, prudence, and excellence. Brave, Eagle-tis-ti-cal dreamers, naturally enjoy trustworthiness. Saving souls from hell's furnace demand courage. "That the trial of your faith, being much more precious than of gold that perisheth, though it be tried with fire, might be found unto praise and honour and glory at the appearing of Jesus Christ…Receiving the end of your faith, *even* the salvation of *your* souls." I Peter 1:7, 9. Daily work, in God's vineyard, requires serious, whole-hearted, business. His holy vineyard is not a playground. Players, get serious, before time expires.

Dreamers perform godly, assigned, duties. Nondreamers' disinterest, out-of-step, attitudes decry divine work. Schedules are man-made and sin-oriented. Time is misspent and void of valuableness. Foolishness appointments cause various mismanagements. Hopefully, before time expiration, clear thinking emerges changing minds and resource allocations for goodwill.

Arrogantly, compassion is sometimes described as weakness. Actually, compassion signifies courage. Unfortunately, nondreamers waddle in backwardness and chaos. Faithfully and emphatically, God's work, in His plenteous vineyard (harvest), is urgent. "And Jesus went about all the cities and villages, teaching…and preaching the gospel of the kingdom, and healing every sickness and every disease among the people. But when he saw the multitudes, he was moved with compassion on them, because they fainted, and were scattered abroad, as sheep having no shepherd." St. Matthew 9:35-36.

Christian Eagle-tis-ti-cal dreamers show compassion. Helping people is part of God's Work. Pitifully, silence, and withholding goods and services, neglect impoverished people. Bravery is sometimes misdiagnosed as forwardness. Genuine (dreamers) leaders are strong and smart. Regardless of consequences, dreamers practice righteousness.

Unbiased workers are employed in godly vineyards. Truthfully and eloquently, godly vineyards reflect equal opportunity for all peoples. Dreamers use fair balances.

Nondreamers use unfairness, questionable balances, etc., for filling self-measures. Without regard for others' well-being, their scales are intentionally, unfairly, tilted. Inequality encourages respect of persons' stances. God's Word teaches against partiality (injustice). In God's vineyard, everyone receives fairness – fair shot at opportunities and pay scales. God's ambassadors treat everyone fairly. Justice-minded ambassadors work in God's vineyard. "Then saith he unto his disciples, The harvest truly *is* plenteous, but the labourers *are* few; pray ye therefore the Lord of the harvest, that he will send forth labourers into his harvest." St. Matthew 9:37-38.

Live God-appointed dreams. Too many people focus on earthly happiness. When God is not center, misery is mainstay. Dreamers focus on God and are eternally saved. "If ye then be risen with Christ, seek those things which are above, where Christ sitteth on the right hand of God. Set your affection on things above, not on things on the earth." Colossians 3:1-2.

Many nondreamers' mental capacities bitterly stress and despond thus spending lifetimes in dismal states, trying to attain joy and fulfillment. According to worldly protocols, as in the days of No'-e, many die unhappy, forever lost. Happiness originates, and continues, with God. Worldliness cannot satisfy, only medicates. Comprehensively, the Holy Bible teaches righteous lifestyles.

"...But Jesus said unto them, A prophet is not without honour, save in his own country, and in his own house." St. Matthew 13:57. "...a man's enemies are the men of his own house." Micah 7:6. Still, Joseph's calling is fulfilled.

6

Satan's Psychological Profile

ALTHOUGH WILDERNESS EXPERIENCES come, some may not be lifetime journeys. For talebearers, confusion is a distressful lifestyle. Inwards clutter with affliction and guilt; because of atrocities committed against others. Satan relishes chaos. By composing heresies and pandemonium, Satan plots evil everywhere. Talebearers attack calmness. Nondreamers' jealousy and covetousness tears them apart; so, they proceed with attempted dream destruction toward dreamers. When peace is not in hearts, giving grief comes natural. Nondreamers dish out as much misery as possible.

The Bible teaches confession of sins, not cover-ups. Talebearing, murmuring, and complaining, indicate brokenness, personal unresolved issues. Intentionally, troublemakers create incriminating gestures/situations hoping to deflect attention from themselves to innocents.

Psychologically, after living in wildernesses so long, the devil encourages talebearers' lying, plotting, stealing, and scheming, tendencies. Sadly, deep comfortableness settles in. Nondreamers' minds and bodies stay busy doing Satan's devious harassments.

Satan profiles people using valuable time, attention, and efforts, for constant, chilling, chaos. Unquestionably, the devil swirls talebearers until they are unable to escape his grip. When talebearers become hooked, basking in confusion erase normalcy. Most likely, company-keepers become victims. Claims and disclaimers are untrue. Truth-disfigurement damages, and destroys, reputations and lives. "False witnesses did rise up; they laid to my charge *things* that I knew not." Psalm 35:11.

Pew villains manufacture (plant, grow, and harvest) full-service hurt dispensaries. Dismissive behavior implies remorselessness, making their ungodly deeds more painful and dangerous. Realization of talebearers' problem-making attitudes and sly opposition tactics batter lives.

Profusely, this book emphasizes talebearers' conduct against dreamers specifically, and society, as a whole. Dysfunction – in churches and society – is disgraceful. Talebearers cause enormous problems, not only in churches but also in societies, and globally. Physical attendance is unnecessary; because, set-ups and cover-ups use numerous undercovers. Simply, talebearers are problem-oriented.

In order to escape devil workings, dreamers need godly realizations. Opposition tactics are real, sinful, and painful. Jesus is dreamers' only escape. Jesus wants to consume mankind with His Holy Spirit, breaking impurity grips. God's grace impassions us with holiness.

Hard times are here. Harder times are coming. In changing societies, young people play gigantic roles whether good or bad. Holy Bible teachings, and following, ensure planet betterment. Otherwise, the planet risk self-inflicted, needless calamites, pitfalls. Innately, mankind (human race) links. The world is full of temporal detractions. Knowingly, Jesus originates success, lasting success and happiness. Satan dislikes Jesus' name, His gospel, and His followers. Also, the devil angers because traps set, and holes dug, do not capture dreamers. He and cronies fail.

In spite of persecutors, Christian Eagle-tis-ti-cal dreamers live righteously. Inspiration never dies. When this earthly journey ends, eternal journey begins; but, never ends. Earthly, light, afflictions and tribulations will be replaced with eternal salvation – heavenly accommodations. Save yourself. Encourage others to save themselves. Each individual is responsible for their soul salvation. In the midst of corruptness, dreamers live, share, and fulfill God's Word. Dreamers give. As others wander wicked paths, Christian Eagle-tis-ti-cal dreamers gallop with their blessed call of Jesus Christ. God is the only One Who can help and save souls.

Satan Endorsements

Jesus owns The Universe. Satan tempted Him. Satan also tempts His followers. Followers have steadfastness to Holy Bible teachings, telling Satan as Jesus told him, "...Get thee behind me..." St. Luke 4:8. "And Jesus being full of the Holy Ghost...was led by the Spirit...Being forty days tempted of the devil. And in those days he did eat nothing: and when they were ended, he afterward hungered. And the devil said unto him, If thou be the Son of God, command this stone that it be made bread. And Jesus answered him, saying, It is written, That man shall not live by bread alone, but by every word of God. And the devil, taking him up into an high mountain, shewed unto him all the kingdoms of the world...And the devil said unto him, All this power will I give thee, and the glory of them: for that is delivered unto me; and to whomsoever I will give it. If thou therefore wilt worship me, all shall be thine. And Jesus answered and said unto him, Get thee behind me, Satan: for it is written, Thou shalt worship the Lord thy God, and him only shalt thy serve...It is said, Thou shalt not tempt the Lord thy God." St. Luke 4:1-8, 12.

Unfortunately, Satan tempts daily, offering food, money, resources, employment, luxuries, and other worldly opportunities. Satan's temporalities keep souls out of heaven. Are the aforementioned items worth your soul? After all, nothing goes. All items stay behind.

Dreamers realize Satan intends to sabotage God's vision for mankind's lives. Holiness and alertness is vital for snare, pit, avoidances. Although San was created by God, he strayed. He possessed beauty but desired to become likened to God. He lured several angels. They followed him. God cast Satan out of heaven. During vulnerabilities, Satan entices and attacks. God's followers' forewarnings lead away from temptations, persecutions, snares, liars, slanderers, complicities and duplicities. God teaches His followers watchfulness and prayfulness, which gives steadfastness, joyfulness, and peacefulness. When Satan presents enticements, tell him to "Get thee behind..." St. Luke 4:8.

Act on God's Word. Satan is, and will always be mankind's enemy. His agenda is totally dishonorable. Assessing motivations is wise and practical. "Be sober, be vigilant; because your adversary the devil, as a roaring lion, walketh about, seeking whom he may devour." I Peter 5:8. Satan's beauty should not be overlooked; because, he uses it for soul stealing. Defeatism drives the devil to grab every soul who listens to his wicked, worldly offers. He employs evil cohorts. He flashes worldly temporalities – money, goods, services, kingdoms, and nations. His lies deceive. Satan offers one hot, permanent place – hell. Wrongly, Satan influences many people and situations. Unsealing his fate is impossible. He, and all his associates, is slated for eternal punishment missing out on Jesus' loving kindness and tender mercies. Jesus loves you. Do not go, with Satan, to everlasting torment. His evil deeds cannot be discounted. Satan aims for souls' destruction. God says, Come. The devil says, don't go. The decision is yours. Who do you believe? God is Truth. Believing in anyone else leads to eternal damnation, separation from God forever. This decision is eternally irreversible.

It is hard to believe that anyone dreams of spending eternity in a hot furnace with fire and brimstone. While making wicked offers, Satan does not advertise his fatal fate. But, God's Word publishes His desires for souls to prosper and live with Him in peace. Streets are paved with gold. Heaven's beauty and rest never ends. Wouldn't you rather have peace with God than Satan's sinful offers, along with fire and brimstone eternity? Remember, the devil lies, steals, entices and makes worthless, temporal, offers. The devil's, ongoing, recruitment persuade fragile, naive souls. As the devil's time steadily shortens, he hurries to ruin lives. He is angry because he cannot save him himself from the mess he made; so, he destroys others.

Confess sins. Come to God. God forgives. Apparently, we are living in perilous times. Discernment prevents cave-ins, pitfalls, to temporalities. "*Favor is* deceitful, and beauty *is* vain: but *a* woman *that* feareth the Lord, she shall be praised. Give her of the fruit of her hands; and let her own works praise her in the gates." Proverbs 30:31-32. God's Word lets us know that Satan has come down in great wrath. As a result, Satan uses his limited time with broader, wilder, and meaner activities. With God's strength, his opposition tactics fail. Mistakenly, many souls take Satan lightly, thinking beauty and smartness add up to holiness.

Constant, fabricated, schemes entice some souls into hot, eternal fire. By accepting Satan's offers, he welcomes souls to eternal fire and brimstone. Jesus' salvation saves souls from wrath. "Therefore rejoice, *ye* heavens, and ye that dwell in them. Woe to the inhabiters of the earth and of the seal for the devil is come down unto you, having great wrath, because he knoweth that he hath but a short time." Revelation 12:12.

Far-sighted, heaven-bound, warriors fight evil. When life's race ends, God's people go home – heaven – to be with Him forever. Holy celebration for God's ambassadors' homegoing! Christians (winners) endure until the end! The Grand Prize is HEAVEN ETERNAL!!!

"Come unto me, all *ye* that labour and are heavy laden, and I will give you rest." St. Matthew 11:28. Listen to Jesus!

Build dreams. Dreamers' focus and steadfastness help prevent evil plots, takeovers. Carelessness resides in nondreamland, mediocrity, circles. Sadly, everyone does not desire to soar. Anyone can settle for triviality. Nondreamers are unstable runaways, lacking honor to pursue their calling – dreams.

When Joseph's brothers threw him in the pit, God knew he is headed to Pharaoh's place to reign over them. Life lessons, sacrifices, beauties, leaderships, derived from pit experience(s), build patience. Dreamers' innate discernibility see them through, and around, problems and dire circumstances. Moving in His plan facilitates victory. Complacency divulges vulnerability.

Satan, family, pew villains, inhumane millionaires, unscrupulous pubic administrators, workplace tormentors, or anyone else, cannot stop God's promises, plans. God crushes Satan's opposition. Suffering is – part of life – not life's entirety. Sufferings can be teaching tools – stepping stones – propelling dreamers' goals.

Joseph chose suffering wrong rather than committing wrongness. He maintains his dreams and integrity. Indeed, he came from the valley of despair to dream fulfillment and ruled over his family. Joseph loved Jesus and exhibited Christ-like love. Upon becoming his family's ruler, he treated them with dignity, loving kindness, not holding their sins against them.

Unfortunately, Joseph may have come within moments of life loss. "And Judah said unto his brethren, What profit *is it* if we slay our brother, and conceal his blood? Come, and let us sell him...and let not our hand be upon him; for he is our brother and our flesh. And his brethren were content." Genesis 37:26-27.

Obviously, opposition tactics, used against Joseph, fail; because, he holds God's trust and values dearly. God deserves praise, credit, for his greatness, and grace. In spite of satanic ploys, dreamers emerge victoriously. God's richness flows in all dominions. Godliness displays obedience to God's Word.

In the end, Joseph remains a dream-fulfilled man. He keeps his uprightness edge. He does not commit sin for wealth acquisition. Even though **family betrayals** and tribulations plaque his dream journey, **he focuses on God** and receives authority, wealth, and exaltation, in due time. His family witnesses his momentous status; but, cannot denounce or take it away. God allows dreamers to feast in enemies' presence.

Boldly, dreamers pursue God. Self-thinking, independent, and confident, dreamers do not follow unhealthy flocks for money, prestige, or other worldly treasures. Brainwashing destroys personal identities and considerations. Group mentalities replace individuality. Group mentalities' ideals, and actions suppress individualism. Many spirits are broken, damaged, and/or destroyed. Self gets lost in others' convictions. Some convictions are right; but some are wicked. If self-convictions are right, keep them. If not, change them. Unfortunately, more people follow wickedness than righteousness. When the flood came on the earth, only eight souls were saved. When Jesus Christ returns...As in the days of No'-e... happens again. Dreamers cannot survive in timid, nonthinking, environments. If they choose, nondreamers have opportunity to seek higher callings. God shows ways of escapement, hopefulness, and refinement.

"For a dream cometh through the multitude of business; and a fool's voice is *known* by multitude of words." Ecclesiastes 5:3. Positively, dreamers help people. Dream realizations happen outside boats and boxes. Dreamers dissociate from mediocrity, fearfulness,

hopelessness, negativity, etc., bad influences. "And in the fourth watch of the night Jesus went unto them, walking on the sea...when the disciples saw him...they cried out for fear. But straightway Jesus spake unto them, saying, Be of good cheer; it is I; be not afraid. And Peter answered him and said, Lord, if it be thou, bid me come unto thee on the water. And he said, Come. And when Peter was come down out of the ship, he walked on the water, to go to Jesus." St. Matthew 14:25-29.

Nondreamers sit in fearful, negativism, despair-filled, boats, while gazing and plotting unsavory schemes toward dreamers. Unfortunately, their opposition tactics cause much pain. Even though they stay in boats, their tongues and ungodly conduct inflict chaos in worship sites and communities. "A fool also is full of words: a man cannot tell what shall be; and what shall be after him, who can tell him?" Ecclesiastes 10:14.

Enemies are invited to "eternal life graduation ceremonies." The theme: "From Valley to Dream Fulfillment Hilltop." Firsthand, enemies agonize because their ploys explode (overthrown)! **God works in pitfalls, as well as palaces. God vindicates. God is great.**

"Be not wise in thine own eyes: fear the Lord, and depart from evil."

PROVERBS 3:7.

"Let us hear the conclusion of the matter: Fear God, and keep his commandments: for this *is* the whole *duty* of man. For God shall bring every work into judgment, with every secret thing, whether *it be* good, or whether *it be* evil."

ECCLESIASTES 12:13-14.

ABOUT THE AUTHOR

"For what shall it profit a man, if he shall gain the whole world, and lose his own soul? Or what shall a man give in exchange for his soul? Whosoever therefore shall be ashamed of me and of my words in this adulterous and sinful generation; of him also shall the Son of man be ashamed, when he cometh in the glory of his Father with the holy angels."

St. Mark 8:36-38.

Gaillee Solomon is an undeterred Eagle-tis-ti-cal dreamer, academician, philanthropist, author, book editor, and real estate entrepreneur. She teaches God's Word in forums such as study groups, classes, meetings, etc. Precisely, she shares information on how Christian dreamers can live faith-filled lives in this present world. Happiness happens now. Experience happiness on earth. You do not have to wait, until you get to heaven, for blissfulness.

Leadership, gifted, and talented programs are favorite concentrations. Supports and opportunities are given to literacy efforts, etc. Those truly interested in education (learning) are encouraged to participate in helps programs.

Studies indicate dreamers and nondreamers live life differently. Courageous dreamers live giving. On the other hand, nondreamers talk giving, but instead take from deserving parties. Unfortunately, nondreamers submit to men-pleasing, hype without substance, mediocrity.

God blesses me with assignments like helping the poor and teaching dream fulfillment prerequisites. Leave godly legacies. Dreamers are proud God sellouts.